John Ford

The Works of John Ford

Vol. I

John Ford

The Works of John Ford
Vol. I

ISBN/EAN: 9783744711784

Printed in Europe, USA, Canada, Australia, Japan

Cover: Foto ©Thomas Meinert / pixelio.de

More available books at **www.hansebooks.com**

THE

WORKS OF JOHN FORD,

WITH

NOTES CRITICAL AND EXPLANATORY

BY

WILLIAM GIFFORD, Esq.

A NEW EDITION, CAREFULLY REVISED,

WITH ADDITIONS TO THE TEXT AND TO THE NOTES

BY THE

REV. ALEXANDER DYCE.

IN THREE VOLUMES.

VOL. I.

LONDON:
JAMES TOOVEY, 177 PICCADILLY.
1869.

PREFACE TO THE PRESENT EDITION.

WHEN I assented (rather unwillingly) to the publisher's request that I would re-edit Gifford's edition of Ford, I certainly expected that I should have had a comparatively easy task, believing that little more would be required of me than to see that Gifford's text and notes were carefully followed by the printer. But, to my surprise, I soon discovered that I had ignorantly formed too high an estimate of the merits of his edition.

That Gifford did much for Ford, rectifying *passim* sundry mistakes of the old copies which had baffled the incapacity of Weber, is undeniable: notwithstanding which, however, his edition is far indeed from perfect. To say nothing of the intolerable inaccuracy of his quotations and references in the notes, Gifford sometimes carelessly deviates in minute particulars from the original text; sometimes passes over, without any attempt to correct them, gross errors of the old copies (vol. i. p. 102, p. 291, vol. ii. p. 23, p. 101, p. 195, &c.); and sometimes deliberately alters the readings of the quartos with what seems unaccountable rashness in one who had devoted so much time to the study of our early dramatists (see a remarkable instance of this in his alteration of "a sister's thread" to "a *spider's* thread," vol. iii. p. 54).

Gifford appended to his *Introduction* a list of numerous mistakes committed by his predecessor Weber, and of his own corrections of them: and in p. lxvi. of that *Introduction* he observes; "Of the general nature of this person's [Weber's] notes some idea may be formed by the few (they are but a few[?]) which I have placed as specimens in the Introductory part. My remarks, together with the innumerable corrections of the text, should have been subjoined to the respective pages, had I not indulged a hope that whenever another edition of this poet should be called for, the future editor (as the reading will then probably be considered as established) would remove this part of the *Introduction*, and relieve the work altogether from the name of Weber." In the present edition, therefore, I have omitted, according to his desire, the concluding portion of Gifford's *Introduction*, preserving, however, certain explanations of the text with which it is interspersed, and which I have transferred to the notes on the respective passages in question.

We find our poet's name variously spelt,—*Ford*, *Forde*, and even *Foard* (see vol. iii. p. 102) and *Foord* (see *Introduction*, p. li.): and in the prefatory matter to *The Broken Heart* Gifford remarks; "Ford has prefixed as a motto the words *Fide Honor* [also prefixed to his *Perkin Warbeck* and *The Lady's Trial*], an anagram of his own name, which therefore should perhaps be written, as he sometimes wrote it himself, *John Forde.*" But since, as Gifford elsewhere observes, *Introduction*, p. li., "Few of our old writers could spell their own names correctly, and still fewer followed any standard," I believe that, however Ford may have chosen to write his name on other occasions, he would not have scrupled, when disposed to turn it into an anagram, to spell it, merely "for the nonce," with a final *e*.

The languor and weakness consequent on a very long and serious illness having made it almost impossible for me personally to examine any public records with a view to the biography of Ford, I was fortunate, in that emergency, to meet with friends who kindly undertook to act as my substitute. I accordingly beg to return my best thanks to Mr. John Bruce, who more than once visited the Prerogative Office in order to search out for me the Will of Ford; but his labour was thrown away, and he was forced at last to come to the decided conclusion that it was not extant there, though he lighted on the Wills of several persons bearing the same names as the poet: also to Mr. William Macpherson, who procured for me from the Middle Temple the exact words of the entry of Ford's admission into that society. I have besides to express my obligations to Mr. J. O. Halliwell and Mr. W. J. Thoms, who zealously exerted themselves, though in vain, to ascertain for me where was to be seen a copy of the prose tract about Mother Sawyer, who figures so strikingly in our author's *Witch of Edmonton*.

ALEXANDER DYCE.

33 *Oxford Terrace, Hyde Park.*
 Feb. 15*th*, 1869.

When I made some additions to the complimentary verses by Ford on the writings of his friends (see vol. iii.), I overlooked the following lines. D.

Of Master Richard Brome his ingenious comedy The Northern Lass. To the Reader.

Poets and painters curiously compar'd
Give life to fancy, and achieve reward
By immortality of name: so thrives
Art's glory, that all what it breathes on lives.
Witness this Northern Piece. The court affords
No newer fashion or for wit or words.
The body of the plot is drawn so fair
That the soul's language quickens with fresh air.
This well-limb'd poem by no rate or thought
Too dearly priz'd, being or sold or bought.

JOHN FORD,
The author's very friend.

In the same vol., p. 331, I ought not to have inserted the lines signed "*Johannes Ford, Encomiastes*," which I now believe are from the pen of the poet's cousin. D.

CONTENTS OF VOL. I.

	PAGE
INTRODUCTION BY GIFFORD	xiii
LIST OF PLAYS	lxx
COMMENDATORY VERSES	lxxi
THE LOVER'S MELANCHOLY	1
'TIS PITY SHE'S A WHORE	107
THE BROKEN HEART	209

INTRODUCTION

BY GIFFORD.

It is incidentally observed by Dr. Farmer (*Essay on Shakespeare*) " that play-writing in the poet's days was scarcely thought a creditable employ." To this, perhaps, may in some measure be attributed the slight notice which is taken of the personal history of the dramatic writers by their contemporaries, and the little degree of interest which they appear to have excited. Of the immortal bard himself scarcely anything is known but what is told by Jonson; and Mr. Malone, who had been foraging for anecdotes of him nearly half a century, and had dwelt, over and over, with full conviction, on the reports current about him down to the times of Rowe and Theobald, ends with rejecting the whole of them, and discomfortably but honestly confesses that his life is a blank.[1] The two bulky volumes of Dr. Drake scarcely add a single fact to history or criticism; and we are

---

[1] Even the cherished peccadillo of *deer-stealing*,
"That last infirmity of noble mind,"
the crown and ornament of Shakespeare's youthful vivacity, must now be given up; for Mr. Malone has proved with immense effort that Sir T. Lucy had *no park*, and could therefore have no deer to be stolen!

doomed to the same *crambe recocta* in all who treat on the subject.

It would seem as if the dramatic poets themselves —for the rest are not so chary of names and circumstances—entertained some such idea as Farmer mentions; and either from mortification or humility commonly abstained from dwelling or even entering upon their personal history. Though frequent in dedications, they are seldom explicit; and even their prefaces fail to convey any information except of their wants, or their grievances from evils which are rarely specified.

The stock of the Fords was highly respectable : they appear to have settled at an early period in the north-west of Devonshire, and to have possessed considerable property in the contiguous parishes of Ashburton, Ilsington, &c. Some account, or rather some mention of them may be found in Prince; but that worthy chronicler of nameless names has contrived to perplex the little manual of their pedigree with such indescribable success, that it is scarcely possible to appropriate a single circumstance. To spare the reader, therefore, it will be sufficient to say, that the family mainly consisted of two branches, which ran collateral with each other, and from the junior of which the ancestors of our poet appear to have sprung. Frequent intermarriages, and a singular attachment to the name of John, bewilder the early inquirer from step to step; but thus much may be relied on by those who are content to take up the poet's pedigree from a comparatively modern period.

John Ford of Ashburton, by his fourth wife Joan, daughter of John Trobridge, Esquire, relict of Gilbert St. Clair, had issue John. George Ford of Ilsington, the son of the above John Ford by a former marriage, wedded Joan, a daughter of Gilbert St. Clair (his relation John's wife), and had issue several children, the eldest of whom, Thomas Ford of Ilsington, married the sister (daughter) of the famous Lord Chief-Justice, John Popham, and had issue John (the poet), and several others. John Ford of Bagtor, in Ilsington (the cousin, I take it, of the poet), married the daughter and sole heiress of George Drake Spratshays, Esquire, and had issue Henry Ford of Nutwell Bagtor and Spratshays, whose life is a part of the general history of the times, and who was also a piece of a poet.

John (our author) was the second son of Thomas Ford. His elder brother probably lived in tranquil obscurity, and died on the spot which gave him birth. John was destined to a wider range, and to a life of somewhat more energy.

From an extract of the baptismal register of Ilsington, procured by Mr. Malone from the vicar,[2] it appears that Ford was baptised there on the 17th

---

[2] The Rev. Jonathan Palk. From this worthy man, who was my associate both at the grammar-school and at Exeter College, I indulged a hope of procuring, through the medium of our common schoolfellow the Dean of Westminster [Dr. Ireland], a few additional notices respecting the poet's connections; but the long and severe illness which afflicted him, and which terminated in death a few months since, took away the power of all communication.—[See Malone's *Shakespeare* by Boswell, vol. i. p. 414. D.]

April 1586; and as he became a member of the Middle Temple Nov. 16, 1602,[3] he could scarcely have spent more than a term or two (if any) at either of the Universities: there was, however, more than one grammar-school in the immediate vicinity of his birthplace fully competent to convey all the classical learning which he ever possessed, and of which, to say the truth, he was sufficiently ostentatious in his earliest work, though he became more reserved when age and experience had enabled him to compare his attainments with those of his contemporaries.

It appears from Rymer's *Fœdera*[4] that the father of our poet was in the commission of the peace. Whether this honourable situation was procured for him by the interest of his wife's father cannot be told: it may, however, be reasonably surmised that his connection with one of the first law-officers of the crown led to the course of studies subsequently pursued by both branches of the family. Popham was made Attorney-General in 1581; and in 1592 he was advanced to the rank of Chief-Justice of the King's Bench, which he held for many years; so that his

[3] "1602 Decimo sexto die Novembris anno præd.
fforde Jo. Mr Johannes fforde filius secundus Thome
ad. fforde de Ilsington in Com. Devon. ar.
admissus est in Societatem Medii Templi
Specialiter et Obligatus una cum Mar^{is}
Georgio Hooper et Thoma fforde et dat
pro fine—iij¹ vj• viij^d."—
Mr. Collier, in his *Introduction* to our author's *Honour Triumphant* and *A Line of Life*, reprinted for the Shake. Soc., erroneously states that Ford "had been admitted a student of *Gray's Inn* in 1602." D.

[4] Tom. xviii. p. 575.

patronage, which must have been considerable (as he appears to have been in some favour both with Elizabeth and her successor), probably afforded many facilities to his young relatives in the progress of their studies, and opened advantages of various kinds.

Our poet had been preceded in his legal studies by his cousin John Ford, son of an elder brother of his father's family, to whom he appears to have looked up with much respect, and to have borne an almost fraternal affection. This gentleman was entered at Gray's Inn; but Popham seems to have taken his young relation more immediately under his own care, and placed him at the Middle Temple, of which he had been appointed treasurer in 1581.

It is probable that Ford was not inattentive to his studies; but we hear nothing of him till 1606 (four years after his admission), when he published *Fame's Memorial, or the Earl of Devonshire deceased*, &c., an elegiac poem, in quarto, which he dedicated to the Countess his widow. Why he came forward in so inauspicious a cause cannot now be known. He was a stranger to both parties; yet he appears to bewail the death of the Earl as if it had been attended with some failure of professional hope to himself. "Elegies" and "Memorials" were sufficiently common at that period, and indeed long after it; but the authors steadfastly looked to the surviving heir for pay or patronage in return for their miserable dole of consolation; and our youthful poet sets out with affirming (and he deserves the fullest credit) that his Muse was unfee'd. Be this as it may, it argued no little spirit in him to advocate an unpopular cause, and step forward in the sanguine expectation of stemming the current of general opinion : not to add, that the praise which he lavishes on the Earl of Essex could scarcely fail to be ill received by the Lord Chief-Justice, who was one of those commissioned by the Queen to inquire into the purport of the military assemblage at his house, was detained there by the troops during the crazy attempt of this ill-starred nobleman to raise an insurrection, and was finally a witness against him for the forcible detention.

Fame's Memorial adds little or nothing to the poet's personal history. It would seem, if we might venture to understand him literally (for he writes to the συνετοί, and takes especial pains to keep all but those familiarly acquainted with him in complete ignorance of his story), that he had involved himself in some unsuccessful affair of love, while at home, with a young lady, whom, by an ungallant allusion, I fear, to the Greek, he at one time calls the *cruel Lycia*, and at another the *cruel subtle Lycia*. He wishes that she were less wise; and in truth she does exhibit no unfavourable symptom of good sense in " confining her thoughts to elder merits," instead of " solacing" her youthful admirer, who, at the period of first *taking the infection into his eye*, could not have reached his eighteenth year. Yet he owes something to this pursuit. He had evidently wooed the lady (herself a Muse) in verse, and symptoms of wounded vanity occasionally appear at the inflexibility of this second Lyde, to whose *obstinate ears* he sang in vain :

yet the attempt gave him some facility in composition; for though he evinces little of either taste or judgment, his lines flow smoothly, and it may be said of him, as it was of a greater personage,

"He caught at love, and fill'd his arms with bays."

In consequence of her blindness or obduracy, he declares his intention of "travailing till some comfort reach his wretched heart forlorn." This is merely a rhetorical flourish; for the *travail* which he contemplated appears to be the labour and pains employed, to divert the current of his thoughts, on the "lamentation for this great lord."

He found, however, better resources against ill-requited love than "perpetual lamentation" for one who was not unwillingly forgotten by his contemporaries, in the pursuit of the law, to which he prudently adhered; a circumstance which he never forgets, nor ever suffers his patrons to forget, as if he feared to pass with them more for a poet than a man of business.

But he had yet another resource. He had apparently contracted a strong and early passion for the stage, to which he devoted most of his *horæ subsecivæ;* and, without prematurely grasping at a name, wrote, as the custom then was, in conjunction with the regular supporters of the minor theatres. That he published nothing, we are warranted to conclude from the assertion in the dedication to the *Lover's Melancholy* (given to the press in 1629), that this was "the first" (dramatic) "piece of his that ever courted *reader*." But in the twenty-three years which had elapsed since the appearance of his elegy, he had more than once courted the favour of the *spectator*,[5] and "stood rubric" with others in the title-page of several plays which have come down to us, and in more, perhaps, which remain to be discovered. The late Mr. G. Chalmers gave to the public the names of three pieces hitherto unnoticed, in which he was concerned: *The Fairy Knight* and *The Bristowe Merchant*, written in conjunction with Decker; and *A late Murther of the Sonne upon the Mother*,[6] in which he was assisted by Webster: and Isaac Reed, in the interleaved copy of his Langbaine (now in the possession of Mr. Heber), has given from the Stationers' books the title of several others, entered under our poet's name, among which are *Sir Thomas Overbury's Life and untimely Death*, 25th November 1615; *The Line of Life*,[7] 10th October 1620; *An ill Beginning has a good End*, &c., which is known to have been brought on the stage as early as 1613. When to these we add the four plays[8] which were among the manuscript dramas destroyed by Mr. Warburton's servant,

---

[5] We have the authority of Singleton for the fact, who, in the lines prefixed to this very play (*The Lover's Melancholy*), says,

"Nor seek I praise for thee, when thine own pen
Hath forc'd a praise *long since* from knowing men."

[6] "Letter of O. Gilchrist, Esquire, to W. Gifford, on the late edition of Ford's Plays." 1811, [p. 17].

[7] Gifford, not having seen this production, erroneously supposed that it was a play. It is included in the present edition, vol. iii. p. 381. D.

[8] But *An ill Beginning*, &c. was one of the *four plays* by Ford which Warburton's servant destroyed; the other three being *Beauty in a Trance, The London Merchant*, and *The Royal Combat:* see *List of Ford's Plays* at the end of this *Introduction*. D.

and recollect that this is still but an imperfect list of his dramatic labours, we may venture to appreciate the just force of the expression quoted in the preceding page [but one]; and, at all events, to admit that, though new to the press, he came before the public well graduated to the stage.

This will be yet more apparent when the two pieces, *The Sun's Darling*, vol. iii. p. 101, and *The Witch of Edmonton*, vol. iii. p. 171, are taken into the account.

The first of these, in the composition of which Ford joined with Decker, is termed a "moral masque." For a moral masque, however, it sets the main business of life sufficiently low: there is nothing worthy of a wise and good man; nothing, in short, beyond what one of the herd of Epicurus might desire—sensual pleasures and gross enjoyments. The plot may be briefly dispatched. "Raybright (the Sun's Darling) is roused from a pleasant dream, and informed that his great progenitor, the Sun, will descend from his sphere to gratify his wildest longings for enjoyment. Accordingly, at his imperial command, he is entertained by the Four Seasons in succession, all of whom endeavour to recommend themselves to his affection, and to all of whom he vows eternal fidelity; but abruptly abandons each of them in turn, at the instigation of Humour and her attendant, Folly."

The result may be anticipated. The youth recognises his error, and determines to be very wise and virtuous for the residue of his days; when he is told, in strains not unworthy of the subject, that his days are already numbered, and that the inevitable hour is fast closing upon all his earthly prospects.

Indifferent as is the execution of this piece, it is still far superior to its conception. Passages of considerable beauty, especially in the last two acts, frequently occur; but there is nothing to redeem the absurdity of the plot. Instead of taking up an inexperienced, unsophisticated youth, and opening the world to him for the first time, for the instruction of others, the authors have inconsiderately brought forward a kind of modern Virbius,—a character who had previously run through life, and its various changes, and seen and enjoyed infinitely more than is tendered to him in his new career.

The Sun's Darling, in its present state, was performed in 1624, but not printed till 1658 [wrong:— see vol. iii. p. 102], when the long persecution of the stage (fortunately for the lovers of the old drama) compelled the actors to have recourse to the press with such of the prompters' copies as remained in their hands, for a temporary relief. In the dedication to the Earl of Southampton we are told that "the poem lived by the breath of general applause;" and it might have attained some degree of popularity, from the quick succession of characters, the songs, the dances, and other incidental entertainments, which, though rude and homely, were yet all that the theatres could give, and such as the audiences of those days were well content to admire.

Langbaine tells us that the greatest part of *The Sun's Darling* was written by Ford; but he quotes no authority for the assertion. A piece with this name [? see vol. iii. p. 102] is mentioned in Henslowe's MSS. as having once belonged to the Rose Theatre. I suspect that this was the foundation of the present masque, and that Decker was the author of it. If it be so, the incongruous nature of the fable is easily accounted for, by the additions which other poets, and above all our author, were called upon to supply, as occasions presented themselves; for we deceive ourselves greatly if we suppose, from the combination of names which sometimes appears on the old title-pages, that those who are specified were always simultaneously employed in the production of the same play.

The second piece, *The Witch of Edmonton*, was brought out about the same period as the former, and printed in 1658, probably at the suggestion of Bird, whose name appears to a few introductory lines, which he calls a Prologue. If I understand him, he says that it was favourably received on the stage; and he therefore argues well of its reception from the general reader;

> " But as the year doth with his plenty bring
> As well a latter as a former spring,
> So hath this Witch enjoy'd the first; and reason
> Presumes she may partake the other season."

In the title-page it is called "a known true story." All my acquaintance with it is derived from the following passages in Caulfield's popular collection of *Portraits, Memoirs, and Characters of Remarkable Persons*, 1794. " Elizabeth Sawyer, executed in 1621 for witchcraft."

"The following title," Mr. Caulfield adds, "is prefixed to a 4to pamphlet printed in London, 1621;
"The wonderfull discoverie of Elizabeth Sawyer, a witch, late of Edmonton; her conviction, and condemnation and death; together with the [relation of the] divel's accesse to her, and their conference together. Written by Henry Goodcole, minister of the word of God, and her constant [continual] visitor in the gaole at [of] Newgate."

I have not been able to procure a sight of this pamphlet,[9] and therefore can only venture to speak from conjecture; but I am disposed to believe that it furnished our poets with little more than a title-page. It is apparently a story made up for the occasion, and though it is highly probable that a woman of this name was executed for a witch, yet I place no reliance on the date, though, in compliance with the general supposition, I have fixed its first appearance in 1623. *The Witch of Islington*[10] appears among the

[9] Neither have I. But in Robinson's *History and Antiquities of the Parish of Edmonton*, &c. is the following article; "*Mother Sawyer, the Witch of Edmonton* (with a woodcut of her 'from a rare print in the collection of W. Beckford, Esq.'). Elizabeth Sawyer was a poor woman, that in the superstitious reign of James the First probably incurred the displeasure of some more potent neighbour, who, having no just cause of complaint to allege against her, accused her of witchcraft; a crime that, of all others, was at this period most dreaded: very little time was allowed between the accusation, condemnation, and death of a suspected witch; and if a voluntary confession was wanting, they never failed extorting a forced one by tormenting the suspected person. The following title is prefixed to a .quarto pamphlet printed in London in the year 1621; *The Wonderful Discovery of Elizabeth Sawyer*," &c. p. 117. D.

[10] Henslowe's *Diary*, p. 90, ed. Shake. Soc.—I greatly doubt if *The Witch of Edmonton* was founded on it. D.

plays performed by Mr. Henslowe's company [the Lord Admiral's men] in 1597; this was not too early for Decker, and may have been the foundation of the present work, with a more popular name: for Edmonton had already given a " Devil to the delighted stage;" and this may be thought to account in some measure for the " &c." subjoined to the list of writers in the title-page.

And popular, no doubt, the piece was. The sorceress of our times (for they will not be called witches now) is a splendid character; she moves like a volcano amidst smoke and fire, and throws heaven and earth into commotion at every step; but the witch of those days was a miserable creature, enfeebled by age, soured by poverty, and maddened by inveterate persecution and abuse. And what were the scenic adjuncts which gave reality and life to the pranks of this august personage? Briefly, a few hereditary " properties" from the greenroom of old John Heywood's days, the whole of which might *inhabit lax* in a single cloak-bag. No sweet symphonies from viewless harps, no beautiful displays of hell broke-up, and holiday devils dancing *ad libitum* through alternate scenes of terror and delight, were at our poet's command, *call for them* as he might: a black shaggy rug in imitation of a dog's-skin,[11] into which a clever imp was

---

[11] In speaking of the Black Dog of Newgate (vol. iii. p. 245), it escaped me that a piece with this title, by R. Hathway, was performed in 1602. A drama with a similar name, by Luke Hutton, is mentioned by the Editor of Dodsley's *Old Plays* as printed before 1600. I have never seen it. Vol. viii. p. 172. [" Mr. Gifford mis-

thrust, and taught to walk on all fours, with permission to relieve himself occasionally by "standing on his hind legs," and "a mask and visor for a spirit in the shape of Katherine," were all the machinery which the simplicity or poverty of the old theatre allowed him; and these were not regarded without considerable interest by those who knew no superstitions but the legendary ones of long ages, and whose creed was in full accordance with that of the stage. We laugh at all this now; and we do well: but, in justice to the poets, we should try them by the code under which they lived and wrote. Nothing more is required.

If it were worth the pains to enter more at large on the subject, it might be observed that the two parts of this drama (the human and superhuman) are very loosely, not to say unskilfully, combined. If the authors ever had a plan, they made good haste to for-

---

takenly terms Luke Hutton's 'Black Dog of Newgate' a play. That there was a drama with this title cannot be doubted: it is mentioned in Henslowe's *Diary* as the authorship of R. Hathway [Day, Smith, and another poet]; but Hutton's tract is quite of a different character, being an attack, in prose and verse, chiefly upon the vices prevalent in London. The supposed author was hanged at York in 1598 for robbery, so that 'The Black Dog of Newgate' must have appeared about that date; and we may presume that it was not penned by Hutton, but by some pamphleteer of the time, who wished to take advantage of the highwayman's notoriety. It was reprinted in 1638, with various changes and some additions, in order to give the work the appearance of novelty. An account of this impression is inserted in the 'Bridgewater Catalogue,' 4to, 1837, p. 149, and a copy of the original edition is in the British Museum."
COLLIER. D.]

get it. Mother Sawyer becomes a witch to revenge herself on Old Banks, who had ill treated her; yet she passes him without injury to wreak her malice on Carter, who had never wronged her, nor even come into contact with her. In addition to which, it may be noticed that not a single circumstance takes place in the serious part which calls for the intervention of supernatural aid. Young Thorney required no instigation to perpetrate any mischief: he carried the fiend (a far more awful demon than the stage could supply) in his own breast, and the meddling of Mother Sawyer's familiar was altogether superfluous. Skilfully disencumbered of this poor traditionary juggling, the fable would form a beautiful whole, and prove one of the most tender and affecting of our domestic tragedies.

It has been observed (p. xvii.) that the poet entertained a high degree of love and respect for his cousin John Ford, of Gray's Inn; and he took the earliest opportunity of showing it, by prefixing his name, with that of one or two others of "his honoured friends of that noble society,"[12] to his first acknowledged piece, *The Lover's Melancholy*. There is an affectation of modesty in the dedication, which, when the writer's age is considered (for he was now in the full maturity of life), might be wished away; and there is something of unsuspicious pleasantry in following up the timely hint "that printing his works might soon grow *out of fashion* with him," by sending *all* his subsequent ones to the press!

[12] Nathaniel Finch, Esq., Mr. Henry Blunt (probably some relation of the Devonshire family), and Mr. Rob. Ellice.

The Lover's Melancholy was published in 1629. It appeared on the stage in the winter of the preceding year; and was probably written not long before, since Burton's popular work, *The Anatomie of Melancholie*, on which the *comic* part (*si Dis placet*) of the story is founded, and to which the title evidently refers, had not been above a year or two, I believe, before the public.

Mr. Campbell speaks favourably of the poetic portion of this play; he thinks, and I fully agree with him, that it has much of the grace and sweetness which distinguish the genius of Ford. It has also somewhat more of the sprightliness in the language of the secondary characters than is commonly found in his plays; and, could we suppose that the idle buffoonery was introduced at a later period, in compliance with the taste of the age, which seems to have found a strange and unnatural delight in the exhibition of these humiliating aberrations of the human mind, we might almost be tempted to surmise that the rest of the drama was of an earlier period than is here set down for it.

Were it my plan to analyse the story of this and the succeeding dramas, and to lengthen-out the introductory matter by extracts, I scarcely know where more favourable specimens of the harmony and unaffected pathos of the writer might be found than in *The Lover's Melancholy*, debased as it is by abortive attempts at humour, and the admission of what the facetious Corax is pleased to term the *Masque of Melancholy*, especially when the author had skilfully presented, in the characters of Meleander and the Prince, two species of melancholy on which the fable hinges, and to which none of the examples introduced from Burton bear the slightest reference. The catastrophe, indeed the whole of the last act, is beautifully written, and exhibits a degree of poetical talent and feeling which few of the dramatic writers of that day surpassed.

Ford had somewhat pettishly observed in the epilogue to this piece, that if it failed to please the audience, he would not trouble them again; and in the same peevish mood he tells his cousin of Gray's Inn, in the dedication, that offering "a play to the reader may soon grow out of fashion with him." He certainly evinced no great degree of earnestness to appear again before the public, as the next play, *'Tis pity she's a Whore*, was not given to the press till nearly four years after the former; when, as if to indemnify himself for his constrained forbearance, he published three of his dramas at short intervals. The present play has neither prologue nor epilogue; but in the dedication to the Earl of Peterborough, who had openly manifested his satisfaction with the piece on its first appearance (when the actors exerted themselves with such success as to call for a separate acknowledgment), Ford terms it "the first-fruits of his leisure." And here, again, we have to lament that indistinctness which everywhere obscures the personal history of the poet. The *first-fruits* of his leisure the play before us could scarcely be; as (to omit all mention of those in which he joined with

Decker) one of his dramas was performed at court nearly twenty years before the date of the present,[13] which bears besides tokens of a mind habituated to deep and solemn musings, and formed by long and severe practice to a style of composition at once ardent and impressive.

The groundwork of this dreadful plot is loosely noticed by Bandello; but it appears, from a note in the last edition of Beaumont and Fletcher (vol. i. p. 239 [179][14]), that the tale is extant in a small collection of French Tales by Rossell [Rosset]; from whom Ford perhaps may have borrowed it. " Rossell [Rosset] relates the story as having actually happened [in France] in the reign of Henry IV." To me, however, it has

---

[13] *An ill Beginning*, &c. See p. xx.

[14] "Histoires Tragiques de notre temps. Paris, 1616. 12mo, p. 174." My attempts to procure this volume, though seconded by the kindness of Mr. Petrie and some other friends, have not proved successful.—[The second edition of *Les Histoires Tragiques de nostre temps, &c., Composées par François de Rosset*, &c., 1615, 12mo, is now before me. The Fifth *Histoire* is entitled "Des amovrs incestueuses d'vn frere et d'vne sœur, et de leur fin malheureuse et tragique :" but though Ford may probably have read it, there are no particular resemblances between it and the play. According to the novel, the guilty pair were the offspring of a gentleman "en vne des meilleures prouinces de France, appellée anciennement Neustrie :" the sister is named Doralice, the brother Lyzaran. The young lady marries a rich old man called Timandre. At last the incestuous lovers "delibererent ensemble du moyen qu'ils pourroient prendre pour iouyr avec plus de liberté de leurs plaisirs. C'est que le lendemain elle prendroit tous ses ioyaux, et puis sur le soir lorsque tout le monde seroit couché, il la monteroit en croupe, et apres cela ils s'en iroient en quelque prouince pour y passer le reste de leurs iours." After wandering about to several places, they take refuge in Paris; where they are arrested, condemned to death, and beheaded : "ce fut en la place de Greue ou l'execution se feit." D.]

not the air of a French adventure. France is not the soil for the production of such fervid and frantic displays of unhallowed desire; her domestic *histoires tragiques*, as far, at least, as they have come under my notice, take their rise principally from avarice and revenge; but I can readily believe that Italy, or even Spain (and Ford has here drawn his characters from both countries), actually furnished materials for the plot, which is laid in Parma, and has not one French name in it.

It is not easy to speak too favourably of the poetry of this play in the more impassioned passages; it is in truth too seductive for the subject, and flings a soft and soothing light over what in its natural state would glare with salutary and repulsive horror.

Somewhat too much indulgence has been shown to the management of the two principal characters: the author has been praised for the skill with which he has marked the progress of their guilt, from the innocence of fraternal intercourse to all the madness of incestuous passion; and said to have "held them up to our admiration at the commencement, the one gifted with every qualification of a generous and philosophical soul, the other interesting for everything which can render a female mind amiable." But is it so? Giovanni comes upon the scene a professed and daring infidel, and, like all other infidels, a fatalist; a shameless avower and justifier of his impure purpose: Annabella is not a jot behind him in precocity of vice, and, as appears from a confession wrung from her with little effort, had long suffered her thoughts to wander in the same polluted path as her brother; and though her conscience, as she subsequently professes, *stood up against her lust*, it was not till the ominous solitude to which she was condemned by her husband convinced her that speedy and fearful vengeance was about to overwhelm her. After all, her repentance is of a very questionable nature; while, on his part, Giovanni continues to accumulate crime on crime till the harassed mind can bear no more.

It is unnecessary to prolong these remarks, as occasional observations on the subject will be found in the notes: it may, however, be added, that the comic characters are simply inoffensive in this drama; a rare merit in our poet.

The Broken Heart was given to the press in the same year as the foregoing piece (1633). It was brought out at the Black Friars; but the date of its appearance is not known. Ford seems to have felt some alarm at the deep tragedy which he was about to develop; and he therefore takes an early opportunity, in the prologue, to inform the audience that the story was a borrowed one, and that "what may be thought a fiction,
   when time's youth
Wanted some riper years, was known a truth."

He could not be so ignorant of history as to suppose that Sparta was ever the scene of a tragedy like this; and he probably means no more than that it was extant in some French or Italian collection of tales.

But whatever may be the groundwork, it must, after all, be admitted that the story derives its main claim on our affections from the poetic powers of the author himself. They are here exerted with wonderful effect: the spell is early laid, and we have scarcely stepped within the circle when we feel the charm too effectual to resist, and abide under it, not without occasional misgivings, till all is dissolved in the awful catastrophe. Ford was not unconscious of its merits; he had, he says [in the prologue], "wrought the piece with the best of his art;" and it will not perhaps be denied that, with respect to the diction, and the deep inherent feeling of the more solemn and tragic scenes, many superior to it will not be found; in truth, it seems scarcely possible to turn back and review the beautiful passages which abound in the three plays of the first volume without placing the author in a very honourable rank among the dramatic writers of his day.

Ford occasionally repeats his characters. The Tecnicus of this drama is an improved copy of the Friar in the preceding one. He is skilfully conceived, and judiciously elevated to the subject: his incidental glances at the moody and ominous meditations of Orgilus prove that the author meant to invest him with something of the prophetic character; and his language, at once pious and monitory, is everywhere worthy of his sacred office. It is observable that both are withdrawn before the catastrophe takes place. In the Friar's case it was undoubtedly a just measure of precaution; but Tecnicus might have witnessed the closing scene with impunity, and even with good effect. He had, however, fairly fulfilled his mission.

The Broken Heart is dedicated (not without the poet's usual glance at his professional industry), in a style highly respectful, yet manly and independent, to the well-known Lord Craven; a nobleman worthy of all praise, and not ill chosen for the patron of a wild, a melancholy, and romantic tale.

The year 1633 must have proved auspicious to our author's fame, for it also gave to the public *Love's Sacrifice*, printed, like the former play, for Hugh Beeston. It appears to have been somewhat of a favourite; and was ushered into the world with more than the usual accompaniments of approbation. That it has many passages of singular merit, many scenes favourable to the display of the writer's powers beautifully executed, it is impossible to deny; but the plot is altogether defective; and the characters proceed from error to error, and from crime to crime, till they exhaust their own interest, and finally expire without care or pity. In the last exquisite drama, the lighter characters, though ill calculated to please, may yet be tolerated; but in this they are gratuitously odious and repellent.

Something, perhaps, should be attributed to the country from which the poet derived his plot (for I have no doubt that it is taken from an Italian novel), and something indulged to the ill-defined manners and language of the age, which, though strictly speaking not licentious, were little polished by the collision of good society, which, indeed, could then be scarcely said to exist. Our poet, however, entertained no misgivings of this kind; he seems, on the contrary, to have been pleased with the management of the story (which, as the title-page informs us, was generally well received); and, as a proof of his satisfaction, dedicates it to "his truest friend and worthiest cousin," John Ford, of Gray's Inn, in a short address highly creditable to his amiable qualities, and full of respectful gratitude and affection. The year before this was written, the indefatigable Prynne had published his ponderous *Histriomastix;* in which he collected and reproduced, with increased bitterness and rancour, all his former invectives against the stage: to this Ford adverts with becoming warmth. "The contempt," he says, "thrown on studies of this kind by such as dote on their own singularity hath almost so outfaced invention and proscribed judgment, that it is more safe, more wise to be suspectedly silent than modestly confident of opinion herein." In this he is supported by Shirley, who has a complimentary poem prefixed to *Love's Sacrifice;* in which, after reproaching Prynne with his *voluminous* ignorance and impudence, he calls upon him to read Ford's tragedy, and then turn to his own interminable farrago, which he had not only termed "the actors' *tragedy*," as if in scorn of them, but divided into acts and scenes.

The admirers of Ford had by this time apparently *supped full of horrors.* Three tragedies of the deepest kind, in rapid succession, were probably as many as the stage would then endure from him; and in an hour not unpropitious to his reputation he turned his thoughts to the historical drama of his own country. *Perkin Warbeck*, which appeared in 1634, and which was accompanied with more than the usual proportion of commendatory verses,[15] is dedicated to the Earl (better known as the Duke) of Newcastle, in a strain which shows that the poet was fully sensible of the " worthiness" as well as the difficulty of the subject, which he had spared no pains to overcome. It is observed, in a critical notice of this drama which appeared in 1812, that "though the subject of it is such as to preclude the author from the high praise of original invention and fancy," a circumstance which he himself notices in the very opening of his dedication, "the play is so admirably conducted, so adorned with poetic sentiment and expression, so full of fine discrimination of character and affecting incidents, that we cannot" (continue the critics) " help regarding that audience as greatly disgraced which, having once witnessed its representation, did not insure its perpetuity on the English stage. If any" (historic) " play in the language can induce us to admit the lawfulness of a comparison with Shakespeare, it is this."[16] There is little to add to this commendation, and I am not aware that much can be taken away from it. It may, however, be observed, that the language of this piece is temperately but uniformly raised; it neither bursts

---

[15] Among them are a few lines from John Ford, of Gray's Inn, who thus returns the kindness with which his cousin had inscribed *Love's Sacrifice* to him.

[16] *Monthly Review.*

into the enthusiasm of passion, nor degenerates into uninteresting whining, but supports the calm dignity of historic action, and accords with the characters of the "graced persons" who occupy the scene.

I have elsewhere noticed the uncommon felicity with which Ford has sustained the part of Warbeck: he could scarcely believe the identity of this youth with the young prince, yet he never permits a doubt of it to escape him, and thus skilfully avoids the awkwardness of shaking the credit and diminishing the interest of his chief character; for Perkin, and not Henry, is the hero of the play. More will be found in the notes on this subject; but it may be added here, that the king was probably less indebted to his armoury than to his craft and his coffers for the suppression of these attempts, which occasionally assumed a very threatening aspect: even the ill-judged attack on the coast, feeble as it undoubtedly was, created a considerable degree of alarm; and it appears from a letter to Sir John Paston,[17] "that a mightie aid of help and succor" was earnestly requested to secure the towns of Sandwich and Yarmouth.

Notwithstanding the warm commendations of his friends on this production, Ford did not renew his acquaintance with the Historic Muse; nor, on the other hand, did he return to the deep and impassioned tone of the preceding dramas. He appears to have fostered the more cheerful feeling which he had recently indulged, and to have adopted a species of serious comedy, which should admit of characters and

[17] *Fenn's Letters*, vol. v. p. 427.

events well fitted for the display of the particular bent of his genius. He was not in haste, however, to court the public; for nothing is heard of him till 1638 (with the single exception of a warm eulogium to the "memory of the best of poets, Ben Jonson," who died in the preceding year), when he published *The Fancies Chaste and Noble*. The date of its first appearance on the stage is not known, but it probably did not long precede its being given to the press. The play is dedicated to the well-known Earl (afterwards Marquis) of Antrim. And here again Ford asserts that his "courtship of greatness" never aimed at any pecuniary advantage. Granted; but he forgets that he had no need of it; and there is something in this implied triumph over his necessitous contemporaries, which, to say the best of it, is to be praised neither for its generosity nor its delicacy.

The poet takes to himself the merit of constructing this comedy with original materials: there is nothing in it, he says, but what he knows to be his own, "without a learned theft." There must surely have been a pretty general notion of Ford's adopting the practice of the dramatic writers of his day, and founding his plots on Spanish or rather Italian fables, to render these frequent abjurations necessary; and when we compare the prologue of *The Lover's Melancholy* with the conduct of that piece, we shall not be inclined to understand such expressions too strictly. If it be as he says, we can only regret that what was conceived with considerable ingenuity, and afforded ample scope for an interesting and amusing story, should produce so little effect. After all, the fable is so probable, when told of a Transalpine magnifico, that I can scarcely avoid thinking Ford found some hint, something analogous to his plot, among the Italian novels of those days. We have a very inadequate idea of the solicitude with which the dramatic and romantic treasures of Spain and Italy were sought for and circulated in this country. The literary intercourse was then far more alive than it is at present, for there were many readers and many translators at hand to furnish them with a succession of novelties; and, though it must be admitted, I fear, that the exchange ran grievously against us—that we imported much, and sent out little,—yet the bare labour of working-up what we received had, as in other cases, a salutary and quickening effect. Meanwhile, I am persuaded that far the greater number of our dramas are founded on Italian novels. This would, perhaps, scarcely be a matter of debate at this time, were it not for the fire of 1666, which destroyed, beyond hope of recovery, no inconsiderable portion of the light and fugitive literature of the preceding age. In the wide and deep vaults under St. Paul's lay thousands and ten thousands of pamphlets, novels, romances, histories, plays, printed and in manuscript; all the amusement and all the satire of Nash and Harvey, of Lodge and Peele and Greene, and innumerable others, which even then made up the principal part of the humble libraries of the day. Here they had been placed for security; and here, when the roof of the cathedral fell in, and the burning beams broke through the floor, they were involved in one general and dreadful conflagration.

I would not willingly be suspected of deeming too lightly of this drama : it is the plot in which I think the poet has failed; the language of the serious parts is deserving of high praise, and the more prominent characters are skilfully discriminated and powerfully sustained. The piece, however, has no medium; all that is not excellent is intolerably bad.

In the prologue to *The Fancies* the poet makes the only allusion to his native county which appears in any part of his works;

" if traduc'd by some,
'Tis well, he says, he's far enough from *home.*"[18]

The succeeding year (1639) gave to the public *The Lady's Trial*, which, it appears, had been performed in May 1638. It is dedicated, in the spirit of true kindness, to Mr. and Mrs. Wyrley; and the poet, though now near the close of his dramatic labours, has not yet conquered his fear of misemploying his time, or rather of being suspected of it, and assures his partial friends that the piece which he has thus placed under their *tuition* is the "issue of some *less serious* hours." There seems but little occasion for this; his patrons must have known enough of his personal concerns to render such apologies unnecessary.

[18] I once thought—or rather, without thinking, followed the prevailing opinion—that Ford was now on his travels: the words quoted prove that this could not be, as the poet speaks in his own person. He probably alludes to the old manor-house at Ilsington, which, though in a dilapidated state, is still standing. It was built as early as Elizabeth's reign.

At fifty-two—and Ford had now reached that age—his professional industry could surely be no subject of doubt; and it requires some little portion of forbearance in the general reader to tolerate this affected and oft-repeated depreciation of the labour to which the genius and inclination of the writer perpetually tended, and overlook the wanton abasement of his own claims to fame.

The Lady's Trial, like *The Fancies*, declines in interest towards the conclusion, in consequence of the poet's imperfect execution of his own plan: that he meditated a more impressive catastrophe for both is sufficiently apparent, but event comes huddling on event, and all is precipitation, weakness, and confusion. It is curious that in the winding-up of each of these pieces the same expedient is employed; and the honour of Adurni in the former, like that of Troylo in the latter, ultimately vindicated by an unlooked-for marriage. Feeble and imperfect, however, as the plot of *The Lady's Trial* is, and trifling as some of the characters will be found, it is not destitute of passages which the lovers of our ancient drama may contemplate with unreproved pleasure.

There is nothing in the dedication, or in the prologue and epilogue to this play, that indicates the slightest inclination of the poet to withdraw from the stage: on the contrary, his mind seems to have attained a cheerful tone and a sprightlier language; yet this was apparently the last of his dramatic labours, and here he suddenly disappears from view.

Much as has been said of the dramatic poets of Elizabeth and James's days, full justice has never yet been rendered to their independence on one another: generally speaking, they stand insulated and alone, and draw, each in his station, from their own stores. Whether it be that poetry in that age

"Wanton'd as in its prime, and play'd at will
Its virgin fancies"—

or that some other fruitful cause of originality was in secret and powerful operation; so it is, that every writer had his peculiar style, and was content with it. At present, we are become an imitative, not to say a mimic, race. A successful poem, a novel, nay even a happy title-page, is eagerly caught at, and a kind of *ombre chinoise* representation of it propagated from one extremity of the kingdom to the other. Invention seems almost extinct among us. That it does not somewhere exist, it would be folly to imagine; but it appears to move, comet-like, in very eccentric orbits, and to have its periods of occultation of more than usual duration. It may, and undoubtedly will, revisit us; meanwhile, as the knight of the enchanted cavern judiciously advises, *patience, and shuffle the cards!*

I have been led into these desultory remarks notwithstanding it may be urged that an exception to the subject of them may be found in Ford. He appears to have discovered, indeed, that one of the nameless charms of Shakespeare's diction consisted in the skill with which he has occasionally vivified it by converting his substantives into verbs; and to have aspired to imitate him. He cannot be complimented on his success; nor, indeed, can much be expected without such a portion of Shakespeare's taste and feeling as it seems almost hopeless to expect:—Ford's grammatical experiments take from the simplicity of his diction, while they afford no strength whatever to his descriptions. Not so with the great original: in his conversions all is life. Take, for example, the following passage. It is not a description that we read; it is a series of events that we hear and see:

> "the quick comedians
> Extemporally will *stage* us, and present
> Our Alexandrian revels; Antony
> Shall be brought drunken forth, and I shall see
> Some squeaking Cleopatra *boy* my greatness
> I' th' posture of a whore."

With this slight exception, which, after all, may be purely visionary, the style of Ford is altogether original and his own. Without the majestic march which distinguishes the poetry of Massinger, and with little or none of that light and playful humour which characterises the dialogue of Fletcher, or even of Shirley, he is yet elegant and easy and harmonious; and though rarely sublime, yet sufficiently elevated for the most pathetic tones of that passion on whose romantic energies he chiefly delighted to dwell. It has (as has been observed) its inherent beauties and defects: among the latter of which may be set down a pedantic affectation of novelty, at one time exhibited in the composition of uncouth phrases, at another (and this is Ford's principal failure) in perplexity of language; frequently too, after perversely labouring with a remote idea till he has confused his meaning, instead of throwing it aside, he obtrudes it upon the reader involved in inextricable obscurity.

Its excellencies, however, far outweigh its defects; but they are rather felt than understood. I know few things more difficult to account for than the deep and lasting impression made by the more tragic portions of Ford's poetry. Whence does it derive that resistless power which all confess, of afflicting, I had almost said harassing, the better feelings? It is not from any peculiar beauty of language,—for in this he is equalled by his contemporaries, and by some of them surpassed; nor is it from any classical or mythological allusions happily recollected and skilfully applied,—for of these he seldom avails himself: it is not from any picturesque views presented to the mind,—for of imaginative poetry he has little or nothing; he cannot conjure up a succession of images, whether grave or gay, to flit across the fancy or play in the eye. Yet it is hardly possible to peruse his passionate scenes without the most painful interest, the most heart-thrilling delight. This can only arise—at least I can conceive nothing else adequate to the excitement of such sensations—from the overwhelming efficacy of intense thought devoted to the embodying of conceptions adapted to the awful situations in which he has, imperceptibly and with matchless felicity, placed his principal characters.

Mr. Campbell observes, that Ford interests us in no other passion than that of *love;* "in which he displays a peculiar depth and delicacy of romantic feeling." Comparatively speaking, this may be admitted; but in justice to the poet it should be added, that he was not insensible to the power of *friendship*, and in more than one of his dramas has delineated it with a master-hand. Had the critic forgotten the noble Dalyell, the generous and devoted Malfato? Nor can it justly be inferred (even setting aside the romantic feelings here alluded to) that the female characters of his second-rate pieces fail to interest us, and occasionally in a high degree, in affections and passions very distinct from those of love. Mr. Campbell, however, terms him "one of the ornaments of our ancient poetry."

So many remarks are incidentally scattered through these pages on the nature of our poet's plots, that little more seems called for here than to remark that in the construction, or rather perhaps in the selection, of his fables there is usually much to commend: like Kent, indeed, he possessed the faculty of *marring a plain tale in the telling;* but this is only saying, in other words, that he planned better than he executed. His besetting error was an unfortunate persuasion that he was gifted with a certain degree of pleasantry, with which it behoved him occasionally to favour the stage; and to this we are indebted for the intrusion of those ill-timed underplots, and those prurient snatches of language, which debase and pollute several of his best dramas. It saddens the heart to see a man, from whom nature has withheld all perception of the tones and attitudes of humour, labouring with all his might to be airy and playful; and it is impossible to contemplate Ford under this strange infatuation without being reminded of the poor maniacs in *The Masque of Corax*, to whom many of the characters that figure in his idle buffooneries might be introduced without ceremony. It is not pleasant to dwell on these defects, though justice requires that they should be noticed. Time has long since avenged them: for it can scarcely be doubted that somewhat of the obscurity into which the poet has fallen should be laid to their charge.

But Ford is *not all alone unhappy*. In his day there was, in fact, no model to work after. The elements of composition, as far as regards taste and judgment, far from being established, were not even arranged; and with the exception of Sir Philip Sidney's *Essay*, nothing can be more jejune and unsatisfactory than the few attempts at poetic criticism then before the public. Add to this, that the scale of ethic as well as of poetic fitness seems to have had few gradations marked on it, and those at remote and uncertain distances; hence the writers suddenly drop from all that is pure in taste and exquisite in feeling to whining imbecility, and from high-toned sentiment and ennobling action to all that is mean and vicious, apparently unconscious of the vast interval through which they have passed, and the depth to which they have fallen. In other respects, they all seem to have acquiesced in the humble station in which prejudice had placed them,[19] and instead of attempting to correct the age, to have sought little more than to in-

[19] See p. xiii.

terest and amuse with the materials so richly provided for them by the extraordinary times on which they were cast. One man[20] indeed there was, one eminent man, who sought from early life to enlist the stage on the side of learning and virtue, and called on the people to view the scene in its genuine light;

> "Attirèd in the majesty of art,
> Set high in spirit with the precious taste
> Of sweet philosophy, and, which is most,
> Crown'd with the rich traditions of a soul
> That hates to have her dignity profan'd
> With any relish of an earthly thought."

But he found few supporters, and no followers; and the stage went on as before; attended, but not honoured; popular, but not influential.

It is not a little mortifying to reflect, that while dramatic poetry *towered in its pride of place*, and long sustained itself at an elevation which it will never reach again, the writers themselves possessed no sway whatever over the feelings of the people; while at a subsequent period, when the power of the stage for good and evil was understood, it was turned wholly to the purposes of the latter, and the greatest men of the age formed themselves into factions for trash that would not now be heard, and names that cannot be pronounced without scorn and shame, that depravity of every kind might be transmitted from the court to the stage, from the stage to the people, and none escape the contagion. And who was the Choragus of this pernicious band? Let Cibber tell. "In this almost general corruption, *Dryden*, whose plays were

---

[20] i.e. Ben Jonson. D.

more famed for their wit than their chastity, led the way; which he fairly confesses, and endeavours to excuse, in his epilogue to *The Pilgrim*, revived in 1700 for his benefit in his declining age and fortune."[20]

Langbaine supposes Ford [and Decker] to be dead when *The Sun's Darling*[21] was published, by Bird and Penneycuicke, in 1657 [see vol. iii. p. 102]. He probably had no better authority than an expression in the dedication, that "the piece was an orphan one." It may, however, be so, for at this period he would have passed his seventieth year; but this still leaves a considerable interval in his history during which nothing is heard of him. Of Decker's decease there can be little doubt; he talks of himself as a worn-out old man in the dedication to *Match me in London*, published in 1631, when Ford was only in his forty-fifth year. "I have been," he says, "a priest in Apollo's temple many years; my voice is decaying with my age," &c. Why it is so generally assumed that our poet died almost immediately after the appearance of *The Lady's Trial*, except that he ceased to write, I have never been able to conjecture. Faint traditions in the neighbourhood of his birthplace lead rather to the supposition that, having from his legal pursuits acquired a sufficient fortune, he retired to his home, to pass the remainder

---

[20] Cibber's *Life*, p. 219, ed. 1750. Such as desire to see what Cibber calls his "excuse" may turn to the passage. For an old man of seventy, it is a very gracious plea. Dryden died a few months after this.

[21] *The Sun's Darling*] Here Gifford carelessly prints "*The Witch of Edmonton.*"—See Langbaine's *Account of the Engl. Dram. Poets*, 1691, p. 222. D.

of his days among the youthful connections whom time had yet spared him.[22]

Nor were there wanting powerful motives for the retirement of one of Ford's lonely and contemplative mood, who watched the signs of the times. Deep and solemn notes of preparation for a tragedy far more terrible than aught the stage could show were audible in the distance; and hollow mutterings, which could not be mistaken, told that the tempest was gathering round the metropolis with fearful acceleration. It is possible that he may have foreseen the approaching storm, and fled from the first efforts of its violence,[23]

> "Apparent diræ facies, inimicaque Trojæ Numina."

The Covenanters were already in arms, and advancing towards the Borders; and at home the stern and uncompromising enemies of all that was graceful and delightful were rapidly ascending in the scale of power.

Of what nature Ford's chief employment at the Temple was we have no means of ascertaining. That he was not called to the bar may be fairly surmised, as he never makes the slightest allusion to his pleadings; and his anxious disavowals to his several patrons

---

[22] I looked into Mr. Carrington's poem on Dartmoor with the hope of finding some memorial of the poet. All that this gentleman says, is; "At Bagtor is a seat of Lord Ashburton, with woods, where was born, in 1586, John Ford, the dramatic writer, whence sprung the family of the same name and place." *Notes, Poems*, vol. i. p. 130.

[23] It fell, indeed, soon after with fatal fury on the dramatic writers. The theatres were closed in 1641.

INTRODUCTION.

of permitting his dramatic labours to encroach upon his proper business, would almost lead to a conclusion that he acted as a kind of auditor or comptroller for the landed property of the nobility, and managed the pecuniary concerns of their estates, for which his knowledge of the law afforded facility on the one side, and security on the other.

Of his social habits there little can be told with certainty. There is sufficient, however, to show that he lived, if not familiarly, yet friendlily, with the dramatic writers of his day, and neither provoked nor felt personal enmities. He speaks, indeed, of opposition; but this is merely the language of the stage; opposition is experienced by every dramatic writer worth criticism, and has nothing in common with ordinary hostility. In truth, with the exception of an allusion to the "voluminous" and rancorous Prynne, nothing can be more general than his complaints. Yet Ford looked not much to the brighter side of life; he could, like Jaques, "suck melancholy out of a song as a weasel sucks eggs;" but he was unable, like this wonderful creation of our great poet, to extract mirth from it. When he touched a lighter string, the tones, though pleasingly modulated, were still sedate; and it must, I think, be admitted that his poetry is rather that of a placid and serene than of a happy mind: he was, in truth, an amiable ascetic amidst a busy world.

Something of this may be attributed to his parents. To take a moody youth from his classical studies, or from his first terms at college, and plunge him at once into the moping drudgery of the law, is not, perhaps, the most approved recipe for enlivening him, especially if he happens also to have fallen in love; and thus our poet's retired and gloomy turn may in some measure be accounted for; but, exclusively of this, it seems clear that

> " Nature in his soul
> Put something of the raven."

In the *Time's Poets*, the first and almost the only place in which he is noticed by his contemporaries,[24] it is said,

> " Deep in a dump John Forde was alone got [gat?],
> With folded arms and melancholy hat."

These "signs of the judicious," as Shirley calls them,

---

[24] In a doggerel list, by Heywood [in his *Hierarchie of the blessed Angels*, 1635, lib. iv. p. 206], of the familiar appellations by which the writers for the stage were known among their acquaintance, he says of our poet;

" And hee's now but *Jacke* Foord, that once was John."*

One word with respect to this disputed name. I inquired of my old friend Mr. Palk, if that which he copied for Mr. Malone was without an *e* final? The answer was in the affirmative. Little, undoubtedly, can be concluded from this, when the lax mode of spelling in that age is considered; but the anagram which is seen on several of the title-pages of Ford's plays—FIDE HONOR—appears to me more like the impress on the armorial bearing of the family than a proud claim set forward by the poet. I am not skilled enough in the mysteries of this profound science to know whether its hierophants admitted of an extra symbol; but, in common parlance, a letter more or less weighs little with our old writers, few of whom could spell their own names correctly, and still fewer followed any standard.

---

* Heywood is singular in his spelling of our poet's name. But Gifford, with his usual unendurable incorrectness of quotation, gives the line thus ;

" And he's *but now Jacke Ford, who* once was John." D.

were undoubtedly assumed by many who, like Master Stephen, aspired to look fashionable as well as wise; but Ford had apparently no affectation of this kind, and they must therefore be taken as genuine indications of his humour. His love of seclusion is here noticed—he was *alone*.

No village anecdotes are told of him, as of his countryman Herrick, nor do any memorials of his private life remain. The troubles which followed, and the confusion which frequently took place in the parish-registers in consequence of the intrusion of ministers little interested in local topics, have flung a veil of obscurity over much of the domestic history of that turbulent and disastrous period. In these troubles the retreat of the Fords is known to have largely shared; and it is more than probable that the family suffered under the Usurpation. The neighbourhood was distinguished for its loyalty; and many of the fugitives who escaped from the field after the overthrow of Lord Wentworth at Bovey-Tracy by Cromwell, unfortunately for the village, took refuge in Ilsington church, whither they were pursued and again driven to flight by the victorious army.

There is no appearance of Ford's being married at the period of his retirement from the Temple, as none of his dedications or addresses make the slightest allusion to any circumstance of a domestic nature; it is probable, therefore, that he *accommodated* himself with a wife at Ilsington. If he withdrew, as I have supposed, about 1639, he was then in his fifty-third year,—no very auspicious period, it must be allowed, for venturing on a matrimonial connection, and yet no uncommon one for those who, like himself, have devoted their time to the arduous and absorbing profession of the law. Be this as it may, there is, or rather was, an indistinct tradition among his neighbours that he married and had children. The cruelty of the flinty Lycia could now affect him but little, as she was probably herself a grandmother; but a person of our poet's character and fortune had not far to seek for a worthy partner, and with such a one it is pleasing to hope that he spent the residue of his blameless and honourable life.

None of his descendants, however, are specified, but Sir Henry Ford (Secretary for Ireland in the reign of Charles II.), who is traditionally reported to be the poet's grandson, or rather son, and in whom, be he who he will (for I suspect that he was òf a more remote branch), the property of the family eventually centered. Sir Henry left no family; and with him, who died in 1684, terminated the line of the Fords, and the property was dispersed. Much of it fell by purchase to Egerton Falconer, Esq., whose descendants held it till within a few years of the present period, when it passed altogether into the hands of strangers.

All that now remain of this once opulent and respectable name are a little charity-school founded at Ashburton by a Mr. John Ford, who endowed it with a few pounds a year for a master "to teach reading and writing;" and a small parcel of land of the annual value of twenty pounds, bequeathed to the parish of Ilsington by a Mrs. Jane Ford, for "instructing the

children of the poor, and for the purchase of Bibles."
What's property, dear Swift?—

It is said by Winstanley that Ford's plays were profitable to the managers. It might be so; though Winstanley, as Langbaine justly observes, is not the best authority for this or any other fact relative to the stage. They seem, however, not to have found many readers, since few if any of them ever reached a second edition. True it is that the civil commotions supplied other employment for men's minds about the close of Ford's dramatic career; but he could at no period of his life have been a popular writer. Not the slightest mention of his name occurs in Wright's excellent Dialogue on the old stage; nor does it once appear in the long lists of Downes the prompter, when, upon the Restoration, the repositories of the playhouses were ransacked for dramas to gratify the rising passion for theatrical performances. Once, and but once, he is mentioned by Pepys (an unwearied frequenter of the stage), who witnessed the representation of *The Lady's Trial*.[25] I have not Pepys before me at this instant, and may therefore have mistaken the piece: whatever it was, however, he passes it over with perfect indifference. From this period (1669) nothing farther is heard of the poet till the year 1714, when an absurd attempt was made to overthrow the Pretender's hopes by a reprint of *Perkin Warbeck!*

[25] Pepys's words are; "March 3, 1668-9. To the Duke of York's playhouse, and there saw an old play, the first time acted these forty years, called 'The Lady's Tryall,' acted only by the young people of the house; but the house very full." D.

and again, in 1745,[26] when, with similar wisdom and similar expectations, that play was brought out at Goodman's Fields!

From this period (with the exception of Macklin's despicable forgery, which took place in 1748), the dramatic works of Ford, together with his name, relapsed into obscurity. He is not mentioned by Mr. G. Ellis nor by Mr. Headley. At length, however, he appears to have attracted the notice of Mr. C. Lamb, who, in his *Specimens of Dramatic Authors*, gave several extracts of considerable length from his best pieces: and to the elaborate and somewhat metaphysical eulogium which was subjoined to one of them, my ingenious friend, Mr. O. Gilchrist,[27] attributed his being finally thought worthy of a reprint.

The person selected by the booksellers for this purpose was Mr. Henry Weber. It would be curious to learn the motives of this felicitous choice. Mr. Weber had never read an old play in his life; he was but imperfectly acquainted with the language; and of the manners, customs, habits—of what was and what was not familiar to us as a nation—he possessed no knowledge whatever; but, secure in ignorance, he entertained a comfortable opinion of himself, and never doubted that he was qualified to instruct and enliven the public. With Ford's quartos, therefore, and a wallet containing Cotgrave's *French Dictionary*, *The Variorum Edition of Shakespeare*, and Dodsley's *Col-*

---

[26] *'Tis pity she's a Whore* had, however, been given to the public the year before by Dodsley.

[27] Letter, &c. p. 15.

lection of Old Plays, he settled himself to his appointed task, and in due time produced the two volumes now before the public, much to the delight of "the judicious admirers of our ancient drama," and so entirely to the satisfaction of his employers, that they wisely resolved to lose no time in securing his valuable services for an edition of Beaumont and Fletcher.

All, however, did not quite agree with "the judicious admirers of the ancient drama" respecting the value of Mr. Weber's labours. In particular, Mr. Octavius Gilchrist, whose memory will long be cherished by the sincere inquirer after truth, for the vigorous and successful stand which he made against the base attacks of the Shakespeare commentators on the moral character of Jonson, came once more forward in the same cause, and was again triumphant.[28]

Mr. Weber seems to have relied for the success of his undertaking not so much on the merits of his author as on the exposition (for the hundredth time) of the "*bitter enmity* of Ben Jonson towards him on account of his close intimacy with Shakespeare." Obtuse as the optics of this person were, they were keen

[28] This gentleman, whom, with Mr. Roscoe, I lament to call "the *late* ingenious Mr. Gilchrist," had not reached the meridian of life when he fell a sacrifice to some consumptive complaint which had long oppressed him. His last labour of love was an attempt to rescue Pope from the rancorous persecution of his editor, the Rev. Mr. Bowles. I know not why this doughty personage gives himself such airs of superiority over Mr. Gilchrist; nor why, unless from pure taste, he clothes them in a diction not often heard out of the purlieus of St. Giles. Mr. Gilchrist was a man of strict integrity; and in the extent and accuracy of his critical knowledge and the patient industry of his researches, as much superior to the Rev. Mr. Bowles as in good manners.

enough to discover that abuse of Jonson, however hackneyed, was still a saleable commodity; and, as recent examples powerfully proved, if seasoned with an additional sprinkling of falsehood and malignity, thankfully received by the public, and *no questions asked*. On this hint *Mr. Weber* spake. He manifests a visible impatience to reach the main subject of his work; and accordingly he has hardly entered upon the Introduction before he brings from *The Variorum Shakespeare* all the baffled trash which Steevens had raked together for a particular purpose; though, as Mr. Gilchrist justly observes, "after its complete overthrow by such a determined champion of Shakespeare as Mr. Malone, it certainly required more than ordinary intrepidity to repeat imputations already refuted, and [in pretended confirmation of them] refer to documents [proofs] which have not, nor ever had, existence."[29]

I have no wish to afflict the reader with the details of this scandalous transaction, and shall therefore merely observe that Macklin, who in 1745 was alike ignorant of Ford and his works (see v. ii. p. 110), shortly became so familiar with both, that in 1748 he fixed upon one of his plays (*The Lover's Melancholy*) for his wife's benefit. As the piece was new to the town, Macklin inserted a letter in *The General Advertiser*, dilating on its surprising merits, which are fully accounted for by the "close intimacy that subsisted between the author and Shakespeare, as appears from several of Ford's sonnets and verses"! As the public did not appear to interest themselves much in this

[20] Letter to W. Gifford, p. 24.

connection, a new stimulant was found necessary. The performance was put off for a week, during which Macklin laboriously exerted himself in fabricating a libel against Jonson, of whom he had not even thought before, in which every calumny that avarice, working on ignorance and impudence, could devise, is brought forward against an innocent man, for the unworthy purpose of disposing of a few additional tickets.[30]

The reader may wonder, perhaps, why this ex-

---

[30] If the reader wishes for more on this subject, let him have the goodness to turn to the introductory remarks on *The New Inn* (*Jonson*, vol. v. p. 314), where sufficient to gratify his curiosity will be found in a connected narrative.

It has not been observed that this republication of Macklin's forgeries might lead in some degree to the fabrications of "young Master Ireland." Macklin, who only wanted his trick to succeed for a night or two, was satisfied with *referring* to "Ford's Sonnets and Poems" as a convincing proof that he lived in strict friendship with Shakespeare; but his more enterprising follower, who saw a fair prospect of raising a fortune on the gullibility of *this great lubber, the town*, prudently chose to take the Shakesperian papers ("Sonnets and Poems and Plays") into his own hands, and bequeath them, in the name of the great poet, to an ancestor of his own—a certain W. H. Ireland, Esq., who, like Ford, "lived in strict friendship with Shakespeare," and was intrusted with the care of his Mss.!

It is mortifying to look back a few years to this disgraceful event, and to see George Chalmers fighting knee-deep in authorities for the authenticity of this most ridiculous stuff; and Dr. Parr on his knees reverently kissing a vulgar scrawl dangling from a dirty piece of red tape, with Dr. Warton close behind him!*

It is still more mortifying to reflect that had this youth, who was a poor illiterate creature, possessed but a single grain of prudence, and known when and where to stop, his worthless forgeries might at this moment be visited by anniversary crowds of devoted pilgrims, in some splendid shrine set apart in his father's house for these pious purposes.

* See "H. Ireland's Confessions."

ploded stuff was admitted into *The Variorum*. It may be easily explained. In reprinting the "Commendatory Poems" on Shakespeare, it became necessary to commence with that of Jonson "to the memory of his beloved friend:" a panegyric, be it said, which was not only the first in date, but which, in warmth of affection and judicious and zealous praise, is worth all that has since appeared on the subject. To leave Jonson with the impression of this most cordial testimony to the talents and virtues of our great poet on the reader's mind was death to Steevens; and he had hardly patience to copy the last word of it before he again burst forth: "What you have just seen is mere hypocrisy; I will now show you Jonson's *real* sentiments:" and accordingly he brings forward the forgeries of Macklin from some old newspapers, where they had lain covered with dust for nearly half a century, "without *entertaining*," as Mr. Weber is pleased to assure us (Introduction, p. xxiv.), "*any suspicion* of their authenticity"!

I have elsewhere called Steevens the *Puck of Commentators;* and I know not that I could have described him more graphically. Yet in this, strict justice, I fear, is hardly done to Puck. Both delighted to mislead, and both enjoyed the fruits of their mischievous activity; but the frank and boisterous laugh, the jolly hoh! hoh! hoh! of the fairy hobgoblin degenerated in his follower to a cold and malignant grin, which he retired to his cell to enjoy alone. Steevens was an acute and apprehensive mind, cankered by envy and debased.

With respect to the *credulity* of this subdolous spirit, for the *sincerity* of which the undoubting Mr. Weber so freely vouches, there is not a syllable of truth in it. Mr. Malone assured me, over and over, that Steevens did not believe one word of it. The last conversation which I had with this gentleman (which took place as we were walking in Piccadilly) turned upon this very subject, when he repeated his assurances; adding that Steevens, exclusively of other causes, espoused the forgery with the insidious hope of deceiving others. With Mr. Malone, who, as he frankly confesses, was prompt to believe the worst of Jonson, he was completely successful at first; but before he could avail himself of his triumph his colleague anticipated his discovery, and with the assistance of Whalley and a few well-ascertained facts and dates, exposed at once the ignorance and impudence of this malicious fabrication.

Had Mr. Weber contented himself with simply copying his predecessor's calumnies, though he would not have gained much as an author, he might have escaped censure; but this was not enough for his ambition; he saw how little was required to insult a man of integrity, learning, and genius, and he aspired to the honour of adding his name to the long list of Jonson's persecutors, and fabricating new charges against him. Could he be suspected of reading the works on which he has been occasionally employed, it might be thought that he had adopted, with regard to Jonson, as too many others have done, the advice and opinion of the old romancer;

> " Hew off his honde, his legge, his theye, his armys :
> *It is the Turk!*—though he be sleyn, noon harm is !"

It is but Jonson !

Here, however, Mr. Weber's better Genius forsook him; for his additional violation of truth called forth that "Letter" to which I have so often alluded, and levelled the whole of his audacious calumnies in the dust. What Mr. Weber thought of this detection of his falsehood, this exposure of his ignorance, is only known to his inmates. To justify himself was impossible; and signals of distress were therefore thrown out on every side ;

> "forthwith to his aid was run"

by some of his early friends; one of whom did everything that kindness could suggest, and prepared a species of apology (defence there could be none), which was subsequently inserted in the prefatory matter and in the notes to the last edition of Beaumont and Fletcher.

The sequel of this transaction is curious. The whole of Macklin, which occupies so large a part of Mr. Weber's Introduction, together with "the authentic documents" in Mr. Weber's possession of the tender friendship of Ford and Shakespeare, and the consequent envy of "the malignant Ben ;" in a word, every syllable of the charge as far as relates to the latter, is flung overboard without ceremony ! Instead, however, of regretting his injustice, and expressing somewhat like contrition for the daring falsehood which he had advanced and the calumnies he had fabricated, the editor returns to the attack, and is permitted by his ill-advised friends to look back thirty years for a proof of Jonson's enmity—not to Ford, but—to Shakespeare! "in *that strong* passage in *The Return from Parnassus* (1606)" which forms the only blot in Shakespeare's character, as it exhibits him wantonly joining a rabble of obscure actors in persecuting Jonson, who was struggling for existence, and who had not offended him even in thought. So besotted is malice!

The note will now be changed, and with an air of affected commiseration I shall be asked—for old experience in these perversities has endued me with *something like prophetic strain*—why, with the sentiments which I am known to entertain of the commentator, I have "condescended"—blessings on the phrase!—to notice him at length? or why, indeed, at all? I reply in the very words which I once heard Macklin himself make use of: they cannot be much praised for their courtesy, it must be admitted; but Macklin was not courteous;

> "I'll not answer that:
> But say it is my humour; is it answer'd?"

Reproof, indeed, does not always profit the object of it; nor is it expected that it should: for what censor was ever vain or mad enough to suppose that he could reform a detractor without feeling, a scribbler without shame! But the example is not lost on others; and on this consideration alone interference is fully justified. It is not, it never can be good, that petulance should find immunity in its wantonness, or malevolence in its excess; and setting aside dramatic criticism for the moment, there are other departments of literature in which the seasonable exposure of the stupendous ears of a *maître âne* (a Hunt or a Hazlitt, for example) frequently relieves the public from the wearisome braying of a drove of less audacious brutes.

And on what particular ground is Mr. Weber entitled to forbearance? Omitting his calumnies and his falsehoods, his insolence is at least as notorious as his ignorance. In the Introduction to Massinger[31] I spoke of Monck Mason *naso adunco*, as I was abundantly warranted in doing; but that gentleman did not always repose in his disgraceful negligence. He saw his error, acknowledged and reformed it. He studied the old editions of our dramatic writers with care and success, and subsequently became one of the most acute and rational commentators on our great poet. It appears that he also meditated an edition of Beaumont and Fletcher, and had prepared a considerable body of notes to accompany it. The extent of the work alarmed him, and he laid it aside, after sending to the press a great number of emendations and elucidatory remarks creditable at once to his industry and his judgment. These fell, of course, into the hands of Mr. Weber, and constitute the only valuable part of his publication, for his own notes are of the most contemptible kind; yet he has the hardihood to speak of Mr. Monck Mason as if he had never advanced a step beyond his Massinger, and of

[31] See *Mass.* vol. i. p. xcix.

every preceding editor of Beaumont and Fletcher with a contempt that, to say the least of it, strangely misbecomes him. Instances of this might be produced from every page. Assuredly, Simpson and Seward were no great champions in the field of criticism; compared with Mr. Weber, however, they were giants, and worthy to be cited by him without a scoff. We have seen with what contempt he speaks of "old Ben;" but he even presumes to treat Dr. Johnson himself without much more ceremony; he calls him in one place a "literary bugbear," and in another sneers at his "superficial contest" with Mr. Steevens! And here—I know not how—but the name recals a little anecdote to my mind, which, as my best atonement, I am tempted to preserve from oblivion.

My friend the late Lord Grosvenor had a house at Salt-Hill, where I usually spent a part of the summer, and thus became a neighbour of that great and good man, Jacob Bryant, who kindly encouraged me to visit him. Here the conversation turned one morning on a Greek criticism by Dr. Johnson, in some volume lying on the table, which I ventured (for I was then young) to deem incorrect, and pointed it out to him. I could not help thinking that he was somewhat of my opinion; but he was cautious and reserved. "But, sir," said I, willing to overcome his scruples, "Dr. Johnson himself," a fact which Mr. Bryant well knew, "admitted that he was not a good Greek scholar." "Sir," he replied, with a serious and impressive air, "it is not easy for us to say what such a man as Johnson would call a good Greek scholar."

I hope that I profited by the lesson; certainly I never forgot it; and if but one of my readers do the same, I shall not repent placing it upon record.

To return to Ford. The tragedy reprinted by Dodsley had both pleased and interested me; and Isaac Reed, to whom I applied, kindly furnished me with a complete collection of the author's works, so that I was prepared to welcome the new edition; for of Mr. Weber I only knew that he was patronised by two of the most liberal and kindhearted of men, and encouraged to copy and reprint some of our old metrical romances.

A slight glance convinced me that the republication was utterly worthless; and I proceeded, with my habitual regard for truth, and reverence for the literary character of my country, to rescue not the worst of its poets from the ignorance which overlaid him and disgraced the national press. I had no distinct notion of giving an edition of Ford myself at that time, for which, in truth, I had little leisure; but I ceased not to look forward to a period of less responsibility, when it might not be incompatible with my ordinary pursuits, and contented myself in the interim with occasional revises of the original text. Even thus I should perhaps have yielded to the pressure of age and ever-recurring disease, and left the task to others, had I not perceived that the booksellers had profited little by experience, and that our old poetry was still foisted upon the public from the modern copies, without improvement, and, in fact, without knowledge: it was therefore morally certain that a reprint of this miserable job would eventually appear; and as I had previously rescued the lovers of our old drama from a verbatim copy of Monck Mason's *Massinger*, I ventured to hope for their liberal construction of my endeavours in the kindred office of relieving them from a second edition of Mr. Weber's *Ford*.

All this may savour of vanity—to those who know me not. About this, however, I give myself no concern, well assured that the most inveterate of my enemies cannot entertain a humbler opinion of this work than I do myself, as far as Mr. Weber and his friends are concerned. If it prove useful to the cause of truth and justice, and tend in any degree to check the unlicensed career of ignorance and presumption, I have all the reward that I ever coveted.

To the text, which will, I flatter myself, be found as correct as that of *Massinger*, a few short notes are subjoined: and here I must bespeak the reader's indulgence if he occasionally observes an explanation when all seems sufficiently clear. In these cases the reference is always to the labours of Mr. Weber, who might, if consulted, still mislead the reader. Of the general nature of this person's notes, some idea may be formed by the few (they are but a few[?]) which I have placed as specimens in the Introductory part. My remarks, together with the innumerable corrections of the text, should have been subjoined to the respective pages, had I not indulged a hope that whenever another edition of this poet should be called for, the future editor (as the reading will then probably be considered as established) would remove this part of the Introduction, and relieve the work altogether from the name of Weber.

To the dramas I have subjoined for the first time *Fame's Memorial*, which had been already given to the press, from the old copy, by Mr. Joseph Haslewood.[32] It requires no comment. A few good lines, and even stanzas, might be selected from it; but as a whole it is little more than the holiday task of an ambitious schoolboy. The elegies and encænias of those days were usually of a formidable length; but the mortuary tribute of our youthful bard outstrips them all. In ten pages he might have said all that he had to say, or his subject required; but he was determined to have fifty, and the inevitable consequence followed: five times he repeats himself, and in every successive repetition becomes more vapid, unnatural, and wearisome. What is still more vexatious, after dragging his reader through an hundred seven-line stanzas, and very pertinently demanding

" What *more* yet unremember'd can I say?"

he bursts forth in a deep and awful strain of pathos, which Old Jeronymo[33] never reached;

[32] The preface to this publication by the editor, the professed admirer of Mr. Weber's talents, is drawn-up with such neatness and perspicuity that it would be a crying injustice to the author to suppress it, were it not morally certain that, like the poem to which it is prefixed, it would never obtain a reader. At the conclusion Mr. Haslewood, who qualifies himself very properly as *an unspleened dove*, has aimed a swashing blow at me—who was even ignorant of his existence—of a most tremendous kind;

" Be merciful, great duke, to men of mould!"

[33] See *The Spanish Tragedy* (which critics agree in assigning to the pen of Kyd), "O eyes! no eyes," &c. act iii. D.

lxviii INTRODUCTION.

> " Life? ah, no life, but soon-extinguish'd tapers ;
> Tapers? no tapers, but a burnt-out light ;
> Light? ah, no light, but exhalation's vapours ;
> Vapours? no vapours, but ill-blinded sight ;
> Sight? ah, no sight, but hell's eternal night ;
> A night? no night, but picture of an elf ;
> An elf? no elf, but very death itself."

He then erects " Nine Tombs" over his *patron's* ashes, upon every one of which he places an epitaph; and, as if this were not sufficient, breaks out once more in a childish rant, which can only excite pity by its hopeless imbecility.

Could it be supposed for an instant that a single person would toil through this *Memorial*, I should have subjoined an observation or two, for which occasion was offered; but to write merely to be overlooked is not very encouraging : I have therefore satisfied myself with the reprint, leaving the notes to be hereafter excogitated by the former editor, who, after innocently confounding the poet with his cousin of Gray's Inn, very feelingly laments that " there yet survives a *puny race* of fastidious readers who will continue to esteem a *naked* text in preference to a page three parts *enriched* by notes critical and illustrative"!

The work closes with an additional poem, composed under better auspices and in a far better taste. It is a warm and cordial tribute of praise to the " best of English poets," written in 1637, and published in the *Jonsonus Virbius* of the following year. Two or three smaller pieces of a complimentary kind might be added,[34] but they are not worth the labour of tran-

[34] I have added two or three, in order to render this edition as complete as possible. D.

scribing; and the reader, who has yet to wade through the corruptions of the last edition,[35] has already been too long detained from the dramatic pieces.

[35] Detailed in a supplement to the present *Introduction;* which supplement I have omitted, according to the wish of Gifford: see p. lxvi., and my Preface. D.

A LIST OF FORD'S PLAYS.

1. *The Lover's Melancholy*, T. C. Acted at the Blackfriars and the Globe, 24th November 1628. Printed 1629.
2. *'Tis Pity she's a Whore*, T. Printed 1633. Acted at the Phœnix.
3. *The Broken Heart*, T. Printed 1633. Acted at the Blackfriars.
4. *Love's Sacrifice*, T. Printed 1633. Acted at the Phœnix.
5. *Perkin Warbeck*, H. T. Printed 1634. Acted at the Phœnix.
6. *The Fancies Chaste and Noble*, C. Printed 1638. Acted at the Phœnix.
7. *The Lady's Trial*, T. C. Acted at the Cockpit in May 1638. Printed 1639.
8. *The Sun's Darling*, M. By Ford and Decker. Acted in March 1623-24, at the Cockpit. Printed 1657 [see vol. iii. p. 102].
9. *The Witch of Edmonton*, T. By Rowley, Decker, Ford, &c. Printed 1658. Probably acted soon after 1622. Acted at the Cockpit and at Court.
10. *Beauty in a Trance*, T. Entered on the Stationers' books September 9th, 1653, but not printed. Destroyed by Mr. Warburton's servant.
11. *The London Merchant*, C.
12. *The Royal Combat*, C.
13. *An ill Beginning has a good End*, &c. C. Played at the Cockpit, 1613.

  Entered on the Stationers' books June 29th, 1660, but not printed. Destroyed by Mr. Warburton's servant.

14. *The Fairy Knight.* By Ford and Decker.
15. *A late Murther of the Sonne upon the Mother.* By Ford and Webster.
16. *The Bristowe Merchant.* By Ford and Decker.

These are given from the researches of Mr. G. Chalmers. For other pieces attributed to our author see p. xx.

COMMENDATORY VERSES ON FORD.

To my honoured Friend, Master John Ford, on his Lover's Melancholy.

IF that thou think'st these lines thy worth can raise,
Thou dost mistake: *my* liking is no praise;
Nor can I think thy judgment is so ill
To seek for bays from such a barren quill.
Let your true critic, that can judge and mend,
Allow thy scenes and style: I, as a friend
That knows thy worth, do only stick my name
To show my love, not to advance thy fame.

       GEORGE DONNE.[1]

[1] *George Donne.*] Mr. Weber felicitates the poet on the success of this drama, which had the good fortune, he says, to be recommended to the public by "the celebrated Dr. Donne"! That anyone who pretended to the slightest acquaintance with the writers of Ford's time should be so incomprehensibly ignorant of their style and manner as to attribute this feeble doggerel to *John* Donne the dean of St. Paul's—but I dare not trust myself with the subject. At the moment when this unfortunate blunderer supposes Dr. Donne anxious to ply *his barren quill* and *stick his name* here, purely " to show his *love*," that great man was fallen into a dangerous sickness (which eventually carried him off), and was pressing forward with the zeal of a martyr and the purity of a saint to the crown that was set before him. *George* Donne seems to have been a constant attendant at the theatres. He was apparently a kind-hearted, friendly man, who had his little modicum of praise ready upon all occasions. He has verses to Jonson, Massinger, and others.

*To his worthy Friend the Author [of The Lover's
Melancholy], Master John Ford.*

I write not to thy play: I'll not begin
To throw a censure upon what hath bin[2]
By th' best approv'd: it can nor fear nor want
The rage or liking of the ignorant.
Nor seek I fame for thee, when thine own pen
Hath forc'd a praise long since from knowing men.
I speak my thoughts, and wish unto the stage
A glory from thy studies; that the age
May be indebted to thee for reprieve
Of purer language, and that spite may grieve
To see itself outdone. When thou art read,
The theatre may hope arts are not dead,
Though long conceal'd; that poet-apes may fear
To vent their weakness, mend, or quite forbear.
This I dare promise; and keep this in store,
As thou hast done enough, thou canst do more.
       WILLIAM SINGLETON.[3]

---

[2] The old ed. has "been." D.

[3] In a copy of verses prefixed to Massinger's *Emperor of the East* Singleton calls himself "the friend and kinsman" of that poet. I know nothing more of him. It will be time enough to speak of his immediate follower, Hum. Howorth, when I know what he means. It must be admitted that Mr. Weber has placed Dr. Donne at the head of a most illustrious quartetto.

To the Author [of The Lover's Melancholy], Master John Ford.

Black choler, reason's overflowing spring,
Where thirsty lovers drink, or anything,
Passion, the restless current of dull plaints
Affords their thoughts, who deem lost beauties saints;
Here their best lectures read, collect, and see
Various conditions of humanity,
Highly enlighten'd by thy Muse's rage;
Yet all so couch'd that they adorn'd the stage.
Shun Phocion's blushes thou; for, sure, to please
It is no sin; then what is thy disease?
Judgment's applause? effeminated smiles?
Study's delight? thy wit mistrust beguiles:
Establish'd fame will thy physician be,
(Write but again) to cure thy jealousy.

HUM. HOWORTH.

Of The Lover's Melancholy.

'Tis not the language, nor the fore-plac'd rhymes
Of friends, that shall commend to after-times
The Lover's Melancholy: its own worth
Without a borrow'd praise[4] shall set it forth.

‘Ο φίλος.[5]

[4] *praise*] Gifford printed "phrase." D.
[5] Macklin, with a degree of learning which quite perplexes Mr. Malone, has daringly (but happily) ventured to put these profound symbols into English characters and subscribe the quatrain *Philos*. Mr. Malone thinks he must have had the assistance of some learned friend.

To my Friend, the Author [*of 'Tis Pity she's a Whore*].

With admiration I beheld this Whore,
Adorn'd with beauty such as might restore
(If ever being, as thy Muse hath fam'd)
Her Giovanni, in his love unblam'd :
The ready Graces lent their willing aid;
Pallas herself now play'd the chambermaid,
And help'd to put her dressings on. Secure
Rest thou that thy name herein shall endure
To th' end of age; and Annabella be
Gloriously fair, even in her infamy.

THOMAS ELLICE.[6]

To my Friend, Master John Ford [*on his Love's Sacrifice*].

Unto this altar, rich with thy own spice,
I bring one grain to thy *Love's Sacrifice;*
And boast to see thy flames ascending, while
Perfumes enrich our air from thy sweet pile.
Look here, thou that hast malice to the stage,
And impudence enough for the whole age;
Voluminously-ignorant,[7] be vext
To read this tragedy, and thy own be next.

JAMES SHIRLEY.

[6] A relative, perhaps, of Mr. Robert Ellice, one of "the three respected friends" to whom our poet inscribed *The Lover's Melancholy*.

[7] *Voluminously*-ignorant, &c.] Antony Wood has adopted and justified this characteristic designation of Prynne. He may as well be called "*voluminous* Prynne," he says, "as Tostatus Abulensis was, two hundred years before him, called *voluminous* Tostatus," &c.

*To my own Friend, Master John Ford, on his justifi-
able poem of Perkin Warbeck, this ode.*

They who do know me know that I,
                     Unskill'd to flatter,
Dare speak this piece, in words, in matter,
A work, without the danger of the[8] lie.

Believe me, friend, the name of this and thee
                     Will live, your story:
Books may want faith, or merit glory;
This neither, without judgment's lethargy.

When the arts dote, then some sick poet may
                     Hope that his pen,
In new-stain'd paper, can find men
To roar " He is the wit;"[9] his noise doth sway:

But such an age cannot be known; for all
                     Ere that time be
Must prove such truth, mortality:
So, friend, thy honour stands too fix'd to fall.
                   GEORGE DONNE.[10]

---

[8] Gifford printed " a,"—rightly perhaps. D.

[9] *wit;*] The old ed. has " Wit's." D.

[10] *George Donne.*] Here again credit is given to Ford for the praises of such a celebrated pen as Dr. Donne's, who, as the commentator is not afraid to assert, was "*the steady friend of the poet, and peculiarly attached to him.*" Between Jonson and Donne, indeed, there was a warm and lasting attachment; their studies lay much in the same way at one period of their lives. Ben, like himself, was a profound scholar, and deeply versed in his favourite pursuit, a knowledge of the early Fathers of the Church. But it is more than probable that Ford was not even known to him by name. It is one of the most venial of Mr. Weber's oscitancies to be igno-

*To his worthy Friend, Master John Ford, upon his
Perkin Warbeck.*

Let men who are writ poets lay a claim
To the Phœbean hill, I have no name
Nor art in verse: true, I have heard some tell
Of Aganippe, but ne'er knew the well;
Therefore have no ambition with the times
To be in print, for making of ill rhymes;
But love of thee, and justice to thy pen,
Hath drawn me to this bar with other men,
To justify, though against double laws,
Waving the subtle business of his cause,
The glorious Perkin, and thy poet's art,
Equal with his in playing the king's part.
    RA. EURE, *baronis primogenitus.*[11]

To my faithful, no less deserving Friend, the Author [*of
Perkin Warbeck*], *this indebted oblation.*

Perkin is rediviv'd by thy strong hand,
And crown'd a king of new; the vengeful wand
Of greatness is forgot; his execution
May rest unmention'd, and his birth's collusion
Lie buried in the story; but his fame
Thou hast eternis'd, made a crown his game.

rant that Dr. Donne had at the time this was written been two years in his grave.

[11] "The son of William, Lord Eure." Of the *Miles* who follows I can say nothing. I have, however, corrected his verses, which were shamefully misprinted in the former edition.

His lofty spirit soars yet: had he bin[12]
Base in his enterprise as was his sin
Conceiv'd, his title, doubtless prov'd unjust,
Had but for thee been silenc'd in his[13] dust.

GEORGE CRYMES, *miles.*

*To the Author, his Friend, upon his Chronicle History
[of Perkin Warbeck].*

These are not to express thy wit,
But to pronounce thy judgment fit,
In full-fil'd[14] phrase, those times to raise
When Perkin ran his wily ways.
Still let the method of thy brain
From error's touch and envy's stain
Preserve thee free, that ever thy quill
Fair truth may wet, and fancy fill.
Thus Graces are with Muses met,
And practic critics on may fret;
For here thou hast produc'd a story
Which shall eclipse their future glory.

JOHN BROGRAVE, *ar.*

*To my Friend and Kinsman, Master John Ford, the
Author [of Perkin Warbeck].*

Dramatic poets, as the times go now,
Can hardly write what others will allow;

---

[12] *bin*] The old ed. has "been." D.
[13] *his*] Gifford printed "the,"—rightly perhaps. D.
[14] *full-fil'd*] Gifford printed "*full*-filled." D.

The cynic snarls, the critic howls and barks,
And ravens croak to drown the voice of larks:
Scorn those stage-harpies! This I'll boldly say,
Many may imitate, few match thy play.

JOHN FORD, *Graiensis*.

To Master John Ford, of the Middle Temple, on his Bower of Fancies [or Fancies Chaste and Noble].

I follow fair example, not report,
Like wits of th' university or court,
    To show how I can write
At mine own charges, for the time's delight,
    But to acquit a debt
Due to right poets, not the counterfeit.

These *Fancies Chaste and Noble* are no strains
Dropt from the itch of overheated brains;
    They speak unblushing truth,
The guard of beauty and the care of youth;
    Well relish'd might repair
An académy for the young and fair.

Such labours, friend, will live; for though some new
Pretenders to the stage in haste pursue
    Those laurels which of old
Enrich'd the actors, yet I can be bold
    To say their hopes are starv'd;
For they but beg what pens approv'd deserv'd.

EDW. GREENFIELD.

Upon the Sun's Darling.

Is he, then, found? Phœbus, make holiday,
Tie up thy steeds, and let the Cyclops play;
Mulciber, leave thy anvil, and be trim,
Comb thy black muzzle, be no longer grim;
Mercury, be quick, with mirth furnish the heavens;
Jove, this day let all run at six and sevens;
And, Ganymede, be nimble, to the brim
Fill bowls of nectar, that the gods may swim,
To solemnise their healths[15] that did discover
The obscure being of the Sun's fond lover;
That from th' example of their liberal mirth
We may enjoy like freedom [here] on earth.

JOHN TATHAM.[16]

Upon Ford's two Tragedies, Love's Sacrifice and The Broken Heart.

Thou cheat'st us, Ford; mak'st one seem two by art:
What is Love's Sacrifice but the Broken Heart?

RICHARD CRASHAW.[17]

---

[15] *healths*] Gifford printed "health." D.

[16] "John Tatham was a poet of the reign of Charles I., and author of four plays enumerated in the *Biographia Dramatica*. From 1657 to 1663 he furnished pageants for the Lord Mayor's day, in the quality of city poet." Had the poets lived to publish their own drama, it can scarcely be imagined that they would have suffered this deplorable balderdash to be prefixed to it.

[17] *The Delights of the Muses*, 1646.

To Master John Ford,[18] *of the Middle Temple, upon his Fame's Memorial, this madrigal.*

If that renowmèd lord—whose powerful fame
In strength of wars and calms of peace exceeded—
Hath after death purchas'd so great a name
   That it must prosper as it hath proceeded,
   Then must in time those spiteful plants be weeded,
Which living, yet him living would have chok'd;
   And those sweet wits, touch'd with a sacred flame
Of his rich virtues, shall advance the same.
But thou, by those deserts in him provok'd,
   That sung his honours which so much exceeded,
Whose pleasant pen, in sacred water soak'd
   Of Castaly, did register his worth,
Reapest much part of honour for thy pen
Through him, fair mirror of our Englishmen,
   Whom with due dignity thy Muse set forth.
                    BAR[NABY] BARNES.

IN EUNDEM.

Vivit, in æternum vivet dux inclytus armis,
   Mountjoyus; vivet, Forde, poema tuum;
Major uterque suo genio: vi carminis heros,
   Materiæ felix nobilis autor ope.
                    T. P.

[18] *To Master John Ford*, &c.] Not reprinted by Gifford. D.

THE LOVER'S MELANCHOLY.

VOL. I. B

This piece, the author tells us, was "the first of his that ever courted reader." It was licensed by Sir Henry Herbert in 1628, and brought out on the 24th of November in that year: in 1629 it was given to the press, accompanied (as the manner was) by several recommendatory poems. It seems to have been favourably received. The title of the 4to is "The Lovers Melancholy. Acted at the Private House in the Blacke Friers, and publikely at the Globe by the Kings Maiesties seruants. London, Printed for H. Seile, and are to be sold at the Tygers head in Saint Pauls Church-yard. 1629."

It was revived at Drury Lane in 1748, by Macklin, for his wife's benefit; but apparently without success.

TO

MY WORTHILY RESPECTED FRIENDS,

NATHANIEL FINCH, JOHN FORD, Esquires;

Master HENRY BLUNT, Master ROBERT ELLICE,

AND ALL THE REST OF THE

NOBLE SOCIETY OF GRAY'S INN.

———◆———

MY HONOURED FRIENDS,

THE account of some leisurable hours is here summed up, and offered to examination. Importunity of others, or opinion of mine own, hath not urged on any confidence of running the hazard of a censure. A plurality hath reference to a multitude, so I care not to please many; but where there is a parity of condition, there the freedom of construction makes the best music. This concord hath equally held between you the patrons and me the presenter. I am cleared of all scruple of disrespect on your parts; as I am of too slack a merit in myself. My presumption of coming in print in this kind[1] hath hitherto been unreprovable,

---

[1] *in this kind*] i. e. the drama: he had previously printed "Fame's Memorial," and, probably, other poems, now lost.

this piece being the first that ever courted reader; and it is very possible that the like compliment with me may soon grow out of fashion.[2] A practice of which that I may avoid now, I commend to the continuance of your loves the memory of his, who, without the protestation of a service, is readily your friend.

JOHN FORD.

[2] *and it is very possible that the like* compliment *with* me *may soon grow out of fashion.*] This, as the author says, is the first time of his appearing in print as a dramatic writer; and yet he comes before the reader with all the querulous cant of an old professor. Fortunately, this language of routine means nothing; and the present publication was, in course, followed by others, as leisure or opportunity offered.

DRAMATIS PERSONÆ.

PALADOR, prince of Cyprus.
AMETHUS, cousin to the Prince.
MELEANDER, an old lord.
SOPHRONOS, brother to Meleander.
MENAPHON, son of Sophronos.
ARETUS, tutor to the Prince.
CORAX, a physician.
PELIAS,
CUCULUS, } two foolish courtiers.
RHETIAS (a reduced courtier), servant to Eroclea.
TROLLIO, servant to Meleander.
GRILLA, a page of Cuculus, in woman's dress.

THAMASTA, sister of Amethus, and cousin to the Prince.
EROCLEA (as PARTHENOPHIL),
CLEOPHILA, } daughters of Meleander.
KALA, waiting-maid to Thamasta.

Officers, Attendants, &c.

SCENE—*Famagosta in Cyprus.*

The names of such as acted.

JOHN LOWIN.
JOSEPH TAYLOR.
ROBERT BENFIELD.
JOHN SHANCK.
EYLYARDT SWANSTON.
ANTHONY SMITH.
RICHARD SHARPE.
THOMAS POLLARD.
WILLIAM PENN.

CURTEISE GRIVILL.
GEORGE VERNON.
RICHARD BAXTER.
JOHN TOMSON.
JOHN HONYMAN.
JAMES HORNE.
WILLIAM TRIGG.
ALEXANDER GOUGH.

For this list see *Massinger*, vol. ii. p. 230, where references to several of the more celebrated names will be found. [See also, for an account of several of these players, Collier's *Memoirs of the Principal Actors in the Plays of Shakespeare*, printed for the Shake. Soc. D.]

PROLOGUE.

To tell ye, gentlemen, in what true sense
The writer, actors, or the audience
Should mould their judgments for a play, might draw
Truth into rules; but we have no such law.
Our writer, for himself, would have ye know
That in his following scenes he doth not owe
To others' fancies, nor hath lain in wait
For any stol'n invention, from whose height
He might commend his own, more than the right
A scholar claims,[1] may warrant for delight.
It is art's scorn, that some of late have made
The noble use of poetry a trade.
For your parts, gentlemen, to quit his pains,
Yet you[2] will please, that as you meet with strains
Of lighter mixture,[3] but to cast your eye
Rather upon the *main* than on the *bye*,
His hopes stand firm, and we shall find it true,
The LOVER'S MELANCHOLY cur'd by you.

---

[1] *more than the right A scholar claims*, &c.] Ford appears anxious, in this place, to anticipate the objections that might be raised against his plagiarisms. That he has borrowed largely there can be no doubt; but he has, certainly, nowhere abused *the right of a scholar:* had he been more familiar with the press, he would, perhaps, have scarcely thought that his freedom with his predecessors required much apology. The confession, however, was not unwise; for Burton (to whom, among others, he alludes) was in every one's hand; and Strada's charming apologue was scarcely less familiar.

[2] *Yet you*] Gifford printed "You yet." D.

[3] *mixture*,] The 4to has "mixtures." D.

THE LOVER'S MELANCHOLY.

ACT I.

SCENE I. *A room in the palace.*

Enter MENAPHON *and* PELIAS.

Men. Dangers! how mean you dangers? that so courtly
You gratulate my safe return from dangers?
　Pel. From travels, noble sir.
　Men.　　　　　　　　These are delights;
If my experience hath not, truant-like,
Misspent the time, which I have strove to use
For bettering my mind with observation.
　Pel. As I am modest, I protest 'tis strange.
But is it possible?
　Men.　　　What?
　Pel.　　　　　　　To bestride
The frothy foams of Neptune's surging waves,
When blustering Boreas tosseth up the deep
And thumps a thunder-bounce?
　Men.　　　　　　　Sweet sir, 'tis nothing:
Straight comes a dolphin, playing near your ship,
Heaving his crookèd back up, and presents

A feather-bed, to waft ye to the shore
As easily as if you slept i' th' court.
  Pel. Indeed! is't true, I pray?
  Men.   I will not stretch
Your faith upon the tenters.—Prithee, Pelias,
Where didst thou learn this language?
  Pel.   I this language!
Alas, sir, we that study words and forms
Of compliment must fashion all discourse
According to the nature of the subject.
But I am silent :—now appears a sun,
Whose shadow I adore.

   Enter AMETHUS, SOPHRONOS, *and* Attendants.
  Men.   My honour'd father!
  Soph. From mine eyes, son, son of my care, my
              love,
The joys that bid thee welcome do too much
Speak me a child.
  Men.   O princely sir, your hand.
  Amet. Perform your duties where you owe them
              first;
I dare not be so sudden in the pleasures
Thy presence hath brought home.
  Soph.   Here thou still find'st
A friend as noble, Menaphon, as when[1]
Thou left'st at thy departure.
  Men.   Yes, I know it,
To him I owe more service—
  Amet.   Pray give leave :
He shall attend your entertainments soon,

---

[1] *as* when
   Thou left'st at thy departure.] I suspect that we should read here " as *whom* Thou left'st." I have not ventured to change anything; though the expression would be in the author's manner.

Next day, and next day: for an hour or two
I would engross him only.
  Soph.   Noble lord!
  Amet. Ye're both dismiss'd.
  Pel.   Your creature and your servant.
    [*Exeunt all but Amethus and Menaphon.*
  Amet. Give me thy hand. I will not say, "Thou'rt
    welcome;"
That is the common road of common friends.
I'm glad I have thee here—O, I want words
To let thee know my heart!
  Men.   'Tis piec'd to mine.
  Amet. Yes, 'tis; as firmly as that holy thing
Call'd friendship can unite it. Menaphon,
My Menaphon, now all the goodly blessings
That can create a heaven on earth dwell with thee!
Twelve months we have been sunder'd; but hence-
    forth
We never more will part, till that sad hour
In which death leaves the one of us behind,
To see the other's funerals perform'd.
Let's now a while be free.—How have thy travels
Disburthen'd thee abroad of discontents?
  Men. Such cure as sick men find in changing beds
I found in change of airs: the fancy flatter'd
My hopes with ease, as theirs do; but the grief
Is still the same.
  Amet.   Such is my case at home.
Cleophila, thy kinswoman, that maid
Of sweetness and humility, more pities
Her father's poor afflictions than the tide
Of my complaints.
  Men.   Thamasta, my great mistress,
Your princely sister, hath, I hope, ere this

Confirm'd affection on[2] some worthy choice.
 Amet. Not any, Menaphon. Her bosom yet
Is intermur'd with ice; though, by the truth
Of love, no day hath ever pass'd wherein
I have not mention'd thy deserts, thy constancy,
Thy—Come, in troth, I dare not tell thee what,
Lest thou mightst think I fawn'd on [thee]—a sin[3]
Friendship was never guilty of; for flattery
Is monstrous in a true friend.
 Men. Does the court
Wear the old looks too?
 Amet. If thou mean'st the prince,
It does. He's the same melancholy man
He was at's father's death; sometimes speaks sense,
But seldom mirth; will smile, but seldom laugh;
Will lend an ear to business, deal in none;
Gaze upon revels, antic fopperies,
But is not mov'd; will sparingly discourse,
Hear music; but what most he takes delight in
Are handsome pictures. One so young and goodly,
So sweet in his own nature, any story
Hath seldom mention'd.
 Men. Why should such as I am
Groan under the light burthens of small sorrows,

---

[2] Confirm'd *affection on*, &c.] So the 4to reads, but, I suspect, erroneously. Perhaps the author's word was "*conferr'd.*"
[3] *Lest thou mightst think I fawn'd on* [*thee*]—*a sin*] This is the best conjecture which I can form of the speaker's meaning. The old copy reads,

"Lest thou mightst think I *fawn'd upon* a sin
Friendship was never guilty of."

I once conjectured,

"Lest thou mightst think I'd *fallen* upon a sin:"

but I prefer the first. [Qy. is the old reading "fawn'd upon" right, and equivalent to the simple "fawn'd"? So our early writers use "look upon" without any substantive following it: see my *Gloss. to Shakespeare.* D.]

Whenas a prince so potent cannot shun
Motions of passion? To be man, my lord,
Is to be but the exercise of cares
In several shapes: as miseries do grow,
They alter as men's forms; but how none know.
 Amet. This little isle of Cyprus sure abounds
In greater wonders both for change and fortune
Than any you have seen abroad.
 Men.   Than any
I have observ'd abroad: all countries else
To a free eye and mind yield something rare;¹
And I, for my part, have brought home one jewel
Of admirable value.⁴
 Amet.   Jewel, Menaphon!
 Men. A jewel, my Amethus, a fair youth;
A youth, whom, if I were but superstitious,
I should repute an excellence more high
Than mere creations are: to add delight,
I'll tell ye how I found him.
 Amet.   Prithee do.
 Men. Passing from Italy to Greece, the tales
Which poets of an elder time have feign'd
To glorify their Tempe, bred in me
Desire of visiting that paradise.
To Thessaly I came; and living private,
Without acquaintance of more sweet companions
Than the old inmates to my love, my thoughts,
I day by day frequented silent groves
And solitary walks. One morning early
This accident encounter'd me: I heard
The sweetest and most ravishing contention
That art and⁵ nature ever were at strife in.⁶

---

⁴ *value.*] Gifford printed "virtue." D.
⁵ *and*] The 4to has "or." D.,
⁶ Vide (Ford says) *Fami. Stradam,* lib. ii. Prolus. 6. Acad. 2.

Amet. I cannot yet conceive what you infer
By art and nature.
 Men. I shall soon resolve ye.
A sound of music touch'd mine ears, or rather
Indeed entranc'd my soul. As I stole nearer,
Invited by the melody, I saw
This youth, this fair-fac'd youth, upon his lute,
With strains of strange variety and harmony,
Proclaiming, as it seem'd, so bold a challenge
To the clear quiristers of the woods, the birds,
That, as they flock'd about him, all stood silent,
Wondering at what they heard. I wonder'd too.
 Amet. And so do I; good, on!
 Men. A nightingale,
Nature's best-skill'd musician, undertakes
The challenge, and for every several strain
The well-shap'd youth could touch, she sung her
 own;[7]
He could not run division with more art
Upon his quaking instrument than she,
The nightingale, did with her various notes
Reply to: for a voice and for a sound,
Amethus, 'tis much easier to believe
That such they were than hope to hear again.
 Amet. How did the rivals part?
 Men. You term them rightly;
For they were rivals, and their mistress, harmony.—
Some time thus spent, the young man grew at last
Into a pretty anger, that a bird,
Whom art had never taught cliffs, moods, or notes,

Imitat. Claudian. This story, as Mr. Lamb observes, has been paraphrased by Crashaw, Ambrose Philips, and others: none of those versions, however, can at all compare for harmony and grace with this before us.

[7] *own;*] The 4to has "down." D.

Should vie with him for mastery, whose study
Had busied many hours to perfect practice :
To end the controversy, in a rapture
Upon his instrument he plays so swiftly,
So many voluntaries and so quick,
That there was curiosity and cunning,
Concord in discord, lines of differing method
Meeting in one full centre of delight.

    Amet. Now for the bird.

    Men.   The bird, ordain'd to be
Music's first martyr, strove to imitate
These several sounds; which when her warbling throat
Fail'd in, for grief down dropp'd she on his lute,
And brake her heart. It was the quaintest sadness,
To see the conqueror upon her hearse
To weep a funeral elegy of tears ;
That, trust me, my Amethus, I could chide[8]
Mine own unmanly weakness, that made me
A fellow-mourner with him.

    Amet.   I believe thee.

    Men. He look'd[9] upon the trophies of his art,
Then sigh'd, then wip'd his eyes, then sigh'd and cried,
"Alas, poor creature! I will soon revenge
This cruelty upon the author of it;
Henceforth this lute, guilty of innocent blood,
Shall never more betray a harmless peace
To an untimely end :" and in that sorrow,
As he was pashing it against a tree,[10]
I suddenly stept in.

    Amet.   Thou hast discours'd

---

[8] *I could chide,* &c.] It should rather be, " I could *not* chide;" unless the speaker means to insinuate that his grief was too poignant and profuse for a man.

[9] *look'd*] The 4to has "lookes." D.

[10] *As he was* pashing *it against a tree,*] i.e. *dashing* it. See *Massinger,* vol. i. p. 38.

A truth of mirth and pity.[11]
Men. I repriev'd
Th' intended execution with entreaties
And interruption.—But, my princely friend,
It was not strange the music of his hand
Did overmatch birds, when his voice and beauty,
Youth, carriage, and discretion must, from men
Endu'd with reason, ravish admiration :
From me they did.
  Amet. But is this miracle
Not to be seen ?
  Men. I won him by degrees
To choose me his companion. Whence he is,
Or who, as I durst modestly inquire,
So gently he would woo not to make known ;
Only—for reasons to himself reserv'd—
He told me, that some remnant of his life
Was to be spent in travel : for his fortunes,
They were nor mean nor riotous ; his friends
Not publish'd to the world, though not obscure ;
His country Athens, and his name Parthenophil.
  Amet. Came he with you to Cyprus ?
  Men. Willingly.
The fame of our young melancholy prince,
Meleander's rare distractions, the obedience
Of young Cleophila, Thamasta's glory, .
Your matchless friendship, and my desperate love,
Prevail'd with him ; and I have lodg'd him privately

---

[11] *Thou hast discours'd*
A truth *of mirth and pity.*] This is evidently corrupt ; but I can suggest no remedy. The sense might be somewhat improved by reading "*tale*" for "*truth,*" or, with less violence, "*I' truth,*" of," &c. : but what can be done with "*mirth*"? Pathetic, indeed, this most beautiful tale is, but it certainly contains nothing of merriment. [I am inclined to think that there is no corruption here,—that "*A truth of mirth and pity*" may mean "A true story which both affords amusement and excites pity." D.]

SCENE II.   THE LOVER'S MELANCHOLY.

In Famagosta.
Amet.   Now thou'rt doubly welcome:
I will not lose the sight of such a rarity
For one part of my hopes. When d'ye intend
To visit my great-spirited sister?
Men.   May I
Without offence?
Amet.   Without offence.—Parthenophil
Shall find a worthy entertainment too.
Thou art not still a coward?
Men.   She's too excellent,
And I too low in merit.
Amet.   I'll prepare
A noble welcome; and, friend, ere we part,
Unload to thee an overchargèd heart.   [*Exeunt.*

SCENE II. *Another room in the palace.*

Enter RHETIAS, *carelessly attired.*

Rhe. I will not court the madness of the times;
Nor fawn upon the riots that embalm
Our wanton gentry, to preserve the dust
Of their affected vanities in coffins
Of memorable shame. When commonwealths
Totter and reel from that nobility
And ancient virtue which renowns the great,
Who steer the helm of government, while mushrooms
Grow up, and make new laws to license folly;
Why should not I, a May-game,[12] scorn the weight

---

[12] *Why should not I, a* May-game, &c.] i.e. an unconsidered trifle, a jest, a piece of mirth. This expression occurs in the same sense in the next piece; "Wilt make thyself a *May-game* to all the world?" The motive which Rhetias assigns for assuming the part of an *all-licensed fool* is not very creditable to him; nor does he

Of my sunk fortunes? snarl at the vices[13]
Which rot the land, and, without fear or wit,[14]
Be mine own antic? 'Tis a sport to live
When life is irksome, if we will not hug
Prosperity in others, and contemn
Affliction in ourselves. This rule is certain,
"He that pursues his safety from the school
Of state must learn to be madman or fool."
Ambition, wealth, ease, I renounce—the devil
That damns ye here on earth. Or I will be
Mine own mirth, or mine own tormentor.—So!
Here comes intelligence; a buzz o' the court.

Enter PELIAS.

Pel. Rhetias, I sought thee out to tell thee news,
New, excellent new news. Cuculus, sirrah,
That gull, that young old gull, is coming this way.
 Rhe. And thou art his forerunner?
 Pel. Prithee, hear me.
Instead of a fine guarded page[15] we've got him
A boy, trick'd up in neat and handsome fashion;
Persuaded him that 'tis indeed a wench,
And he has entertain'd him: he does follow him,
Carries his sword and buckler, waits on 's trencher,

---

turn the character to much account. Some part of what he here says, however, though it might be expressed with less effort, is the result of sound observation.

[13] snarl *at the vices*] *Snarl* (as well as *girl*) is commonly made a dissyliable by our poet: he passed his youth in the neighbourhood of Dartmoor, and probably adopted the practice of that wild district. This mode of enunciation still prevails in the northern counties, at least in poetry, where what to an English ear sounds like a soft *d* is interposed between *r* and *l* in such monosyllables as end with these two letters.

[14] *without fear or wit,*] For *boldly, desperately, without care of consequences.*

[15] *Instead of a fine* guarded *page*] i.e. of a page with a livery richly laced, or turned up. The expression is common to all our old writers.

Fills him his wine, tobacco; whets his knife,
Lackeys his letters, does what service else
He would employ his man in. Being ask'd
Why he is so irregular in courtship,
His answer is, that since great ladies use
Gentlemen-ushers to go bare before them,
He knows no reason but he may reduce
The courtiers to have women wait on them;
And he begins the fashion: he is laugh'd at
Most complimentally. Thou'lt burst to see him.

Rhe. Agelastus, so surnamed for his gravity,[16] was a very wise fellow, kept his countenance all days of his life as demurely as a judge that pronounceth sentence of death on a poor rogue for stealing as much bacon as would serve at a meal with a calf's head. Yet he smiled once, and never but once:—thou art no scholar?

Pel. I have read pamphlets dedicated to me.— Dost call him Agelastus? Why did he laugh?

Rhe. To see an ass eat thistles. Puppy, go study to be a singular coxcomb. Cuculus is an ordinary ape; but thou art an ape of an ape.

Pel. Thou hast a patent to abuse thy friends.— Look, look, he comes! observe him seriously.

Enter CUCULUS, *followed by* GRILLA, *both fantastically dressed.*

Cuc. Reach me my sword and buckler.
Gril. They are here, forsooth.

---

[16] Agelastus, *so surnamed for his gravity*, &c.] Thus Jonson, in the *New Inn;*
      "The Roman alderman,
    Old Master Gross, surnamed 'Ἀγέλαστος,
     Was never seen to laugh but at an ass."

The story is in Pliny, who tells it of Crassus, the grandfather of the unfortunate Crassus who fell the victim of his rapacity in Parthia.

Cuc. How now, minx, how now! where is your duty, your distance? Let me have service methodically tendered; you are now one of us. Your curtsy. [GRILLA *curtsies.*] Good! remember that you are to practise courtship.[17] Was thy father a piper, sayest thou?

Gril. A sounder of some such wind-instrument, forsooth.[18]

Cuc. Was he so?—Hold up thy head. Be thou musical to me, and I will marry thee to a dancer; one that shall ride on his footcloth,[19] and maintain thee in thy muff and hood.

Gril. That will be fine indeed.

Cuc. Thou art yet but simple.

Gril. D'ye think so?

Cuc. I have a brain, I have a head-piece: o' my conscience, if I take pains with thee, I should raise thy understanding, girl, to the height of a nurse, or a court-midwife at least: I will make thee big in time, wench.

Gril. E'en do your pleasure with me, sir.

Pel. [*coming forward*] Noble, accomplished Cuculus!

Rhe. [*coming forward*] Give me thy fist, innocent.

Cuc. Would 'twere in thy belly! there 'tis.

---

[17] *courtship.*] The behaviour necessary to be observed at court; the manners of a courtier. *Steevens.* Thus the word is used in the preceding page—"so irregular in *courtship.*"

[18] Gril. *A sounder of some such wind-instrument, forsooth.*] Grilla's answer is meant to intimate that her father was a sow-gelder. [Sow-gelders, it appears, used formerly to blow a horn. So in Fletcher's *Beggars' Bush*, act iii. sc. 1;

"*Enter Higgen disguised as a sow-gelder, singing as follows.*
Have ye any work for the sow-gelder, ho?
My horn goes to high, to low, to high, to low." D.]

[19] *footcloth,*] i.e. housings of cloth, hanging down on each side of the horse. D.

Pel. That's well; he's an honest blade, though he be blunt.

Cuc. Who cares? We can be as blunt as he, for's life.

Rhe. Cuculus, there is, within a mile or two, a sow-pig hath sucked a brach,[20] and now hunts the deer, the hare, nay, most unnaturally, the wild-boar, as well as any hound in Cyprus.

Cuc. Monstrous sow-pig! is't true?

Pel. I'll be at charge of a banquet on thee for a sight of her.

Rhe. Every thing takes after the dam that gave it suck. Where hadst thou thy milk?

Cuc. I? Why, my nurse's husband was a most excellent maker of shittlecocks.

Pel. My nurse was a woman-surgeon.[21]

Rhe. And who gave thee pap, mouse?

Gril. I never sucked, that I remember.

Rhe. La now, a shittlecock-maker! all thy brains are stuck with cork and feather, Cuculus. This learned courtier takes after the nurse too; a she-surgeon; which is, in effect, a mere matcher of colours. Go learn to paint and daub compliments, 'tis the next step to run into a new suit. My Lady Periwinkle here never sucked: suck thy master, and bring forth mooncalves, fop, do! This is good philosophy, sirs; make use on't.

Gril. Bless us, what a strange creature this is!

Cuc. A gull, an arrant gull by proclamation.

---

[20] *brach,*] The kennel term for a bitch-hound. See *Mass.* vol. i. p. 210. The late Sir Harry Mildmay had a "sow-pig" that would apparently do all that Cuculus thinks so monstrous, without having *sucked a brach* for the matter. [And see note, p. 52. D.]

[21] *woman-surgeon.*] i.e. as Rhetias presently explains it, a dealer in paints and cosmetics for the ladies.

Enter CORAX, *passing over the stage.*

Pel. Corax, the prince's chief physician! What business speeds his haste?—Are all things well, sir?

Cor. Yes, yes, yes.

Rhe. Phew! you may wheel about, man; we know you're proud of your slovenry and practice; 'tis your virtue. The prince's melancholy fit, I presume, holds still.

Cor. So do thy knavery and desperate beggary.

Cuc. Aha! here's one will tickle the ban-dog.

Rhe. You must not go yet.

Cor. I'll stay in spite of thy teeth. There lies my gravity. [*Throws off his gown.*]²² Do what thou darest; I stand thee.

Rhe. Mountebank[s], empirics, quack - salvers, mineralists, wizards, alchemists, cast-apothecaries, old wives and barbers, are all suppositors to the right worshipful doctor, as I take it. Some of ye are the head of your art, and the horns too—but they come by nature. Thou livest single for no other end but that thou fearest to be a cuckold.

Cor. Have at thee! Thou affectest railing only for thy health; thy miseries are so thick and so lasting, that thou hast not one poor denier to bestow on opening a vein: wherefore, to avoid a pleurisy, thou'lt be sure to prate thyself once a month into a whipping, and bleed in the breech instead of the arm.

---

²² *There lies my* gravity. [*Throws off his gown.*] Thus Prospero, when he throws off his mantle, exclaims,
　　　　"Lie there, my *art.*"
And Fuller tells us that the great Lord Burleigh, when he put off his gown at night, used to say,
　　　　"Lie there, *Lord Treasurer.*"
[Here Gifford borrows from Steevens's note on *The Tempest*, act i. sc. 2.—For some similar expressions see my *Gloss. to Shakespeare*, sub "*Lie there, my art.*" D.]

Rhe. Have at thee again!
Cor. Come!
Cuc. There, there, there! O brave doctor!
Pel. Let 'em alone.
Rhe. Thou art in thy religion an atheist, in thy condition a cur, in thy diet an epicure, in thy lust a goat, in thy sleep a hog; thou takest upon thee the habit of a grave physician, but art indeed an impostorous empiric. Physicians are the cobblers, rather the botchers, of men's bodies;[23] as the one patches our tattered clothes, so the other solders our diseased flesh. Come on!

Cuc. To't, to't! hold him to't! hold him to't! to't, to't, to't!

Cor. The best worth in thee is the corruption of thy mind, for that only entitles thee to the dignity of a louse, a thing bred out of the filth and superfluity of ill humours. Thou bitest anywhere, and any man who defends not himself with the clean linen of secure honesty; him thou darest not come near. Thou art fortune's idiot, virtue's bankrupt, time's dunghill, manhood's scandal, and thine own scourge. Thou wouldst hang thyself, so wretchedly miserable thou art, but that no man will trust thee with as much money as will buy a halter; and all thy stock to be sold is not worth half as much as may procure it.

Rhe. Ha, ha, ha! this is flattery, gross flattery.

Cor. I have employment for thee, and for ye all. Tut, these are but good-morrows between us.

Rhe. Are thy bottles full?

---

[23] *Physicians are the cobblers, rather the botchers, of men's bodies;*] I have omitted the word "*bodies*," which seems to have slipped in before "*cobblers*." This is not, I suspect, the only error; but 'tis to little purpose to waste time on what, after all, will scarcely be thought worth mending. In the opening of this speech the poet uses *condition*, like all the writers of his time, for *disposition, nature*, &c.

Cor. Of rich wine; let's all suck together.
Rhe. Like so many swine in a trough.
Cor. I'll shape ye all for a device before the prince: we'll try how that can move him.
Rhe. He shall fret or laugh.
Cuc. Must I make one?
Cor. Yes, and your feminine page too.
Gril. Thanks, most egregiously.
Pel. I will not slack my part.
Cuc. Wench, take my buckler.
Cor. Come all unto my chamber: the project is cast; the time only we must attend.
Rhe. The melody must agree[24] well and yield sport,
When such as these are, knaves and fools, consort.[25]

[*Exeunt.*

SCENE III. *An apartment in the house of* THAMASTA.

Enter AMETHUS, THAMASTA, *and* KALA.

Amet. Does this show well?
Tha.   What would you have me do?
Amet. Not like a lady of the trim, new crept
Out of the shell of sluttish sweat and labour
Into the glittering pomp of ease and wantonness,
Embroideries, and all these antic fashions
That shape a woman monstrous; to transform
Your education and a noble birth
Into contempt and laughter. Sister, sister,

---

[24] *agree*] Here probably Ford wrote "gree" (which is very common in our old authors). D.

[25] The audience must be *light o' the sere* to whom such "melody could yield sport." It is generally a relief to escape from the sad efforts of the author's attempts at pleasantry. To do him justice, he appears to entertain some suspicion of his success in this part of the plot, and has therefore besought the audience, when "they met some *lighter* strain, rather to look at the *main* than the *bye.*"

She who derives her blood from princes ought
To glorify her greatness by humility.
    Tha. Then you conclude me proud?
    Amet.   Young Menaphon,
My worthy friend, has lov'd you long and truly:
To witness his obedience to your scorn,
Twelve months, wrong'd gentleman, he undertook
A voluntary exile. Wherefore, sister,
In this time of his absence have you not
Dispos'd of your affections on some monarch?
Or sent ambassadors to some neighbouring king
With fawning protestations of your graces,
Your rare perfections, admirable beauty?
This had been a new piece of modesty
Would have deserv'd a chronicle!
    Tha.   You're bitter;
And, brother, by your leave, not kindly wise.[26]
My freedom is my birth's;[27] I am not bound
To fancy your approvements, but my own.
Indeed, you are an humble youth! I hear of
Your visits and your loving commendation
To your heart's saint, Cleophila, a virgin
Of a rare excellence. What though she want
A portion to maintain a portly greatness?
Yet 'tis your gracious sweetness to descend
So low; the meekness of your pity leads ye!
She is your dear friend's sister! a good soul!
An innocent!—
    Amet.   Thamasta!
    Tha.   I have given
Your Menaphon a welcome home, as fits me;
For his sake entertain'd Parthenophil,

---

[26] *not kindly wise.*] i.e. your wisdom has not the *natural* tenderness of a brother in it.
[27] *birth's,*] Gifford printed "birth." D.

The handsome stranger, more familiarly
Than, I may fear, becomes me; yet, for his part,
I not repent my courtesies : but you—
 Amet. No more, no more ! be affable to both ;
Time may reclaim your cruelty.
 Tha. I pity
The youth ; and, trust me, brother, love his sadness :
He talks the prettiest stories ; he delivers
His tales so gracefully, that I could sit
And listen, nay, forget my meals and sleep,
To hear his neat discourses. Menaphon
Was well advis'd in choosing such a friend
For pleading his true love.
 Amet. Now I commend thee ;
Thou'lt change at last, I hope.
 Tha. I fear I shall. [*Aside.*

Enter MENAPHON *and* PARTHENOPHIL.

 Amet. Have ye survey'd the garden ?
 Men. 'Tis a curious,
A pleasantly contriv'd delight.
 Tha. Your eye, sir,
Hath in your travels often met contents
Of more variety?
 Par. Not any, lady.
 Men. It were impossible, since your fair presence
Makes every place, where it vouchsafes to shine,
More lovely than all other helps of art
Can equal.
 Tha. What you mean by "helps of art,"
You know yourself best : be they as they are ;
You need none, I am sure, to set me forth.
 Men. 'Twould argue want of manners, more than
 skill,
Not to praise *praise itself.*

Tha.   For your reward,
Henceforth I'll call you servant.[28]
   Amet.   Excellent sister!
   Men. 'Tis my first step to honour.   May I fall
Lower than shame, when I neglect all service
That may confirm this favour!
   Tha.   Are you well, sir?
   Par. Great princess, I am well.   To see a league
Between an humble love, such as my friend's is,
And a commanding virtue, such as yours is,
Are sure restoratives.
   Tha.   You speak ingeniously.—[29]
Brother, be pleas'd to show the gallery
To this young stranger.   Use the time a while,
And we will all together to the court:
I will present ye, sir, unto the prince.
   Par. You're all compos'd of fairness and true
           bounty.
   Amet. Come, come.—We'll wait thee,[30] sister.
           This beginning
Doth relish happy process.
   Men.   You have bless'd me.
           [*Exeunt Men., Amet., and Par.*
   Tha. Kala, O, Kala!
   Kal.   Lady?
   Tha.   We are private;
Thou art my closet.
   Kal.   Lock your secrets close, then:
I am not to be forc'd.
   Tha.   Never till now
Could I be sensible of being traitor
To honour and to shame.

---

[28] *Henceforth I'll call you servant.*] i.e. acknowledge you as a lover.   See *Mass.* vol. i. p. 185.
[29] *ingeniously.*] i.e. wittily.
[30] *thee,*] Gifford printed "you." D.

Kal.   You are in love.
Tha. I am grown base.—Parthenophil—
Kal.   He's handsome,
Richly endow'd; he hath a lovely face,
A winning tongue.
    Tha.   If ever I must fall,
In him my greatness sinks : Love is a tyrant,
Resisted. Whisper in his ear, how gladly
I would steal time to talk with him one hour :
But do it honourably; prithee, Kala,
Do not betray me.
    Kal.   Madam, I will make it
Mine own case; he shall think I am in love with him.
    Tha. I hope thou art not, Kala.
    Kal.   'Tis for your sake :
I'll tell him so; but, 'faith, I am not, lady.
    Tha. Pray, use me kindly; let me not too soon
Be lost in my new follies. 'Tis a fate
That overrules our wisdoms; whilst we strive
To live most free, we're caught in our own toils.
Diamonds cut diamonds; they who will prove
To thrive in cunning must cure love with love.
                                    [*Exeunt.*

ACT II.

SCENE I. *An apartment in the palace.*

Enter SOPHRONOS *and* ARETUS.

Soph. Our commonwealth is sick : 'tis more than time
That we should wake the head thereof, who sleeps
In the dull lethargy of lost security.

The commons murmur, and the nobles grieve;
The court is now turn'd antic, and grows wild,
Whiles all the neighbouring nations stand at gaze,
And watch fit opportunity to wreak
Their just-conceivèd fury on such injuries
As the late prince, our living master's father,
Committed against laws of truth or honour.
Intelligence comes flying in on all sides;
Whilst the unsteady multitude presume
How that you, Aretus, and I engross,
Out of particular ambition,
Th' affairs of government; which I, for my part,
Groan under and am weary of.
 Are.   Sophronos,
I am as zealous too of shaking off
My gay state-fetters, that I have bethought
Of speedy remedy; and to that end,
As I have told ye, have concluded with
Corax, the prince's chief physician.
 Soph. You should have done this sooner, Aretus;
You were his tutor, and could best discern
His dispositions, to inform them rightly.
 Are. Passions of violent nature, by degrees
Are easiliest reclaim'd. There's something hid
Of his distemper, which we'll now find out.

   Enter CORAX, RHETIAS, PELIAS, CUCULUS, *and*
      GRILLA.

You come on just appointment. Welcome, gentlemen!
Have you won Rhetias, Corax?
 Cor.   Most sincerely.
 Cuc. Save ye, nobilities! Do your lordships take notice of my page? 'Tis a fashion of the newest

edition, spick and span new, without example.—Do your honour, housewife.

Gril. There's a curtsy for you,—and a curtsy for you.

Soph. 'Tis excellent: we must all follow fashion, And entertain she-waiters.

Are. 'Twill be courtly.

Cuc. I think so; I hope the chronicles will rear me one day for a headpiece—

Rhe. Of woodcock,[1] without brains in't! Barbers shall wear thee on their citterns,[2] and hucksters set thee out in gingerbread.

Cuc. Devil take thee! I say nothing to thee now; canst let me be quiet?

Gril. You're too perstreperous, saucebox.

Cuc. Good girl!—If we begin to puff once—

Pel. Prithee, hold thy tongue; the lords are in the presence.

Rhe. Mum, butterfly!

Pel. The prince ![3] stand and keep silence.

Cuc. O, the prince !— Wench, thou shalt see the prince now. [*Soft music.*

Enter PALADOR *with a book.*

Soph. Sir!

---

[1] Of *woodcock*, &c.] A cant term for a simpleton. See *Jonson*, vol. ii. p. 127.

[2] Barbers *shall wear thee on their* citterns,] For an explanation of this passage the reader may refer to *Jonson*, vol. iii. p. 411, where he will find all that is necessary to be said on the subject. The head of the cittern, like that of the harp, occasionally terminated, I suppose, in some grotesque kind of ornament. [In the note on Jonson above referred to, Gifford observes; "It appears from innumerable passages in our old writers, that barbers' shops were furnished with some musical instrument (commonly a cittern or guitar), for the amusement of such customers as chose to strum upon it while waiting for their turn to be shaved, &c."—Here Gifford might have omitted "I suppose:" citterns were usually ornamented with grotesque heads carved at the extremity of the neck and finger-board. D.]

[3] *The prince!*] I have omitted "O," which was probably adopted from the next speech.

  Are.   Gracious sir!
  Pal.   Why all this company?
  Cor. A book! is this the early exercise
I did prescribe? instead of following health,
Which all men covet, you pursue disease.[4]
Where's your great horse, your hounds, your set at tennis,
Your balloon-ball, the practice of your dancing,
Your casting of the sledge, or learning how
To toss a pike? all chang'd into a sonnet!
Pray, sir, grant me[5] free liberty to leave
The court; it does infect me with the sloth
Of sleep and surfeit: in the university
I have employments, which to my profession
Add profit and report; here I am lost,
And in your wilful dulness held a man
Of neither art nor honesty. You may
Command my head:—pray, take it, do! 'twere better
For me to lose it than to lose my wits,
And live in Bedlam;[6] you will force me to't;
I'm almost mad already.
  Pal.   I believe it.
  Soph. Letters are come from Crete, which do require
A speedy restitution of such ships
As by your father were long since detain'd;
If not, defiance threaten'd.
  Are.   These near parts
Of Syria that adjoin muster their friends;
And by intelligence we learn for certain

---

 [4] *you pursue disease.*] The old copy reads "*your* disease." This word, which spoils the measure, seems to have crept in from the passage immediately following it.
 [5] *Pray, sir, grant me*] Qy. "*Pray*, grant me, sir"? D.
 [6] *And live in* Bedlam;] As there were mad folks in Famagosta, there were doubtless receptacles for them. Ford, however, was thinking of Moorfields.

The Syrian will pretend an ancient interest
Of tribute intermitted.
 Soph.   Through your land
Your subjects mutter strangely, and imagine
More than they dare speak publicly.
 Cor.   And yet
They talk but oddly of you.
 Cuc.   Hang 'em, mongrels!
 Pal. Of me! my subjects talk of me!
 Cor.   Yes, scurvily,
And think worse, prince.
 Pal.   I'll borrow patience
A little time to listen to these wrongs;
And from the few of you which are here present
Conceive the general voice.
 Cor.   So! now he's nettled. [*Aside.*
 Pal. By all your loves I charge ye, without fear
Or flattery, to let me know your thoughts,
And how I am interpreted: speak boldly.
 Soph. For my part, sir, I will be plain and brief.
I think you are of nature mild and easy,
Not willingly provok'd, but withal headstrong
In any passion that misleads your judgment:
I think you too indulgent to such motions
As spring out of your own affections;
Too old to be reform'd, and yet too young
To take fit counsel from yourself of what
Is most amiss.
 Pal.   So!—Tutor, your conceit?
 Are. I think you dote—with pardon let me speak it—
Too much upon your pleasures; and these pleasures
Are so wrapt up in self-love, that you covet
No other change of fortune; would be still
What your birth makes you; but are loth to toil

SCENE I.   THE LOVER'S MELANCHOLY.   33

In such affairs of state as break your sleeps.
 Cor. I think you would be by the world reputed
A man in every point complete; but are
In manners and effect[7] indeed a child,
A boy, a very boy.
 Pel.   May't please your grace,
I think you do contain within yourself
The great elixir, soul, and quintessence
Of all divine perfections; are the glory
Of mankind, and the only strict example
For earthly monarchs[8] to square out their lives by;
Time's miracle, Fame's pride; in knowledge, wit,
Sweetness, discourse, arms, arts—
 Pal.   You are a courtier.
 Cuc. But not of the ancient fashion, an't like your highness. 'Tis I; I that am the credit of the court, noble prince; and if thou wouldst, by proclamation or patent, create me overseer of all the tailors in thy dominions, then, then the golden days should appear again; bread should be cheaper, fools should have more wit, knaves more honesty, and beggars more money.
 Gril. I think now—
 Cuc. Peace, you squall!
 Pal. [*to Rhetias*] You have not spoken yet.
 Cuc. Hang him! he'll nothing but rail.
 Gril. Most abominable;—out upon him!
 Cor. Away, Cuculus; follow the lords.
 Cuc. Close, page, close.
  [*They all silently withdraw but Pal. and Rhe.*
 Pal. You are somewhat long a' thinking.
 Rhe. I do not think at all.
 Pal. Am I not worthy of your thought?

---

[7] *effect*] Qy. "affect"? D.
[8] *monarchs*] The 4to has "Monarchies." D.

Rhe. My pity you are, but not my reprehension.
Pal. Pity!
Rhe. Yes, for I pity such to whom I owe service, who exchange their happiness for a misery.
Pal. Is it a misery to be a prince?
Rhe. Princes who forget their sovereignty, and yield to affected passion, are weary of command.—• You had a father, sir.
Pal. Your sovereign, whiles he liv'd: but what of him?
Rhe. Nothing. I only dared to name him; that's all.
Pal. I charge thee, by the duty that thou ow'st us, Be plain in what thou mean'st to speak: there's something
That we must know: be free; our ears are open.
Rhe. O, sir, I had rather hold a wolf by the ears than stroke a lion; the greatest danger is the last.
Pal. This is mere trifling.—Ha! are all stol'n hence?
We are alone: thou hast an honest look;
Thou hast a tongue, I hope, that is not oil'd
With flattery: be open. Though 'tis true
That in my younger[9] days I oft have heard
Agenor's name, my father, more traduc'd
Than I could then observe; yet I protest
I never had a friend, a certain friend,
That would inform me throughly of such errors
As oftentimes are incident to princes.
Rhe. All this may be. I have seen a man so curious in feeling of the edge of a keen knife, that

---

[9] *younger*] So a copy of the 4to in the King's Library, British Museum, and a copy in my possession. Another copy in my possession has "young."—N.B. Copies of old plays *of the same edition* occasionally differ in minute particulars, certain alterations having been made in the text as the edition was passing through the press. D.

he has cut his fingers. My flesh is not of[10] proof against the metal I am to handle; the one is tenderer than the other.

Pal. I see, then, I must court thee. Take the word
Of a just prince; for any thing thou speakest
I have more than a pardon,—thanks and love.

Rhe. I will remember you of an old tale that something concerns you. Meleander, the great but unfortunate statesman, was by your father treated with for a match between you and his eldest daughter, the Lady Eroclea: you were both near of an age. I presume you remember a contract, and cannot forget *her*.

Pal. She was a lovely beauty. Prithee, forward!

Rhe. To court was Eroclea brought; was courted by your father, not for Prince Palador, as it followed, but to be made a prey to some less noble design. With your favour, I have forgot the rest.

Pal. Good, call it back again into thy memory;
Else, losing the remainder, I am lost too.

Rhe. You charm me.[11] In brief, a rape by some bad agents was attempted; by the Lord Meleander her father rescued, she conveyed away; Meleander accused of treason, his land seized, he himself distracted and confined to the castle, where he yet lives. What had ensued was doubtful; but your father shortly after died.

Pal. But what became of fair Eroclea?

Rhe. She never since was heard of.

Pal. No hope lives, then,
Of ever, ever seeing her again?

---

[10] *of*] Omitted by Gifford. D.

[11] *You charm me.*] You overpower my reluctance to speak; and accordingly Rhetias feels no further difficulty in disclosing himself.

Rhe. Sir, I feared[12] I should anger ye. This[13] was, as I said, an old tale :—I have now a new one, which may perhaps season the first with a more delightful relish.

Pal. I am prepar'd to hear ; say what you please.

Rhe. My Lord Meleander falling,—on whose favour my fortunes relied,—I furnished myself for travel, and bent my course to Athens ; where a pretty accident, after a while, came to my knowledge.

Pal. My ear is open to thee.

Rhe. A young lady contracted to a noble gentleman, as the lady we[14] last mentioned and your highness were, being hindered by their jarring parents, stole from her home, and was conveyed like a shipboy in a merchant[15] from the country where she lived, into Corinth first, afterwards to Athens ; where in much solitariness she lived, like a youth, almost two years, courted by all for[16] acquaintance, but friend to none by familiarity.

Pal. In habit of a man ?

Rhe. A handsome young man—till, within these three months or less,—her sweetheart's father[17] dying some year before or more,—she had notice of it, and with much joy returned home, and, as report voiced it at Athens, enjoyed her happiness she was long an exile for. Now, noble sir, if you did love the Lady Eroclea, why may not such safety and fate direct her as directed the other ? 'tis not impossible.

---

[12] *feared*] The 4to has "feare." D.
[13] *This*] The 4to has "There ;" which perhaps Gifford need not have altered. D.
[14] *we*] Omitted by Gifford. D.
[15] *in a merchant*] i. e. a merchantship, a trader. This is the expression which so greatly perplexed Steevens, who has made woful work with it in *The Tempest*.
[16] *for*] Gifford printed "her." D.
[17] *her sweetheart's father*] The 4to has "*her* sweet hearty *Father*." D.

Pal. If I *did* love her, Rhetias! Yes, I did.
Give me thy hand: as thou didst serve Meleander,
And art still true to these, henceforth serve me.
 Rhe. My duty and my obedience are my surety;
but I have been too bold.
 Pal. Forget the sadder story of my father,
And only, Rhetias, learn to read me well ;[18]
For I must ever thank thee: thou'st unlock'd
A tongue was vow'd to silence; for requital,
Open my bosom, Rhetias.
 Rhe. What's your meaning?
 Pal. To tie thee to an oath of secrecy.
Unloose the buttons, man: thou dost it faintly.
What find'st thou there?
 Rhe. A picture in a tablet.
 Pal. Look well upon 't.
 Rhe. I do—yes—let me observe it—
'Tis hers, the lady's.
 Pal. Whose?
 Rhe. Eroclea's.
 Pal. Hers that was once Eroclea. For her sake
Have I advanc'd Sophronos to the helm
Of government; for her sake will restore
Meleander's honours to him; will, for her sake,
Beg friendship from thee, Rhetias. O, be faithful,
And let no politic lord work from thy bosom
My griefs: I know thou wert put on to sift me;
But be not too secure.
 Rhe. I am your creature.
 Pal. Continue still thy discontented fashion,
Humour the lords, as they would humour me;
I'll not live in thy debt.—We are discover'd.

---

[18] *to read me well;*] To *understand,* to *comprehend* me.

Enter AMETHUS, MENAPHON, THAMASTA, KALA, *and*
PARTHENOPHIL.

Amet. Honour and health still wait upon the
prince !
Sir, I am bold with favour to present
Unto your highness Menaphon my friend,
Return'd from travel.
Men. Humbly on my knees
I kiss your gracious hand.
Pal. It is our duty
To love the virtuous.
Men. If my prayers or service
Hold any value, they are vow'd yours ever.
Rhe. I have a fist for thee too, stripling; thou'rt
started up prettily since I saw thee. Hast learned any
wit abroad? Canst tell news and swear lies with a
grace, like a true traveller?—What new ouzle's this?[19]
Tha. Your highness shall do right to your own
judgment
In taking more than common notice of
This stranger, an Athenian, nam'd Parthenophil;
One who,[20] if mine opinion do not soothe me
Too grossly, for the fashion of his mind
Deserves a dear respect.
Pal. Your commendations,
Sweet cousin, speak him nobly.
Par. All the powers
That sentinel just thrones double their guards[21]
About your sacred excellence!

[19] *What new* ouzle's *this?*] Parthenophil, whom he pretends not to know. If anything be necessary on so common a word, it may be briefly observed that "*ouzle* is a generic term, in which the species blackbird (one among many) is contained."
[20] *who,*] The 4to has "whom." D.
[21] *double their guards*] The old copy reads "double *these* guards;" which seems hardly intelligible.

SCENE I.   THE LOVER'S MELANCHOLY.   39

Pal.   What fortune
Led him to Cyprus?
Men.   My persuasions won him.
Amet. And if your highness please to hear the entrance
Into their first acquaintance, you will say—
  Tha. It was the newest, sweetest, prettiest accident
That e'er delighted your attention :
I can discourse it, sir.
  Pal.   Some other time.
How is he call'd?
  Tha.   Parthenophil.
  Pal.   Parthenophil!
We shall sort time to take more notice of him. [*Exit.*
  Men. His wonted melancholy still pursues him.
  Amet. I told you so.
  Tha.   You must not wonder at it.
  Par. I do not, lady.
  Amet.   Shall we to the castle?
  Men. We will attend ye both.
  Rhe. All three,—I'll go too. Hark in thine ear, gallant; I'll keep the old madman[22] in chat, whilst thou gabblest to the girl: my thumb's upon my lips; not a word.
  Amet. I need not fear thee, Rhetias.—Sister, soon Expect us: this day we will range the city.
  Tha. Well, soon I shall expect ye.—Kala ![23]
                                    [*Aside to Kala.*
  Kal.   Trust me.
  Rhe. Troop on !—Love, love, what a wonder thou art !   [*Exeunt all but Par. and Kala.*

---

[22] *madman*] Gifford printed "*man.*" D.
[23] *Kala!*] This is a hint to her attendant to take the present opportunity of conveying her message "honourably" to Parthenophil. See p. 28.

Kal. May I not be offensive, sir?
Par.   Your pleasure?
Yet, pray, be brief.
Kal.   Then, briefly; good, resolve me;
Have you a mistress or a wife?
Par.   I've neither.
Kal. Nor did you ever love in earnest any
Fair lady, whom you wish'd to make your own?
Par. Not any, truly.
Kal.   What your friends or means are
I will not be inquisitive to know,
Nor do I care to hope for. But admit
A dowry were thrown down before your choice,
Of beauty, noble birth, sincere[24] affection,
How gladly would you entertain it! Young man,
I do not tempt you idly.
Par.   I shall thank you,
When my unsettled thoughts can make me sensible
Of what 'tis to be happy; for the present
I am your debtor; and, fair gentlewoman,
Pray give me leave as yet to study ignorance,
For my weak brains conceive not what concerns me.
Another time—   [*Going.*

Re-enter THAMASTA.

Tha.   Do I break off your parley,
That you are parting? Sure, my woman loves you:
Can she speak well, Parthenophil?
Par.   Yes, madam,
Discreetly chaste she can; she hath much won
On my belief, and in few words, but pithy,
Much mov'd my thankfulness. You are her lady;
Your goodness aims, I know, at her preferment;

---

[24] *sincere*] The 4to has "and *sincere.*" D.

Therefore I may be bold to make confession
Of truth : if ever I desire to thrive
In woman's favour, Kala is the first
Whom my ambition shall bend to.
 Tha.   Indeed !
But say a nobler love should interpose.
 Par. Where real worth and constancy first settle
A hearty truth, there greatness cannot shake it;
Nor shall it mine : yet I am but an infant
In that construction, which must give clear light
To Kala's merit; riper hours hereafter
Must learn me how to grow rich in deserts.
Madam, my duty waits on you.   [*Exit*.
 Tha.   Come hither :—
" If ever henceforth I desire to thrive
In woman's favour,[25] Kala is the first
Whom my ambition shall bend to." 'Twas so !
 Kal. These very words he spake.
 Tha.   These very words
Curse thee, unfaithful creature, to thy grave.
Thou woo'dst him for thyself?
 Kal.   You said I should.
 Tha. My name was never mention'd?
 Kal.   Madam, no;
We were not come to that.
 Tha.   Not come to that!
Art thou a rival fit to cross my fate?
Now poverty and a dishonest fame,
The waiting-woman's wages, be thy payment,
False, faithless, wanton beast! I'll spoil your car-
   riage;[26]

---

 [25] *favour*,] The 4to has "fauours;" but see above. D.
 [26] *I'll spoil your* carriage;] So the 4to reads. From the sequel of the speech it appears not improbable that the poet's word was "*marriage*."

There's not a page, a groom, nay, not a citizen
That shall be cast [away] upon ye, Kala;
I'll keep thee in my service all thy lifetime,
Without hope of a husband or a suitor.

Kal. I have not verily deserv'd this cruelty.

Tha. Parthenophil shall know, if he respect
My birth, the danger of a fond neglect.[27]   [*Exit.*

Kal. Are you so quick? Well, I may chance to cross
Your peevishness. Now, though I never meant
The young man for myself, yet, if he love me,
I'll have him, or I'll run away with him;
And let her do her worst then! What! we're all
But flesh and blood; the same thing that will do
My lady good will please her woman too.[28]   [*Exit.*

SCENE II. *An apartment at the castle.*

Enter CLEOPHILA *and* TROLLIO.

Cleo. Tread softly, Trollio; my father sleeps still.

Trol. Ay, forsooth; but he sleeps like a hare, with his eyes open, and that's no good sign.

Cleo. Sure, thou art weary of this sullen living;
But I am not; for I take more content
In my obedience here than all delights
The time presents elsewhere.

Mel. [*within*] O!

Cleo.   Dost hear that groan?

Trol. Hear it! I shudder: it was a strong blast, young mistress, able to root up heart, liver, lungs, and all.

[27] *of a* fond *neglect.*] i.e. the danger of slighting the *love* of a lady of my rank.
[28] Kala bears some resemblance to Valeria in Shirley's tragedy of *The Cardinal.*

Cleo. My much-wrong'd father! let me view his face.

[*Draws the arras.*[29] *Meleander discovered in a chair, sleeping.*

Trol. Lady mistress, shall I fetch a barber to steal away his rough beard whiles he sleeps? In's naps[30] he never looks in a glass—and 'tis high time, on conscience,[31] for him to be trimmed; 'has not been under the shaver's hand almost these four years.

Cleo. Peace, fool!

Trol. [*aside*] I could clip the old ruffian; there's hair enough to stuff all the great codpieces in Switzerland. 'A begins to stir; 'a stirs. Bless us, how his eyes roll!—A good year keep your lordship in your right wits, I beseech ye!

Mel. Cleophila!

Cleo. Sir, I am here; how d'ye, sir?

Trol. Sir, is your stomach up yet? get some warm porridge in your belly; 'tis a very good settle-brain.

Mel. The raven croak'd, and hollow shrieks of owls
Sung dirges at her funeral; I laugh'd
The whiles, for 'twas no boot to weep. The girl
Was fresh and full of youth: but, O, the cunning
Of tyrants, that look big! their very frowns
Doom poor souls guilty ere their cause be heard.—
Good, what art thou?—and thou?

Cleo. I am Cleophila,
Your woful daughter.

---

[29] *the arras:*] Arras was used precisely as a curtain: it hung (on tenters or lines) from the rafters, or from some temporary stay, and was opened, held up, or drawn aside, as occasion required.

[30] *whiles he sleeps? In's naps,* &c.] The 4to reads "whiles he sleeps in's naps?" which is not easily understood; unless by *naps* the facetious Trollio means in his *rough state*. I believe, however, that the error lies in the pointing.

[31] *on conscience,*] Gifford printed "o' my *conscience*." D.

Trol. I am Trollio,
Your honest implement.
　　Mel. I know ye both. 'Las, why d'ye use me thus?
Thy sister, my Eroclea, was so gentle,
That turtles in their down do feed more gall
Than her spleen mix'd with: yet, when winds and storm
Drive dirt and dust on banks of spotless snow,
The purest whiteness is no such defence
Against the sullying foulness of that fury.
So rav'd Agenor, that great man, mischief
Against the girl: 'twas a politic trick!
We were too old in honour. I am lean,
And fall'n away extremely; most assuredly
I have not din'd these three days.
　　Cleo. Will you now, sir?
　　Trol. I beseech ye heartily, sir: I feel a horrible puking myself.
　　Mel. Am I stark mad?
　　Trol. [*aside*] No, no, you are but a little staring; there's difference between staring and stark mad. You are but whimsied yet; crotcheted, conundrumed, or so.
　　Mel. Here's all my care; and I do often sigh
For thee, Cleophila; we are secluded
From all good people. But take heed; Amethus
Was son to Doryla, Agenor's sister;
There's some ill blood about him, if the surgeon
Have not been very skilful to let all out.
　　Cleo. I am, alas, too griev'd to think of love;
That must concern me least.
　　Mel. Sirrah, be wise! be wise!
　　Trol. Who, I? I will be monstrous and wise immediately.

SCENE II. THE LOVER'S MELANCHOLY.

Enter AMETHUS, MENAPHON, PARTHENOPHIL, *and* RHETIAS.

Welcome, gentlemen; the more the merrier. I'll lay the cloth, and set the stools in a readiness, for I see here is some hope of dinner now. [*Exit.*

Amet. My Lord Meleander, Menaphon, your kinsman,
Newly return'd from travel, comes to tender
His duty t'ye;—to you his love, fair mistress.

Men. I would I could as easily remove
Sadness from your remembrance, sir, as study
To do you faithful service.—My dear cousin,
All best of comforts bless your sweet obedience!

Cleo. One chief of 'em, [my] worthy cousin, lives
In you and your well-doing.

Men.   This young stranger
Will well deserve your knowledge.

Amet.   For my friend's sake,
Lady, pray give him welcome.

Cleo.   He has met it,
If sorrows can look kindly.

Par.   You much honour me.

Rhe. [*aside*] How he eyes the company! sure my passion will betray my weakness.—O my master, my noble master, do not forget me; I am still the humblest and the most faithful in heart of those that serve you.

Mel. Ha, ha, ha!

Rhe. [*aside*] There's wormwood in that laughter; 'tis the usher to a violent extremity.

Mel. I am a weak old man. All these are come
To jeer my ripe calamities.

Men.   Good uncle!

Mel. But I'll outstare ye all : fools, desperate fools !

You're cheated, grossly cheated; range, range on,
And roll about the world to gather moss,
The moss of honour, gay reports, gay clothes,
Gay wives, huge empty buildings, whose proud roofs
Shall with their pinnacles even reach the stars.
Ye work and work like blind moles,[32] in the paths
That are bor'd through the crannies of the earth,
To charge your hungry souls with such full surfeits
As, being gorg'd once, make ye lean with plenty;
And when ye've skimm'd the vomit of your riots,
Ye're fat in no felicity but folly:
Then your last sleeps seize on ye; then the troops
Of worms crawl round and feast; good cheer, rich
 fare,
Dainty, delicious!—Here's Cleophila;
All the poor stock of my remaining thrift:
You, you, the prince's cousin, how d'ye like her?
Amethus, how d'ye like her?
 Amet. My intents
Are just and honourable.
 Men. Sir, believe him.
 Mel. Take her.—We two must part; go to him,
 do.
 Par. This sight is full of horror.
 Rhe. There is sense yet
In this distraction.
 Mel. In this jewel I have given away
All what I can call mine. When I am dead,
Save charge; let me be buried in a nook:
No guns, no pompous whining; these are fooleries.
If, whiles we live, we stalk about the streets
Jostled by carmen, footposts, and fine apes
In silken coats, unminded and scarce thought on,

---

[32] *like blind moles,*] The 4to has "*like* Moles, blind." D.

It is not comely to be hal'd to th' earth,³³
Like high-fed jades upon a tilting-day,
In antic trappings. Scorn to useless tears!
Eroclea was not coffin'd so; she perish'd,
And no eye dropp'd save mine—and I am childish;
I talk like one that dotes: laugh at me, Rhetias,
Or rail at me. They will not give me meat,
They've starv'd me; but I'll henceforth be mine own
                cook.
Good morrow! 'tis too early for my cares
To revel; I will break my heart a little,
And tell ye more hereafter. Pray be merry. [*Exit.*

    Rhe. I'll follow him. — My Lord Amethus, use your time respectively; few words to purpose soonest prevail: study no long orations; be plain and short.— I'll follow him.   [*Exit.*

    Amet. Cleophila, although these blacker clouds
Of sadness thicken and make dark the sky
Of thy fair eyes, yet give me leave to follow
The stream of my affections: they are pure,
Without all mixture of unnoble thoughts.
Can you be ever mine?
    Cleo.   I am so low
In mine own fortunes and my father's woes,
That I want words to tell ye you deserve
A worthier choice.
    Amet.   But give me leave to hope.
    Men. My friend is serious.
    Cleo. Sir, this for answer. If I ever thrive
In any³⁴ earthly happiness, the next
To my good father's wish'd recovery

---

    ³³ *hal'd to th' earth,*] i.e. drawn to the grave. The allusion is to the pomp and parade of a funeral procession, and to the rich heraldic trophies with which the hearse was covered.
    ³⁴ *any*] The 4to has "an." D.

Must be my thankfulness to your great merit,
Which I dare promise: for the present time
You cannot urge more from me.
Mel. [*within*]   Ho, Cleophila!
Cleo. This gentleman is mov'd.
Amet.   Your eyes, Parthenophil,
Are guilty of some passion.
Men.   Friend, what ails thee?
Par. All is not well within me, sir.
Mel. [*within*]   Cleophila!
Amet. Sweet maid, forget me not; we now must part.
Cleo. Still you shall have my prayer.
Amet.   Still you my truth.
[*Exeunt.*

ACT III.

Scene I. *A room in the palace.*

Enter Cuculus *and* Grilla ; *the former in a black velvet cap and a white feather, with a paper in his hand.*

Cuc. Do not I look freshly, and like a youth of the trim?

Gril. As rare an old youth as ever walked cross-gartered.

Cuc. Here are my mistresses mustered in white and black. [*Reads*] "Kala, the waiting-woman"—I will first begin at the foot: stand thou for Kala.

Gril. I stand for Kala; do your best and your worst.

Cuc. I must look big, and care little or nothing for her, because she is a creature that stands at livery. Thus I talk wisely, and to no purpose:—Wench, as it is not fit that thou shouldst be either fair or honest, so, considering thy service, thou art as thou art, and so are thy betters, let them be what they can be. Thus, in despite and defiance of all thy good parts, if I cannot endure thy baseness, 'tis more out of thy courtesy than my deserving; and so I expect thy answer.

Gril. I must confess—
Cuc. Well said.
Gril. You are—
Cuc. That's true too.
Gril. To speak you right, a very scurvy fellow.
Cuc. Away, away!—dost think so?
Gril. A very foul-mouth'd and misshapen coxcomb.
Cuc. I'll never believe it, by this hand.
Gril. A maggot, most unworthy to creep in
To the least wrinkle of a gentlewoman's—
What d'ye call—good conceit, or so, or what
You will else,—were you not refin'd by courtship
And education, which in my blear eyes
Makes you appear as sweet as any nosegay,
Or savoury cod of musk new fall'n from the cat.

Cuc. This shall serve well enough for the waiting-woman. My next mistress is Cleophila, the old madman's daughter. I must come to her in whining tune; sigh, wipe mine eyes, fold my arms, and blubber out my speech as thus:—Even as a kennel of hounds, sweet lady, cannot catch a hare when they are full-paunched on the carrion of a dead horse; so, even so, the gorge of my affections being full-crammed with the garboils of your condolements doth tickle me with the prick, as it were, about me, and fellow-feeling of howling outright.

Gril. This will do't, if we will hear.[1]

Cuc. Thou seest I am crying ripe, I am such another tender-hearted fool.

Gril. Even as the snuff of a candle that is burnt in the socket goes out, and leaves a strong perfume behind it; or as a piece of toasted cheese next the heart in a morning is a restorative for a sweet breath; so, even so, the odoriferous savour of your love doth perfume my heart—heigh-ho!—with the pure scent of an intolerable content, and not to be endured.

Cuc. By this hand, 'tis excellent! Have at thee, last of all, for the Princess Thamasta, she that is my mistress indeed. She is abominably proud, a lady of a damnable high, turbulent, and generous spirit: but I have a loud-mouthed cannon of mine own to batter her, and a penned speech of purpose: observe it.

Gril. Thus I walk by, hear, and mind you not.

Cuc. [*reads*]
"Though haughty as the devil or his dam
  Thou dost appear, great mistress, yet I am
  Like to an ugly firework, and can mount
  Above the region of thy sweet ac—count.
  Wert thou the moon herself, yet having seen
    thee,
  Behold the man ordain'd to move within thee."
Look to yourself, housewife! answer me in strong lines, you're best.

Gril. Keep off, poor fool, my beams will strike
    thee blind;
Else, if thou touch me, touch me but behind.
In palaces, such as pass in before
Must be great princes; for at the back-door

---

[1] *if* we *will hear.*] Probably a misprint for "*she.*" If Grilla answered in the name of Cleophila, *we* had already heard.

Tatterdemalions wait, who know not how
To get[2] admittance; such a one—art thou.
    Cuc. 'Sfoot, this is downright roaring.[3]
    Gril. I know how to present a big lady in her own cue. But, pray, in earnest, are you in love with all these?
    Cuc. Pish! I have not a rag of love about me; 'tis only a foolish humour I am possessed with, to be surnamed the Conqueror. I will court anything; be in love with nothing, nor no—thing.
    Gril. A rare man you are, I protest.
    Cuc. Yes, I know I am a rare man, and I ever held myself so.

    Enter PELIAS *and* CORAX.

    Pel. In amorous contemplation, on my life;
Courting his page, by Helicon!
    Cuc.   'Tis false.
    Gril. A gross untruth; I'll justify it, sir,
At any time, place, weapon.
    Cuc.   Marry, shall she.
    Cor. No quarrels, Goody Whisk! lay-by your trumperies, and fall-to your practice. Instructions are ready for you all. Pelias is your leader; follow him: get credit now or never. Vanish, doodles, vanish!
    Cuc. For the device?
    Cor. The same; get ye gone, and make no bawling.   [*Exeunt all but Corax.*
To waste my time thus, drone-like, in the court,
And lose so many hours as my studies
Have hoarded up, is to be like a man

---

    [2] *get*] Gifford printed "gain." D.
    [3] *this is downright* roaring.] i. e. the language of *bullies*, affecting a quarrel. See *Jonson*, vol. iv. p. 483.

That creeps both on his hands and knees to climb
A mountain's top; where, when he is ascended,
One careless slip down-tumbles him again
Into' the bottom, whence he first began.
I need no prince's favour; princes need
My art: then, Corax, be no more a gull;
The best of 'em cannot fool thee, nay, they shall not.

Enter SOPHRONOS *and* ARETUS.

Soph. We find him timely now; let's learn the cause.

Are. 'Tis fit we should.—Sir, we approve you learn'd,
And, since your skill can best discern the humours
That are predominant in bodies subject
To alteration, tell us, pray, what devil
This Melancholy is, which can transform
Men into monsters.

Cor.   You're yourself a scholar,
And quick of apprehension. Melancholy
Is not, as you conceive, indisposition
Of body, but the mind's disease. So Ecstasy,
Fantastic Dotage, Madness, Frenzy, Rapture[4]
Of mere imagination, differ partly
From Melancholy;[5] which is briefly this,
A mere commotion of the mind, o'ercharg'd

---

[4] *Rapture*] The 4to has "Rupture," which Gifford retained. D.

[5] "Vide," Ford says, "*Democritus Junior.*" He alludes to the *Anatomy of Melancholy*, by Robert Burton; from which not only what is here said, but the descriptions and personifications of the various affections of the mind in the Interlude (scene iii.) are imitated, or rather copied; for the poet has added little or nothing of his own to what he found in that popular volume. To say the truth, the stupendous and undistinguishing diligence of our "Democritus the Younger" almost precluded the possibility of adding to any topic which he had previously made the object of his researches. I omitted to observe that the anecdote of the "sow-pig that sucked a brach," p. 21, is taken from that writer, who found it in Giraldus Cambrensis.

With fear and sorrow; first begot i' th' brain,
The seat of reason, and from thence deriv'd
As suddenly into the heart, the seat
Of our affection.
 Are.   There are sundry kinds
Of this disturbance?
 Cor.   Infinite: it were
More easy to conjecture every hour
We have to live than reckon up the kinds
Or causes of this anguish of the mind.
 Soph. Thus you conclude that, as the cause is doubtful,
The cure must be impossible; and then
Our prince, poor gentleman, is lost for ever
As well unto himself as to his subjects.
 Cor. My lord, you are too quick: thus much I dare
Promise and do; ere many minutes pass
I will discover whence his sadness is,
Or undergo the censure of my ignorance.
 Are. You are a noble scholar.
 Soph.   For reward
You shall make your own demand.
 Cor.   May I be sure?
 Are. We both will pledge our truth.
 Cor.   'Tis soon perform'd:
That I may be discharg'd from my attendance
At court, and never more be sent for after;
Or—if I be, may rats gnaw all my books,
If I get home once, and come here again!
Though my neck stretch a halter for't, I care not.
 Soph. Come, come, you shall not fear it.
 Cor.   I'll acquaint ye
With what is to be done; and you shall fashion it.
            [*Exeunt.*

SCENE II. *A room in* THAMASTA'S *house.*

Enter KALA *and* PARTHENOPHIL.

Kal. My lady does expect ye, thinks all time
Too slow till you come to her: wherefore, young man,
If you intend to love me, and me only,
Before we part, without more circumstance,
Let us betroth ourselves.
 Par.   I dare not wrong ye;—
You are too violent.
 Kal.   Wrong me no more
Than I wrong you; be mine, and I am yours:
I cannot stand on points.
 Par.   Then, to resolve
All further hopes, you never can be mine,
Must not, and—pardon though I say—you shall not.
 Kal. [*aside*] The thing is sure a gelding.—Shall
  not! Well,
You're best to prate unto my lady now,
What proffer I have made.
 Par.   Never, I vow.
 Kal. Do, do! 'tis but a kind heart of mine own,
And ill luck can undo me.—Be refus'd!
O scurvy!—Pray walk on, I'll overtake ye. [*Exit Par.*
What a green-sickness-liver'd boy is this!
My maidenhead will shortly grow so stale
That 'twill be mouldy:—but I'll mar her market.[6]

Enter MENAPHON.

 Men. Parthenophil pass'd this[7] way: prithee, Kala,
Direct me to him.
 Kal.   Yes, I can direct ye;

---

[6] *but I'll mar her market.*] Her mistress's, whom she accordingly betrays to Menaphon.
[7] *this*] The 4to has "the." D.

But you, sir, must forbear.
  Men.   Forbear!
  Kal.   I said so.
Your bounty has engag'd my truth: receive
A secret, that will, as you are a man,
Startle your reason; 'tis but mere respect
Of what I owe to thankfulness. Dear sir,
The stranger whom your courtesy receiv'd
For friend is made your rival.
  Men.   Rival, Kala!
Take heed; thou art too credulous.
  Kal.   My lady
Dotes on him. I will place you in a room
Where, though you cannot hear, yet you shall see
Such passages as will confirm the truth
Of my intelligence.
  Men.   'Twill make me mad.
  Kal. Yes, yes.
It makes me mad too, that a gentleman
So excellently sweet, so liberal,
So kind, so proper, should be so betray'd
By a young smooth-chinn'd straggler: but, for love's
    sake,
Bear all with manly courage. Not a word;
I am undone then.
  Men.   That were too much pity:
Honest, most honest Kala, 'tis thy care,
Thy serviceable care.
  Kal.   You have even spoken
All can be said or thought.
  Men.   I will reward thee:
But as for him, ungentle boy, I'll whip
His falsehood with a vengeance.
  Kal.   O, speak little.
Walk up these stairs; and take this key; it opens

A chamber-door, where, at that window yonder,
You may see all their courtship.
   Men.   I am silent.
   Kal. As little noise as may be, I beseech ye:
There is a back-stair to convey ye forth
Unseen or unsuspected.   [*Exit Menaphon.*
                     He that cheats
A waiting-woman of a free good turn
She longs for must expect a shrewd revenge.
Sheep-spirited boy! although he had not married me,
He might have proffer'd kindness in a corner,
And ne'er have been the worse for't.—They are come:
On goes my set of faces most demurely.

      Enter THAMASTA *and* PARTHENOPHIL.

   Tha. Forbear the room.
   Kal.   Yes, madam.
   Tha.   Whosoever
Requires access to me, deny him entrance
Till I call thee; and wait without.
   Kal.   I shall.—
Sweet Venus, turn his courage to a snow-ball;
I heartily beseech it!   [*Aside, and exit.*
   Tha.   I expose
The honour of my birth, my fame, my youth,
To hazard of much hard construction,
In seeking an adventure of a parley,
So private, with a stranger: if your thoughts
Censure me not with mercy, you may soon
Conceive I have laid by that modesty
Which should preserve a virtuous name unstain'd.
   Par. Lady,—to shorten long excuses,—time
And safe experience have so throughly arm'd
My apprehension with a real taste
Of your most noble nature, that to question

The least part of your bounties, or that freedom
Which heaven hath with a plenty made you rich in,
Would argue me uncivil;[8] which is more,
Base-bred; and, which is most of all, unthankful.
   Tha. The constant loadstone and the steel are found
In several mines; yet is there such a league
Between these minerals as if one vein
Of earth had nourish'd both. The gentle myrtle
Is not engraft upon an olive's stock,
Yet nature hath between them lock'd a secret
Of sympathy, that, being planted near,
They will, both in their branches and their roots,
Embrace each other: twines of ivy round
The well-grown oak; the vine doth court the elm;
Yet these are different plants. Parthenophil,
Consider this aright; then these slight creatures
Will fortify the reasons I should frame
For that ungrounded[9]—as thou think'st—affection
Which is submitted to a stranger's pity.
True love may blush, when shame repents too late;
But in all actions nature yields to fate.
   Par. Great lady, 'twere a dulness must exceed
The grossest and most sottish kind of ignorance
Not to be sensible of your intents;
I clearly understand them. Yet so much
The difference between that height and lowness
Which doth distinguish our unequal fortunes
Dissuades me from ambition, that I am
Humbler in my desires than love's own power
Can any way raise up.

   [8] *Would argue me* uncivil;] i.e. unacquainted with the language and manners of good society. In this sense, the word frequently occurs in our old dramas.
   [9] *ungrounded*] Gifford printed "unguarded." D.

Tha.   I am a princess,
And know no law of slavery; to sue,
Yet be denied!
    Par.   I am so much a subject
To every law of noble honesty,
That to transgress the vows of perfect friendship
I hold a sacrilege as foul and curs'd
As if some holy temple had been robb'd,
And I the thief.
    Tha.   Thou art unwise, young man,
T' enrage a lioness.
    Par.   It were unjust
To falsify a faith, and ever after,
Disrob'd of that fair ornament, live naked,
A scorn to time and truth.
    Tha.   Remember well
Who I am, and what thou art.
    Par.   That remembrance
Prompts me to worthy duty. O, great lady,
If some few days have tempted your free heart
To cast away affection on a stranger;
If that affection have so oversway'd
Your judgment, that it, in a manner, hath
Declin'd your sovereignty of birth and spirit;
How can ye turn your eyes off from that glass
Wherein you may new-trim and settle right
A memorable name?
    Tha.   The youth is idle.[10]
    Par. Days, months, and years are past since Menaphon
Hath lov'd and serv'd you truly; Menaphon,
A man of no large distance in his blood
From yours; in qualities desertful, grac'd

---

[10] *The youth is* idle.] i.e. talks from the purpose.

With youth, experience, every happy gift
That can by nature or by education
Improve a gentleman: for him, great lady,
Let me prevail, that you will yet at last
Unlock the bounty which your love and care
Have wisely treasur'd up, t'enrich his life.

   Tha. Thou hast a moving eloquence, Parthenophil!—

Parthenophil, in vain we strive to cross
The destiny that guides us. My great heart
Is stoop'd so much beneath that wonted pride
That first disguis'd it, that I now prefer
A miserable life with thee before
All other earthly comforts.

   Par.   Menaphon,
By me, repeats the self-same words to you:
You are too cruel, if you can distrust
His truth or my report.

   Tha.   Go where thou wilt,
I'll be an exile with thee; I will learn
To bear all change of fortunes.

   Par.   For my friend
I plead with grounds of reason.

   Tha.   For thy love,
Hard-hearted youth, I here renounce all thoughts
Of other hopes, of other entertainments,—

   Par. Stay, as you honour virtue.

   Tha.   When the proffers
Of other greatness,—

   Par.   Lady!

   Tha.   When entreats
Of friends,—

   Par.   I'll ease your grief.

   Tha.   Respect of kindred,—

   Par. Pray, give me hearing.

Tha.   Loss of fame,—
Par.   I crave
But some few minutes.
   Tha.   Shall infringe my vows,
Let Heaven,—
   Par.   My love speaks[11] t'ye : hear, then go on.
   Tha. Thy love! why, 'tis a charm to stop a vow
In its most violent course.
   Par.   Cupid has broke
His arrows here ; and, like a child unarm'd,
Comes to make sport between us with no weapon
But feathers stolen from his mother's doves.
   Tha. This is mere trifling.
   Par.   Lady, take a secret.
I am as you are—in a lower rank,
Else of the self-same sex—a maid, a virgin.
And now, to use your own words, "if your thoughts
Censure me not with mercy, you may soon
Conceive I have laid by that modesty
Which should preserve a virtuous name unstain'd.
   Tha. Are you not mankind, then ?
   Par.   When you shall read
The story of my sorrows, with the change
Of my misfortunes, in a letter printed[12]
From my unforg'd relation, I believe
You will not think the shedding of one tear
A prodigality that misbecomes
Your pity and my fortune.
   Tha.   Pray, conceal
The errors of my passion.[13]
   Par.   Would I had

---

[11] *speaks*] The 4to has "speake." D.

[12] *printed*] By *printed* no more is meant than *set down*, recounted, &c. It was the language of the times.

[13] *passion.*] The 4to has "passions:" and so Gifford. D.

Much more of honour—as for life, I value't not—
To venture on your secrecy!
Tha.   It will be
A hard task for my reason to relinquish
Th' affection which was once devoted thine;
I shall awhile repute thee still the youth
I lov'd so dearly.
Par.   You shall find me ever
Your ready faithful servant.
Tha.   O, the powers
Who do direct our hearts laugh at our follies!
We must not part yet.
Par.   Let not my unworthiness
Alter your good opinion.
Tha.   I shall henceforth
Be jealous of thy company with any:
My fears are strong and many.[14]

Re-enter KALA.

Kal.   Did your ladyship
Call me?
Tha. For what?
Kal.   Your servant Menaphon
Desires admittance.

Enter MENAPHON.

Men.   With your leave, great mistress,
I come,—So private! is this well, Parthenophil?
Par. Sir, noble sir,—
Men.   You are unkind and treacherous;
This 'tis to trust a straggler!
Tha.   Prithee, servant,—

---

[14] This scene, at once dignified and pathetic, is happily conceived, delicately conducted, and beautifully written. It places Ford's powers of language and command of feeling in a very eminent rank.

Men. I dare not question you; you are my mistress,
My prince's nearest kinswoman: but he—
Tha. Come, you are angry.
Men. Henceforth I will bury
Unmanly passion in perpetual silence :
I'll court mine own distraction, dote on folly,
Creep to the mirth and madness of the age,
Rather than be so slav'd again to woman,
Which in her best of constancy is steadiest
In change and scorn.
Tha. How dare ye talk to me thus?
Men. Dare! Were you not own sister to my friend,
Sister to my Amethus, I would hurl ye
As far off from mine eyes as from my heart;
For I would never more look on ye. Take
Your jewel t'ye !—And, youth, keep under wing,
Or—boy !—boy !—
Tha. If commands be of no force,
Let me entreat thee, Menaphon.
Men. 'Tis naught.
Fie, fie, Parthenophil ! have I deserv'd
To be thus us'd ?
Par. I do protest—
Men. You shall not:
Henceforth I will be free, and hate my bondage.

Enter AMETHUS.

Amet. Away, away to court ! The prince is pleas'd
To see a masque to-night; we must attend him :
'Tis near upon the time.—How thrives your suit?
Men. The judge, your sister, will decide it shortly.
Tha. Parthenophil, I will not trust you from me.
[*Exeunt.*

SCENE III. *A room in the palace.*

Enter PALADOR, SOPHRONOS, ARETUS, *and* CORAX; Servants
with torches.

Cor. Lights and attendance!— I will show your highness
A trifle of mine own brain. If you can,
Imagine you were now in the university,
You'll take it well enough ; a scholar's fancy,
A quab—'tis nothing else—a very quab.[15]

Pal. We will observe it.

Soph. Yes, and grace it too, sir,
For Corax else is humorous and testy.

Are. By any means ; men singular in art
Have always some odd whimsey more than usual.

Pal. The name of this conceit?

Cor. Sir, it is call'd
The Masque of Melancholy.

Are. We must look for
Nothing but sadness here, then.

Cor. Madness rather
In several changes.[16] Melancholy is
The root as well of every apish frenzy,

---

[15] *A quab—a very quab.*] An unfledged bird, a nestling: metaphorically, anything in an imperfect, unfinished state. In the first sense the word is still used in that part of Devonshire where Ford was born, and perhaps in many other places.—It is undoubtedly (among other things) a small fish of some kind; but I have given it a meaning more familiar to me, as I am persuaded it was to Ford.

[16] Ford has here introduced one of those interludes in which the old stage so much delighted. The various characters of these "apish frenzies," as he calls them, he has taken from Burton's *Melancholy;* the book to which he refers in a former scene. He cannot be said to have improved what he has borrowed, which, on the contrary, reads better in Burton's pages than his own. What delight the audience may have gathered from the fantastic garb and action of his crazy monologists, I know not; but even here they must have missed the wild and tumultuous extravagance of Beaumont and Fletcher's *Love's Pilgrimage,* and even the more impressive moodiness of Brome's *Northern Lass.*

Laughter, and mirth, as dulness. Pray, my lord,
Hold, and observe the plot [*gives Pal. a paper*]: 'tis
　　there express'd
In kind, what shall be now express'd in action.

Enter AMETHUS, MENAPHON, THAMASTA, *and* PAR-
THENOPHIL.

No interruption; take your places quickly;
Nay, nay, leave ceremony.—Sound to th' entrance!
　　　　　　　　　　　　　　　　　　[*Flourish.*

Enter RHETIAS, *his face whited, with black shag hair
and long nails, and with a piece of raw meat.*

Rhe. *Bow, bow! wow, wow! the moon's eclipsed;
I'll to the churchyard and sup. Since I turned wolf, I
bark, and howl, and dig up graves; I will never have
the sun shine again: 'tis midnight, deep dark midnight,
—get a prey, and fall to—I have catched thee now—
Arre!—*

Cor. This kind is called Lycanthropia, sir; when
men conceive themselves wolves.[17]

Pal. Here I find it. 　　　[*Looking at the paper.*

Enter PELIAS, *with a crown of feathers and anticly rich.*

Pel. *I will hang 'em all, and burn my wife. Was
I not an emperor? my hand was kissed, and ladies lay
down before me; in triumph did I ride with my nobles
about me till the mad dog bit me: I fell, and I fell,*

---

[17] "*Lycanthropia*, which Avicenna calls *Cucubuth*, others *Lupi-
nam insaniam*, or Wolf-madness, when men run howling about
graves and fields in the night, and will not be perswaded but that
they are Wolves, or some such beasts," &c. *Anatomy of Melancholy*,
p. 6, ed. 1676. This and the extracts which follow are all taken
from what Burton calls "the fourth subsection of the first partition
of his Synopsis." Here is more than enough, I suspect, to satisfy
the most curious reader; if not, he may turn to the pages which I
have marked.

and I fell. It shall be treason by statute for any man to name water, or wash his hands, throughout all my dominions. Break all the looking-glasses; I will not see my horns: my wife cuckolds me; she is a whore, a whore, a whore, a whore!

Pal. Hydrophobia[18] term you this?

Cor. And men possess'd so shun all sight of water: Sometimes, if mix'd with jealousy, it renders them Incurable, and oftentimes brings death.

Enter a Philosopher *in black rags, with a copper chain, an old gown half off, and a book.*

Phi. Philosophers dwell in the moon. Speculation and theory girdle the world about like a wall. Ignorance, like an atheist, must be damned in the pit. I am very, very poor, and poverty is the physic for the soul: my opinions are pure and perfect. Envy is a monster, and I defy the beast.

Cor. Delirium this is call'd, which is mere dotage,[19]
Sprung from ambition first and singularity,
Self-love, and blind opinion of true merit.

Pal. I not dislike the course.

---

[18] "*Hydrophobia* is a kind of madness, well known in every village, which comes by the biting of a mad dog, or scratching, saith Aurelianus; touching, or smelling alone sometimes, as Sckenkius proves . . . so called, because the parties affected cannot endure the sight of water, or any liquor, supposing still they see a mad dog in it. And which is more wonderful, though they be very dry (as in this malady they are), they will rather dye than drink." Burton's *Anat. of Mel.* p. 6, ed. 1676.

[19] "*Dotage*, Fatuity, or Folly, is a common name to all the following species, as some will have it. Laurentius and Altomarus comprehended [comprehend] Madness, Melancholy, and the rest under this name, and call it the *summum genus* of them all. If it be distinguished from them, it is *natural* or *ingenite*, which comes by some defect of the organs, and over-much brain, as we see in our common fools; and is for the most part intended or remitted in particular men, and thereupon some are wiser than other; or else it is acquisite, an appendix or symptom of some other disease, which comes or goes; or if it continue, a sign of *Melancholy* itself." Burton's *Anat. of Mel.* p. 5, ed. 1676.

Enter GRILLA, *in a rich gown, a great fardingale, a great ruff, a muff, a fan, and a coxcomb*[20] *on her head.*

Gril. *Yes forsooth, and no forsooth; is not this fine? I pray your blessing, gaffer. Here, here, here—did he give me a shough,*[21] *and cut off's tail! Buss, buss, nuncle, and there's a pum for daddy.*

Cor. You find this noted there phrenitis.[22]

Pal. True.

Cor. Pride is the ground on't; it reigns most in women.

Enter CUCULUS *like a Bedlam, singing.*

Cuc. *They that will learn to drink a health in hell*
Must learn on earth to take tobacco well,
To take tobacco well, to take tobacco well;
For in hell they drink nor wine nor ale nor beer,
But fire and smoke and stench, as we do here.[23]

Rhe. *I'll swoop thee up.*

Pel. *Thou'st straight to execution.*

Gril. *Fool, fool, fool! catch me an thou canst.*

---

[20] *coxcomb*] i. e. a fool's cap.

[21] *did he give me a* shough,] A shock-dog, a water-spaniel. It is mentioned in Macbeth's catalogue of dogs, and in Nashe's *Lenten Stuffe*—"a brindle-tail tike, or *shough*, or two."

[22] "*Phrenitis*, which the Greeks derive from the word φρὴν, is a disease of the mind, with a continual madness or dotage, which hath an acute feaver annexed, or else an inflammation of the brain, or the membranes or kells of it, with an acute feaver, which causeth madness and dotage. It differs from *Melancholy* and *Madness*, because their dotage is without an ague: this continual, with waking, or memory decayed, &c. *Melancholy* is most part silent, this clamorous; and many such like differences are assigned by physitians." Burton's *Anat. of Mel.* p. 5, ed. 1676.

[23] This is a sarcastic description of *drinking* tobacco, as the phrase was. The ingredients (stench, smoke, and fire) are thus enumerated in the *Counterblast*.

SCENE II.   THE LOVER'S MELANCHOLY.   67

  Phi. *Expel him the house; 'tis a dunce.*
  Cuc. [sings] *Hark! did ye not hear a rumbling?*
     The goblins are now a tumbling:
     I'll tear 'em, I'll sear 'em,
     I'll roar 'em, I'll gore 'em!
     Now, now, now! my brains are a
      jumbling,—
Bounce! the gun's off.
  Pal. You name this here[24] hypochondriacal?
  Cor. Which is a windy flatuous humour, stuffing
The head, and thence deriv'd to th' animal parts.
To be too over-curious, loss of goods
Or friends, excess of fear, or sorrows cause it.

  Enter a Sea-Nymph *big-bellied, singing and dancing.*
  Nymph. *Good your honours,*
     Pray your worships,
     Dear your beauties,—
  Cuc. *Hang thee!*
     To lash your sides,
     To tame your hides,
     To scourge your prides;
     And bang thee.
  Nymph. *We're pretty and dainty, and I will begin:*
     See, how they do jeer me, deride me, and grin!
     Come sport me, come court me, your topsail advance,

---

[24] *You name this* here] i.e. in the paper which Palador still holds in his hand, and which may be supposed to contain the extracts from Burton; that of the Bedlamite, to which the prince alludes, follows. "The third [species of melancholy] ariseth from the bowels, liver, spleen, or membrane called mesenterium, named *Hypochondriacal or windy Melancholy*," &c. Burton's *Anat. of Mel.* p. 21, ed. 1676.

*And let us conclude our delights in a
    dance!*
All. *A dance, a dance, a dance!*
Cor. This is the Wanton Melancholy. Women
with child, possess'd with this strange fury, often
Have danc'd three days together without ceasing.[25]
Pal. 'Tis very strange: but heaven is full of miracles.

THE DANCE.

[*After which the masquers run out in couples.*
We are thy debtor, Corax,[26] for the gift
Of this invention; but the plot[27] deceives us:
What means this empty space? [*Pointing to the paper.*
Cor. One kind of Melancholy
Is only left untouch'd: 'twas not in art
To personate the shadow of that fancy;
'Tis nam'd Love-Melancholy. As, for instance,
Admit this stranger here,—young man, stand forth—
    [*To Par.*
Entangl'd by the beauty of this lady,
The great Thamasta, cherish'd in his heart

---

[25] "*Chorus Sancti Viti*, or S. Vitus' dance; the lascivious dance Paracelsus cals it, because they that are taken with it can do nothing but dance till they be dead or cured. It is so called, for that the parties so troubled were wont to go to S. Vitus for help, and after they had danced there a while, they were certainly freed. 'Tis strange to hear how long they will dance, and in what manner, over stools, forms, tables; even great-bellied women sometimes (and yet never hurt their children) will dance so long that they can stir neither hand nor foot, but seem to be quite dead." Burton's *Anat. of Mel.* p. 6, ed. 1676.

[26] *We are thy debtor, Corax*, &c.] This good prince is easily pleased; for, to speak truth, a masque more void of invention or merit of any kind never shamed the stage. It is singular that Ford did not recollect how absolutely he had anticipated the boasted experiment of this trifler, and laid open the whole secret of the prince's melancholy in the admirable scene with Rhetias in the second act: but he was determined to have a show, and, in evil hour, he had it.

[27] *the plot*] i.e. the paper, which, as Gifford has observed, p. 67, note 24, "may be supposed to contain the extracts from Burton." D.

The weight of hopes and fears; it were impossible
To limn his passions in such lively colours
As his own proper sufferance could express.
    Par. You are not modest, sir.
    Tha.   Am I your mirth?
    Cor. Love is the tyrant of the heart; it darkens
Reason, confounds discretion; deaf to counsel,
It runs a headlong course to desperate madness.
O, were your highness but touch'd home and throughly
With this—what shall I call it?—devil—
    Pal.   Hold!
Let no man henceforth name the word again.—
Wait you my pleasure, youth.—'Tis late; to rest!
                                                     [*Exit.*
    Cor. My lords,—
    Soph.   Enough; thou art a perfect arts-man.
    Cor. Panthers may hide their heads, not change
            the skin;
And love pent ne'er so close, yet will be seen.
                                                   [*Exeunt.*

ACT IV.

SCENE I. *A room in* THAMASTA'S *house.*

Enter AMETHUS *and* MENAPHON.

    Amet. Dote on a stranger?
    Men.   Court him; plead, and sue to him.
    Amet. Affectionately?
    Men.   Servilely; and, pardon me
If I say, basely.
    Amet.   Women, in their passions,
Like false fires, flash, to fright our trembling senses,

Yet in themselves contain nor light nor heat.
My sister do this! she, whose pride did scorn
All thoughts that were not busied on a crown,
To fall so far beneath her fortunes now!—
You are my friend.
　　Men.　　　　　　　What I confirm is truth.
　　Amet. Truth, Menaphon?
　　Men.　　　　　　　　If I conceiv'd you were
Jealous of my sincerity and plainness,
Then, sir,—
　　Amet.　What then, sir?
　　Men.　　　　　　　I would then resolve
You were as changeable in vows of friendship
As is Thamasta in her choice of love:
That sin is double, running in a blood,
Which justifies another being worse.
　　Amet. My Menaphon, excuse me; I grow wild,
And would not willingly believe the truth
Of my dishonour: she shall know how much
I am a debtor to thy noble goodness
By checking the contempt her poor desires
Have sunk her fame in. Prithee tell me, friend,
How did the youth receive her?
　　Men.　　　　　　　With a coldness
As modest and as hopeless as the trust
I did repose in him could wish or merit.
　　Amet. I will esteem him dearly.

　　　　　　Enter THAMASTA *and* KALA.

　　Men.　　　　　　　Sir, your sister.
　　Tha. Servant, I have employment for ye.
　　Amet.　　　　　　　　　　　Hark ye!
The mask of your ambition is fall'n off;
Your pride hath stoop'd to such an abject lowness,

That you have now discover'd to report
Your nakedness in virtue, honours, shame,—
    Tha. You are turn'd satire.[1]
    Amet.   All the flatteries
Of greatness have expos'd ye to contempt.
    Tha. This is mere railing.
    Amet.   You have sold your birth
For lust.
    Tha. Lust!
    Amet.   Yes; and at a dear expense
Purchas'd the only glories of a wanton.
    Tha. A wanton!
    Amet.   Let repentance stop your mouth;
Learn to redeem your fault.[2]
    Kal. [*aside to Men.*]   I hope your tongue
Has not betray'd my honesty.
    Men. [*aside to Kal.*]   Fear nothing.
    Tha. If, Menaphon, I hitherto have strove
To keep a wary guard about my fame;
If I have us'd a woman's skill to sift
The constancy of your protested love;
You cannot, in the justice of your judgment,
Impute that to a coyness or neglect,
Which my discretion and your service aim'd
For noble purposes.
    Men.   Great mistress, no.
I rather quarrel with mine own ambition,
That durst to soar so high as to feed hope
Of any least desert that might entitle
My duty to a pension from your favours.

    [1] *satire.*] i.e. satirist: see my *Gloss. to Shakespeare.* D.
    [2] It is evident, from what follows in a subsequent scene, that this warmth of language is merely affected by Amethus for the purpose of intimidating his sister, and, by dint of overpowering her supposed coquetry, surprising her into an avowal of her attachment to his friend.

Amet. And therefore, lady,—pray, observe him
   well,—
He henceforth covets plain equality;
Endeavouring to rank his fortunes low,
With some fit partner, whom, without presumption,
Without offence or danger, he may cherish,
Yes, and command too, as a wife,—a wife,
A wife, my most great lady!
   Kal. [*aside*]   All will out.
   Tha. Now I perceive the league of amity,
Which you have long between ye vow'd and kept,
Is sacred and inviolable; secrets
Of every nature are in common to you.
I have trespass'd, and I have been faulty;
Let not too rude a censure doom me guilty,
Or judge my error wilful without pardon.
   Men. Gracious and virtuous mistress!
   Amet.   'Tis a trick;
There is no trust in female cunning, friend.
Let her first purge her follies past, and clear
The wrong done to her honour, by some sure
Apparent testimony of her constancy;
Or we will not believe these childish plots:
As you respect my friendship, lend no ear
To a reply.—Think on't!
   Men.   Pray, love your fame.
      [*Exeunt Men. and Amet.*
   Tha. Gone! I am sure awake.[3]   Kala, I find
You have not been so trusty as the duty
You ow'd requir'd.
   Kal.   Not I? I do protest
I have been, madam.
   Tha.   Be—no matter what.

---

[3] *awake.*] The 4to has "awakt."—Gifford printed "awak'd." D.

I'm paid in mine own coin; something I must,
And speedily.—So!—Seek out Cuculus;
Bid him attend me instantly.
    Kal.   That antic!
The trim old youth shall wait ye.
    Tha. Wounds may be mortal, which are wounds indeed;
But no wound's deadly till our honours bleed.
                                                  [*Exeunt.*

Scene II. *A room in the castle.*

Enter RHETIAS *and* CORAX.

    Rhe. Thou'rt an excellent fellow. Diabolo! O these[4] lousy close-stool empirics, that will undertake all cures, yet know not the causes of any disease! Dog-leeches![5] By the four elements, I honour thee; could find in my heart to turn knave, and be thy flatterer.

    Cor. Sirrah, 'tis pity thou'st not been a scholar;
Thou'rt honest, blunt, and rude enough, o' conscience.
But for thy lord now, I have put him to't.

    Rhe. He chafes hugely, fumes like a stew-pot: is he not monstrously overgone in frenzy?

    Cor. Rhetias, 'tis not a madness, but his sorrows—
Close-griping grief and anguish of the soul—
That torture him; he carries hell on earth
Within his bosom: 'twas a prince's tyranny
Caus'd his distraction;[6] and a prince's sweetness

---

    [4] *these*] The 4to has "this." D.
    [5] *Dog-leeches!*] i.e. Dog-doctors. D.
    [6]   '*twas a prince's tyranny
Caus'd his distraction;* &c.] Here again poor Corax has just stumbled on what the prince had discovered long before. Never, surely, was reputation so cheaply obtained as by this compound of fool and physician.

Must qualify that tempest of his mind.

Rhe. Corax, to praise thy art were to assure
The misbelieving world that the sun shines
When 'tis i' th' full meridian of his beauty:
No cloud of black detraction can eclipse
The light of thy rare knowledge. Henceforth, casting
All poor disguises off, that play in rudeness,
Call me your servant; only, for the present,
I wish a happy blessing to your labours.
Heaven crown your undertakings! and believe me,
Ere many hours can pass, at our next meeting,
The bonds my duty owes shall be full cancell'd.

Cor. Farewell. [*Exit Rhe.*
A shrewd-brain'd whoreson; there is pith
In his untoward plainness.

Enter TROLLIO, *with a morion*[7] *on.*
Now, the news?

Trol. Worshipful Master Doctor, I have a great deal of I cannot tell what to say t'ye. My lord thunders; every word that comes out of his mouth roars like a cannon; the house shook once:—my young lady dares not be seen.

Cor. We will roar with him, Trollio, if he roar.

Trol. He has got a great poleaxe in his hand, and fences it up and down the house, as if he were to make room for the pageants.[8] I have provided me a morion for fear of a clap on the coxcomb.

Cor. No matter for the morion; here's my cap: Thus I will pull it down, and thus outstare him.
[*He produces a frightful mask and headpiece.*

---

[7] *morion*] A headpiece, a helmet.
[8] *to make room for the* pageants.] An allusion to the city-officers, who headed the shows on the Lord-Mayor's day, and opened the passage for the masquers. They must have found occasion for all their *fencing*, if the fierce curiosity of the citizens be considered, and the state of the public streets.

SCENE II.   THE LOVER'S MELANCHOLY.   75

Trol. [*aside*] The physician is got as mad as my lord.—O brave! a man of worship.

Cor. Let him come, Trollio. I will firk his trangdido, and bounce and bounce in metal, honest Trollio.

Trol. [*aside*] He vapours like a tinker, and struts like a juggler.

Mel. [*within*] So ho, so ho!

Trol. There, there, there! look to your right worshipful, look to yourself.

Enter MELEANDER *with a poleaxe.*

Mel. Show me the dog whose triple-throated noise
Hath rous'd a lion from his uncouth den
To tear the cur in pieces.

Cor. [*putting on his mask, and turning to Mel.*]
                    Stay thy paws,
Courageous beast; else, lo, the Gorgon's[9] skull,
That shall transform thee to that restless stone
Which Sisyphus rolls up against the hill,
Whence, tumbling down again, it with his[10] weight
Shall crush thy bones and puff thee into air.

Mel. Hold, hold thy conquering breath; 'tis
                    stronger far
Than gunpowder and garlic. If the fates
Have spun my thread, and my spent clue of life
Be now[11] untwisted, let us part like friends.—
Lay up my weapon, Trollio, and be gone.

Trol. Yes, sir, with all my heart.

Mel.   This friend and I
Will walk, and gabble wisely.

                    [*Exit Trol. with the poleaxe.*

Cor.   I allow
The motion; on!   [*Takes off his mask.*

[9] *Gorgon's*] The 4to has "gorgeous." D.
[10] *his*] Altered by Gifford to "its,"—very unnecessarily. D.
[11] *now*] Gifford printed "not." D.

Mel.   So politicians thrive,
That, with their crabbèd faces and sly tricks,
Legerdemain, ducks, cringes, formal beards,
Crisp'd hairs, and punctual cheats, do wriggle in
Their heads first, like a fox, to rooms of state,
Then the whole body follows.
    Cor.   Then they fill
Lordships; steal women's hearts; with them and theirs
The world runs round; yet these are square men still.[12]
    Mel. There are none poor but such as engross offices.
    Cor. None wise but unthrifts, bankrupts, beggars, rascals.
    Mel. The hangman is a rare physician.
    Cor. [*aside*] That's not so good.—It shall be granted.
    Mel.   All
The buzz of drugs and minerals and simples,
Bloodlettings, vomits, purges, or what else
Is conjur'd up by men of art, to gull
Liege-people, and rear golden piles, are trash
To a strong well-wrought halter; there the gout,
The stone, yes, and the melancholy devil,
Are cur'd in less time than a pair of minutes:
Build me a gallows in this very plot,
And I'll dispatch your business.
    Cor.   Fix the knot
Right under the left ear.
    Mel.   Sirrah, make ready.
    Cor. Yet do not be too[13] sudden; grant me leave

---

[12] *The world runs* round; *yet these are* square *men still.*] The play of words between round and square is not of a very exquisite kind, but it does well enough for Corax. By *square* he means just, unimpeachable.

[13] *too*] Gifford printed "so." D.

To give a farewell to a creature long
Absented from me: 'tis a daughter, sir,
Snatch'd from me in her youth, a handsome girl;
She comes to ask a blessing.
 Mel.   Pray, where is she?
I cannot see her yet.
 Cor.   She makes more haste
In her quick prayers than her trembling steps,
Which many griefs have weaken'd.
 Mel.   . Cruel man!
How canst thou rip a heart that's cleft already
With injuries of time?—Whilst I am frantic,
Whilst throngs of rude divisions huddle on,
And do disrank my brains from peace and sleep,
So long—I am insensible of cares.
As balls of wildfire may be safely touch'd,
Not violently sunder'd and thrown up;
So my distemper'd thoughts rest in their rage,
Not hurried in the air of repetition,
Or memory of my misfortunes past:
Then are my griefs struck home, when they're re-
  claim'd
To their own pity of themselves.—Proceed;
What of your daughter now?
 Cor.   I cannot tell ye,
'Tis now out of my head again; my brains
Are crazy; I have scarce slept one sound sleep
These twelve months.
 Mel.   'Las, poor man! canst thou imagine
To prosper in the task thou tak'st in hand
By practising a cure upon my weakness,
And yet be no physician for thyself?
Go, go, turn over all thy books once more,
And learn to thrive in modesty; for impudence
Does least become a scholar. Thou'rt a fool,

A kind of learnèd fool.
Cor.   I do confess it.
Mel. If thou canst wake with me, forget to eat,
Renounce the thought of greatness, tread on fate,
Sigh out a lamentable tale of things
Done long ago, and ill done; and, when sighs
Are wearied, piece up what remains behind
With weeping eyes, and hearts that bleed to death;
Thou shalt be a companion fit for me,
And we will sit together, like true friends,
And never be divided. With what greediness
Do I hug my afflictions! there's no mirth
Which is not truly season'd with some madness:
As, for example,—   [*Exit hastily.*
Cor.   What new crotchet next?
There is so much sense in this wild distraction,
That I am almost out of my wits too,
To see and hear him: some few hours more
Spent here would turn me apish, if not frantic.

Re-enter MELEANDER *with* CLEOPHILA.

Mel. In all the volumes thou hast turn'd, thou man
Of knowledge, hast thou met with any rarity,
Worthy thy contemplation, like to this?
The model of the heavens, the earth, the waters,
The harmony and sweet consent of times,
Are not of such an excellence, in form
Of their creation, as the infinite wonder
That dwells within the compass of this face:
And yet I tell thee, scholar, under this
Well-order'd sign is lodg'd such an obedience
As will hereafter, in another age,
Strike all comparison into a silence.
She had a sister too;—but as for her,

If I were given to talk, I could describe
A pretty piece of goodness—let that pass—
We must be wise sometimes. What would you with
    her?
    Cor. I with her! nothing, by your leave, sir, I;
It is not my profession.
    Mel.   You are saucy,
And, as I take it, scurvy in your sauciness,
To use no more respect.—Good soul, be patient;
We are a pair of things the world doth laugh at:
Yet be content, Cleophila; those clouds,
Which bar the sun from shining on our miseries,
Will never be chas'd off till I am dead;
And then some charitable soul will take thee
Into protection: I am hasting on;
The time cannot be long.
    Cleo.   I do beseech ye,
Sir, as you love your health, as you respect
My safety, let not passion overrule you.
    Mel. It shall not; I am friends with all the world.
Get me some wine; to witness that I will be
An absolute good fellow, I will drink with thee.
    Cor. [*aside to Cleo.*] Have you prepar'd his cup?
    Cleo. [*aside to Cor.*]   It is in readiness.

          Enter Cuculus *and* Grilla.

    Cuc. By your leave, gallants, I come to speak with a young lady, as they say, the old Trojan's daughter of the house.
    Mel. Your business with my lady-daughter, toss-
    pot?
    Gril. Toss-pot! O base! toss-pot!
    Cuc. Peace! dost not see in what case he is?—
I would do my own commendations to her; that's all.

Mel. Do.—Come, my Genius, we will quaff in wine[14]
Till we grow wise.
  Cor.   True nectar is divine.
     [*Exeunt Mel. and Cor.*
  Cuc. So! I am glad he is gone.—Page, walk aside. —Sweet beauty, I am sent ambassador from the mistress of my thoughts to you, the mistress of my desires.
  Cleo. So, sir! I pray, be brief.
  Cuc. That you may know I am not, as they say, an animal, which is, as they say, a kind of cokes,[15] which is, as the learned term [it], an ass, a puppy, a widgeon, a dolt, a noddy, a—
  Cleo. As you please.
  Cuc. Pardon me for that, it shall be as you please indeed: forsooth, I love to be courtly and in fashion.
  Cleo. Well, to your embassy. What, and from whom?
  Cuc. Marry, *what* is more than I know;[16] for to know *what's what* is to know *what's what* and for *what's what:*—but these are foolish figures and to little purpose.
  Cleo. From whom, then, are you sent?
  Cuc. There you come to me again. O, to be in the favour of great ladies is as much to say as to be great in ladies' favours.

[14] *we will quaff* in *wine*] "To drink *in* wine (Mr. Malone says) always seemed to me a very strange phrase till I met with it in King James's first speech to his parliament, in 1604." Mr. Malone seems to have gone far a-field for a very common expression; but his knowledge of our ancient language was very limited, even at the end of his career. I could produce scores of instances of this mode of speaking from the old dramatists, to every one of whom it was perfectly familiar.—See *Jonson*, vol. ii. 44.

[15] *cokes,*] i. e. a simpleton. The allusion is [certainly *is not*. D.] to a character [Cokes] in [Jonson's] *Bartholomew Fair.*

[16] Cuc. *Marry,* what *is more than I know,* &c.] How is it that the commentators have not discovered a *sneer* at Shakespeare in this speech? But no: Ben Jonson alone "sneers at the poet," of whom Ford, like Fletcher, was the devoted admirer!

SCENE III.   THE LOVER'S MELANCHOLY.   81

Cleo. Good time o' day t'ye! I can stay no longer.

Cuc. By this light, but you must; for now I come to't. The most excellent, most wise, most dainty, precious, loving, kind, sweet, intolerably fair Lady Thamasta commends to your little hands this letter of importance. By your leave, let me first kiss, and then deliver it in fashion to your own proper beauty.
[*Delivers a letter.*

Cleo. To me, from her? 'tis strange! I dare
    peruse it.   [*Reads.*

Cuc. Good.—O, that I had not resolved to live a single life! Here's temptation, able to conjure up a spirit with a witness. So, so! she has read it. [*Aside.*

Cleo. Is't possible? Heaven, thou art great and
    bountiful.—

Sir, I much thank your pains; and to the princess
Let my love, duty, service be remember'd.

Cuc. They shall, mad-dam.[17]

Cleo. When we of hopes or helps are quite be-
    reaven,

Our humble prayers have entrance into heaven.

Cuc. That's my opinion clearly and without doubt.
[*Exeunt.*

SCENE III. *A room in the palace.*

Enter ARETUS *and* SOPHRONOS.

Are. The prince is throughly mov'd.

Soph.   I never saw him
So much distemper'd.

Are.   What should this young man be?
Or whither can he be convey'd?

Soph.   'Tis to me

[17] *mad-dam.*] So Gifford (the 4to having "Mad-dame"). D.

A mystery; I understand it not.
Are.   Nor I.

Enter PALADOR, AMETHUS, *and* PELIAS.

Pal. Ye have consented all to work upon
The softness of my nature; but take heed:
Though I can sleep in silence, and look on
The mockery ye make of my dull patience,
Yet ye shall know, the best of ye, that in me
There is a masculine, a stirring spirit,
Which, [once] provok'd, shall, like a bearded comet,
Set ye at gaze, and threaten horror.
Pel.   Good sir,—
Pal. Good sir! 'tis not your active wit or language,
Nor your grave politic wisdoms, lords, shall dare
To check-mate and control my just commands.[18]

Enter MENAPHON.

Where is the youth, your friend? is he found yet?
Men. Not to be heard of.
Pal.   Fly, then, to the desert,
Where thou didst first encounter this fantastic,
This airy apparition; come no more
In sight! Get ye all from me: he that stays
Is not my friend.
Amet.   'Tis strange.
Are. Soph.   We must obey.
        [*Exeunt all but Pal.*
Pal. Some angry power cheats with rare delusions
My credulous sense; the very soul of reason
Is troubled in me:—the physician
Presented a strange masque, the view of it
Puzzled my understanding; but the boy—

---

[18] *commands.*] Gifford printed "demands." D.

Enter RHETIAS.

Rhetias, thou art acquainted with my griefs:
Parthenophil is lost, and I would see him;
For he is like to something I remember
A great while since, a long, long time ago.

Rhe. I have been diligent, sir, to pry into every corner for discovery, but cannot meet with him. There is some trick, I am confident.

Pal. There is; there is some practice, sleight, or plot.

Rhe. I have apprehended a fair wench in an odd private lodging in the city, as like the youth in face as can by possibility be discerned.

Pal. How, Rhetias!

Rhe. If it be not Parthenophil in long-coats, 'tis a spirit in his likeness; answer I can get none from her: you shall see her.

Pal. The young man in disguise, upon my life,
To steal out of the land.

Rhe.   I'll send him t'ye.

Pal. Do, do, my Rhetias.   [*Exit Rhe.*

As there is by nature
In everything created contrariety,
So likewise is there unity and league
Between them in their kind: but man, the abstract
Of all perfection, which the workmanship
Of heaven hath modell'd, in himself contains
Passions of several qualities.

[*Enter behind Eroclea* (*Parthenophil*) *in female attire.*

The music
Of man's fair composition best accords
When 'tis in consort, not in single strains:
My heart has been untun'd these many months,

Wanting her presence, in whose equal love
True harmony consisted. Living here,
We are heaven's bounty all, but fortune's exercise.
 Ero. Minutes are number'd by the fall of sands,
As by an hourglass; the span of time
Doth waste us to our graves, and we look on it:
An age of pleasures, revell'd out, comes home
At last, and ends in sorrow; but the life,
Weary of riot, numbers every sand,
Wailing in sighs, until the last drop down;
So to conclude calamity in rest.
 Pal. What echo yields a voice to my complaints?
Can I be nowhere private?
 Ero. [*comes forward, and kneels*] Let the substance
As suddenly be hurried from your eyes
As the vain sound can pass [, sir, from] your ear,
If no impression of a troth vow'd yours
Retain a constant memory.
 Pal.   Stand up. [*She rises.*
'Tis not the figure stamp'd upon thy cheeks,
The cozenage of thy beauty, grace, or tongue,
Can draw from me a secret, that hath been
The only jewel of my speechless thoughts.
 Ero. I am so worn away with fears and sorrows,
So winter'd with the tempests of affliction,
That the bright sun of your life-quickening presence
Hath scarce one beam of force to warm again
That spring of cheerful comfort, which youth once
Apparell'd in fresh looks.
 Pal.   Cunning impostor!
Untruth hath made thee subtle in thy trade.
If any neighbouring greatness hath seduc'd
A free-born resolution to attempt
Some bolder act of treachery by cutting
My weary days off, wherefore, cruel-mercy,

Hast thou assum'd a shape that would make treason
A piety, guilt pardonable, bloodshed
As holy as the sacrifice of peace?

 Ero. The incense of my love-desires are flam'd[19]
Upon an altar of more constant proof.
Sir, O, sir, turn me back into the world,
Command me to forget my name, my birth,
My father's sadness, and my death alive,
If all remembrance of my faith hath found
A burial without pity in your scorn!

 Pal. My scorn, disdainful boy, shall soon unweave
The web thy art hath twisted. Cast thy shape off,
Disrobe the mantle of a feignèd sex,
And so I may be gentle: as thou art,
There's witchcraft in thy language, in thy face,
In thy demeanours; turn, turn from me, prithee,
For my belief is arm'd else.—Yet, fair subtilty,
Before we part,—for part we must,—be true:
Tell me thy country.

 Ero.   Cyprus.
 Pal.   Ha!—Thy father?
 Ero. Meleander.
 Pal.   Hast a name?
 Ero.   A name of misery;
Th' unfortunate Eroclea.

 Pal.   There is danger
In this seducing counterfeit. Great Goodness,
Hath honesty and virtue left the time?
Are we become so impious, that to tread

---

[19] *The incense of my love-desires are flam'd*] Gifford printed "—— is *flam'd:*" but in our early authors there are innumerable instances of a verb plural following a nominative singular when a genitive plural intervenes.—Indeed, even modern writers occasionally fall unconsciously, as it were, into the same formula: *e.g.* "Alas, how the dignity of actions *are* lost!" *Letters of Mrs. Eliz. Montagu*, vol. i. p. 231, sec. ed. D.

The path of impudence is law and justice?—
Thou vizard of a beauty ever sacred,
Give me thy name.
 Ero.   Whilst I was lost to memory
Parthenophil did shroud my shame in change
Of sundry rare misfortunes; but, since now
I am, before I die, return'd to claim
A convoy to my grave, I must not blush
To let Prince Palador, if I offend,
Know, when he dooms me, that he dooms Eroclea:
I am that woful maid.
 Pal.   Join not too fast
Thy penance with the story of my sufferings:—
So dwelt simplicity with virgin truth,
So martyrdom and holiness are twins,
As innocence and sweetness on thy tongue.
But, let me by degrees collect my senses;
I may abuse my trust. Tell me, what air
Hast thou perfum'd, since tyranny first ravish'd
The contract of our hearts?
 Ero.   Dear sir, in Athens
Have I been buried.
 Pal.   Buried! Right; as I
In Cyprus.—Come, to trial; if thou beest
Eroclea, in my bosom I can find thee.[20]
 Ero. As I, Prince Palador in mine: this gift
          [*Shows him a tablet.*
His bounty bless'd me with, the only physic
My solitary cares have hourly took,
To keep me from despair.
 Pal.   We are but fools
To trifle in disputes, or vainly struggle

---

[20] *in my bosom I can find thee.*] The allusion is to the miniature which the prince wore, and which he here proposes to compare with the lady before him.

With that eternal mercy which protects us.
Come home, home to my heart, thou banish'd peace!
My ecstasy of joys would speak in passion,
But that I would not lose that part of man
Which is reserv'd to entertain content.
Eroclea, I am thine; O, let me seize thee
As my inheritance! Hymen shall now
Set all his torches burning, to give light
Throughout this land, new-settled in thy welcome.

 Ero. You are still gracious, sir. How I have liv'd,
By what means been convey'd, by what preserv'd,
By what return'd, Rhetias, my trusty servant,
Directed by the wisdom of my uncle,
The good Sophronos, can inform at large.

 Pal. Enough. Instead of music, every night,
To make our sleeps delightful, thou shalt close
Our weary eyes with some part of thy story.

 Ero. O, but my father!

 Pal.   Fear not; to behold
Eroclea safe will make him young again:
It shall be our first task.—Blush, sensual follies,
Which are not guarded with thoughts chastely pure:
There is no faith in lust, but baits of arts;
'Tis virtuous love keeps clear contracted hearts.
              [*Exeunt.*

ACT V.

SCENE I. *A room in the castle.*

Enter CORAX *and* CLEOPHILA.

Cor. 'Tis well, 'tis well; the hour is at hand
Which must conclude the business, that no art
Could all this while make ripe for wish'd content.
O, lady, in the turmoils of our lives,
Men are like politic states, or troubled seas,
Toss'd up and down with several storms and tempests,
Change and variety of wrecks and fortunes;
Till, labouring to the havens of our homes,
We struggle for the calm that crowns our ends.
  Cleo. A happy end heaven bless us with!
  Cor.   'Tis well said.
The old man sleeps still soundly.
  Cleo.   May soft dreams
Play in his fancy, that when he awakes,
With comfort he may, by degrees, digest
The present blessings in a moderate joy!
  Cor. I drench'd his cup to purpose; he ne'er stirr'd
At barber or at tailor. He will laugh
At his own metamorphosis, and wonder.—
We must be watchful. Does the couch[1] stand ready?
  Cleo. All, [all] as you commanded.

Enter TROLLIO.

                        What's your haste for?
  Trol. A brace of big women, ushered by the young old ape with his she-clog at his bum, are entered the castle. Shall they come on?

---

[1] *couch*] The 4to has "Coach." D.

Cor. By any means : the time is precious now.—
Lady, be quick and careful.—Follow, Trollio. [*Exit.*
  Trol. I owe all sir-reverence to your right worship-
fulness. [*Exit.*
  Cleo. So many fears, so many joys encounter
My doubtful expectations, that I waver
Between the resolution of my hopes
And my obedience : 'tis not—O my fate !—
The apprehension of a timely blessing
In pleasures shakes my weakness ; but the danger
Of a mistaken duty that confines
The limits of my reason.   Let me live,
Virtue, to thee as chaste as truth to time !

Enter THAMASTA, *speaking to some one without.*

  Tha. Attend me till I call.—My sweet Cleophila !
  Cleo. Great princess,—
  Tha.   I bring peace, to sue a pardon
For my neglect of all those noble virtues
Thy mind and duty are apparell'd with :
I have deserv'd ill from thee, and must say
Thou art too gentle, if thou canst forget it.
  Cleo. Alas, you have not wrong'd me ; for, indeed,
Acquaintance with my sorrows and my fortune
Were grown to such familiarity,
That 'twas an impudence, more than presumption,
To wish so great a lady as you are
Should lose affection on my uncle's son :
But that your brother, equal in your blood,
Should stoop to such a lowness as to love
A castaway, a poor despisèd maid,
Only for me to hope was almost sin ;—
Yet, 'troth, I never tempted him.
  Tha.   Chide not
The grossness of my trespass, lovely sweetness,

In such an humble language; I have smarted
Already in the wounds my pride hath made
Upon your sufferings: henceforth 'tis in you
To work my happiness.
   Cleo.   Call any service
Of mine a debt; for such it is. The letter
You lately sent me, in the blest contents
It made me privy to, hath largely quitted
Every suspicion of your grace or goodness.
   Tha. Let me embrace thee with a sister's love,
A sister's love, Cleophila; for should
My brother henceforth study to forget
The vows that he hath made thee, I would ever
Solicit thy deserts.[2]
   Amet. Men. [*within*] We must have entrance.
   Tha. Must! Who are they say *must?* you are un-
      mannerly.

          Enter AMETHUS *and* MENAPHON.

Brother, is't you? and you too, sir?
   Amet.   Your ladyship
Has had a time of scolding to your humour:
Does the storm hold still?
   Cleo.   Never fell a shower
More seasonably gentle on the barren
Parch'd thirsty earth than showers of courtesy
Have from this princess been distill'd on me,
To make my growth in quiet of my mind
Secure and lasting.
   Tha.   You may both believe
That I was not uncivil.
   Amet.   Pish! I know
Her spirit and her envy.

   [2] *Solicit thy deserts.*] i.e. plead your merits to my brother; which accordingly she does in pp. 91-2, where Amethus observes, "The ladies are turn'd lawyers."

SCENE I.   THE LOVER'S MELANCHOLY.   91

Cleo.   Now, in troth, sir,—
Pray credit me, I do not use to swear,—
The virtuous princess hath in words and carriage
Been kind, so over-kind, that I do blush
I am not rich enough in thanks sufficient
For her unequall'd bounty.—My good cousin,
I have a suit to you.
    Men.   It shall be granted.
    Cleo. That no time, no persuasion, no respects
Of jealousies, past, present, or hereafter
By possibility to be conceiv'd,
Draw you from that sincerity and pureness
Of love which you have oftentimes protested
To this great worthy lady: she deserves
A duty more than what the ties of marriage
Can claim or warrant; be for ever hers,
As she is yours, and heaven increase your comforts!
    Amet. Cleophila hath play'd the churchman's part;
I'll not forbid the bans.
    Men.   Are you consented?[3]
    Tha. I have one task in charge first, which con-
        cerns me.
Brother, be not more cruel than this lady;
She hath forgiven my follies, so may you.
Her youth, her beauty, innocence, discretion,
Without additions of estate or birth,
Are dower for a prince, indeed. You lov'd her;
For sure you swore you did: else, if you did not,
Here fix your heart; and thus resolve,[4] if now

   [3] *consented?*] Gifford printed "contented."—But compare, in our author's *Broken Heart*, act ii. sc. 2,
                  "'Thad been pity
     To sunder hearts so equally *consented.*" D.

   [4] *and thus* resolve,] i.e. and come to this certain conclusion, that—if now, &c. As the passage was printed before, it was hardly intelligible.

You miss this heaven on earth, you cannot find
In any other choice aught but a hell.
   Amet. The ladies are turn'd lawyers, and plead
      handsomely
Their clients' cases: I'm an easy judge;
And so shalt thou be, Menaphon. I give thee
My sister for a wife; a good one, friend.
   Men. Lady, will you confirm the gift?
   Tha.   The errors
Of my mistaken judgment being lost
To your remembrance, I shall ever strive
In my obedience to deserve your pity.
   Men. My love, my care, my all!
   Amet.   What rests for me?
I'm still a bachelor.—Sweet maid, resolve me,
May I yet call you mine?
   Cleo.   My Lord Amethus,
Blame not my plainness; I am young and simple,
And have not any power to dispose
Mine own will without warrant from my father;
That purchas'd, I am yours.
   Amet.   It shall suffice me.

Enter CUCULUS, PELIAS, *and* TROLLIO, *plucking in*
                  GRILLA.

   Cuc. Revenge! I must have revenge; I will have revenge, bitter and abominable revenge; I will have revenge. This unfashionable mongrel, this linsey-wolsey of mortality—by this hand, mistress, this she-rogue is drunk, and clapper-clawed me, without any reverence to my person or good garments.—Why d'ye not speak, gentlemen?
   Pel. Some certain blows have pass'd, an't like your
      highness.

Trol. Some few knocks of friendship, some love-toys, some cuffs in kindness, or so.

Gril. I'll turn him away; he shall be my master no longer.

Men. Is this your she-page, Cuculus? 'tis a boy, sure.

Cuc. A boy, an arrant boy in long-coats.

Trol. He has mumbled his nose, that 'tis as big as a great codpiece.

Cuc. O, thou cock-vermin of iniquity!

Tha. Pelias, take hence the wag, and school him for't.—
For your part, servant, I'll entreat the prince
To grant you some fit place about his wardrobe.

Cuc. Ever after a bloody nose do I dream of good luck.—I horribly thank your ladyship.—
Whilst I'm in office, th' old garb shall agen
Grow in request, and tailors shall be men.—
Come, Trollio, help to wash my face, prithee.

Trol. Yes, and to scour it too.

[*Exeunt Cuc., Trol., Pel., and Gril.*[5]

Re-enter CORAX *with* RHETIAS.

Rhe. The prince and princess are at hand; give over
Your amorous dialogues.—Most honour'd lady,
Henceforth forbear your sadness: are you ready
To practise your instructions?

Cleo.   I have studied
My part with care, and will perform it, Rhetias,
With all the skill I can.

[5] It is pleasant to witness the departure of this despicable set of buffoons; and Ford has shown more judgment than he was probably aware of (for he seems to take delight in his wretched antics), in dismissing them at a period when they would have broken in on the deep pathos and feeling of his exquisite catastrophe.

Cor. I'll pass my word for her.

A flourish.—Enter PALADOR, SOPHRONOS, ARETUS, *and* EROCLEA.

Pal. Thus princes should be circled, with a guard
Of truly noble friends and watchful subjects.
O, Rhetias, thou art just; the youth thou told'st me
That liv'd at Athens is return'd at last
To her own fortunes and contracted love.
  Rhe. My knowledge made me sure of my report, sir.
  Pal. Eroclea, clear thy fears; when the sun shines
Clouds must not dare to muster in the sky,
Nor shall they here.—   [*Cleo. and Amet. kneel.*
          Why do they kneel?—Stand up;
The day and place is privileg'd.
  Soph.   Your presence,
Great sir, makes every room a sanctuary.
  Pal. Wherefore does this young virgin use such circumstance
In duty to us?—Rise.
  Ero.   'Tis I must raise her.—[*Raises Cleo.*
Forgive me, sister, I have been too private,
In hiding from your knowledge any secret
That should have been in common 'twixt our souls;
But I was rul'd by counsel.
  Cleo.   That I show
Myself a girl,[6] sister, and bewray
Joy in too soft a passion 'fore all these,
I hope you cannot blame me.
       [*Weeps, and falls into the arms of Ero.*
  Pal.   We must part
The sudden meeting of these two fair rivulets

---

[6] Cleo. *That I show Myself a* girl,] See p. 18.

SCENE I.   THE LOVER'S MELANCHOLY.   95

With th' island of our arms. [*Embraces Ero.*]—Cleo-
    phila,
The custom of thy piety hath built,
Even to thy younger years, a monument
Of memorable fame: some great reward
Must wait on thy desert.
    Soph.   The prince speaks t'ye, niece.
    Cor. Chat low, I pray; let us about our business.
The good old man awakes.—My lord, withdraw.—
Rhetias, let's settle here the couch.[7]
    Pal.   Away, then!   [*Exeunt.*

Soft music. — *Re-enter* CORAX *and* RHETIAS *with*
    MELEANDER *asleep on a couch, his hair and beard
    trimmed, habit and gown changed. While they are
    placing the couch, a* Boy *sings without.*

                Song.
    Fly hence, shadows, that do keep
    Watchful sorrows charm'd in sleep!
    Though the eyes be overtaken,
    Yet the heart doth ever waken
    Thoughts, chain'd up in busy snares
    Of continual woes and cares:
    Love and griefs are so exprest
    As they rather sigh than rest.
    Fly hence, shadows, that do keep
    Watchful sorrows charm'd in sleep!

    Mel. [*awakes*] Where am I? ha! What sounds are
        these? 'Tis day, sure.
O, I have slept belike; 'tis but the foolery
Of some beguiling dream. So, so! I will not
Trouble the play of my delighted fancy,

      [7] *couch.*] The 4to has "Coach." D.

But dream my dream out.
Cor. Morrow to your lordship!
You took a jolly nap, and slept it soundly.
Mel. Away, beast! let me alone.
[*The music ceases.*
Cor. O, by your leave, sir,
I must be bold to raise ye; else your physic
Will turn to further sickness.
[*He assists Mel. to sit up.*
Mel. Physic, bear-leech?[8]
Cor. Yes, physic; you are mad.
Mel. Trollio! Cleophila!
Rhe. Sir, I am here.
Mel. I know thee, Rhetias; prithee rid the room
Of this tormenting noise. He tells me, sirrah,
I have took physic, Rhetias; physic, physic!
Rhe. Sir, true, you have; and this most learnèd
    scholar
Applied 't ye.[9] O, you were in dangerous plight
Before he took ye [in] hand.
Mel. These things are drunk,
Directly drunk.—Where did you get your liquor?
Cor. I never saw a body in the wane
Of age so overspread with several sorts
Of such diseases as the strength of youth
Would groan under and sink.
Rhe. The more your glory
In the miraculous cure.
Cor. Bring me the cordial[10]

---

[8] *bear-leech?*] i.e. bear-doctor. D.
[9] *Applied 't ye.*] Weber calls this "remarkably harsh;" and so it is: but he certainly did not improve it when he printed "*Apply'd 't t'you.*" D.
[10] *Bring me the* cordial] He alludes to the successive appearance of the messengers from the prince, to whom the hint was now to be given, and more particularly to the entrance of Eroclea and her sister, who are brought in by Rhetias.

Prepar'd for him to take after his sleep;
'Twill do him good at heart.
    Rhe.   I hope it will, sir. [*Exit.*
    Mel. What dost [thou] think I am, that thou shouldst fiddle
So much upon my patience? Fool, the weight
Of my disease sits on my heart so heavy,
That all the hands of art cannot remove
One grain, to ease my grief. If thou couldst poison
My memory, or wrap my senses up
Into a dulness hard and cold as flints;
If thou couldst make me walk, speak, eat, and laugh
Without a sense or knowledge of my faculties,
Why, then, perhaps, at marts thou mightst make benefit
Of such an antic motion,[11] and get credit
From credulous gazers, but not profit me.
Study to gull the wise; I am too simple
To be wrought on.
    Cor.   I'll burn my books, old man,
But I will do thee good, and quickly too.

        Re-enter ARETUS, *with a patent.*

    Are. Most honour'd Lord Meleander, our great master,
Prince Palador of Cyprus, hath by me
Sent you this patent, in which is contain'd
Not only confirmation of the honours
You formerly enjoy'd, but the addition
Of the Marshalship of Cyprus; and ere long
He means to visit you. Excuse my haste;
I must attend the prince.   [*Exit.*

    [11] *Of such an antic* motion,] i. e. of such a strange *automaton,* or puppet. Exhibitions of this kind formed, in the poet's days, one of the principal attractions of the people on all public occasions.

Cor.   There's one pill works.
Mel. Dost know that spirit? 'tis a grave familiar,
And talk'd I know not what.
Cor.   He's like, methinks,
The prince's tutor Aretus.
Mel.   Yes, yes;
It may be I have seen such a formality;
No matter where or when.

Re-enter AMETHUS, *with a staff.*

Ame.   The prince hath sent ye,
My lord, this staff of office, and withal
Salutes you Grand Commander of the Ports
Throughout his principalities. He shortly
Will visit you himself: I must attend him.   [*Exit.*
Cor. D'ye feel your physic stirring yet?
Mel.   A devil
Is a rare juggler, and can cheat the eye,
But not corrupt the reason, in the throne
Of a pure soul.

Re-enter SOPHRONOS, *with a tablet.*[12]

Another!—I will stand thee;
Be what thou canst, I care not.
Soph.   From the prince,
Dear brother, I present you this rich relic,
A jewel he hath long worn in his bosom:
Henceforth, he bade me say, he does beseech you
To call him son, for he will call you father;
It is an honour, brother, that a subject
Cannot but entertain with thankful prayers.
Be moderate in your joys: he will in person
Confirm my errand, but commands my service. [*Exit.*

[12] *with a tablet.*] i.e. with the *miniature* of Eroclea, which Palador had worn so long in his bosom, and to which he alludes, p. 86.

SCENE I.   THE LOVER'S MELANCHOLY.   99

Cor. What hope now of your cure?
Mel.   Stay, stay!—What earthquakes
Roll in my flesh! Here's prince, and prince, and prince;
Prince upon prince! The dotage of my sorrows
Revels in magic of ambitious scorn :
Be they enchantments deadly as the grave,
I'll look upon 'em. Patent, staff, and relic !
To the last first. [*Taking up the miniature*] Round me,
        ye guarding ministers,
And ever keep me waking, till the cliffs
That overhang my sight fall off, and leave
These hollow spaces to be cramm'd with dust !
   Cor. 'Tis time, I see, to fetch the cordial.[13]—
        Prithee,
Sit down; I'll instantly be here again.   [*Exit.*
   Mel. Good, give me leave; I will sit down : indeed,
Here's company enough for me to prate to.
                      [*Looks at the picture.*
Eroclea!—'tis the same; the cunning arts-man
Falter'd not in a line. Could he have fashion'd
A little hollow space here, and blown breath
T' have made it move and whisper, 't had been excellent :—
But, 'faith, 'tis well, 'tis very well as 'tis,
Passing, most passing well.

   Re-enter CLEOPHILA *leading* EROCLEA, *and followed
        by* RHETIAS.

   Cleo.   The sovereign greatness,
Who, by commission from the powers of heaven,

---

[13] '*Tis time, I see, to fetch the cordial.*] i.e. the prince; with whom he subsequently returns, and whom he terms the *sure* or crowning cordial.

Sways both this land and us, our gracious prince,
By me presents you, sir, with this large bounty,
A gift more precious to him than his birthright.
Here let your cares take end; now set at liberty
Your long-imprison'd heart, and welcome home
The solace of your soul, too long kept from you.
 Ero. [*kneeling*] Dear sir, you know me?
 Mel.   Yes, thou art my daughter,
My eldest blessing. Know thee! why, Eroclea,
I never did forget thee in thy absence.
Poor soul, how dost?
 Ero.   The best of my well-being
Consists in yours.
 Mel.   Stand up: the gods, who hitherto
             [*Ero. rises.*
Have kept us both alive, preserve thee ever!—
Cleophila, I thank thee and the prince:—
I thank thee too, Eroclea, that thou wouldst,
In pity of my age, take so much pains
To live, till I might once more look upon thee,
Before I broke my heart: O, 'twas a piece
Of piety and duty unexampled!
 Rhe. [*aside*] The good man relisheth his comforts
        strangely;
The sight doth turn me child.
 Ero.   I have not words
That can express my joys.
 Cleo.   Nor I.
 Mel.   Nor I:
Yet let us gaze on one another freely,
And surfeit with our eyes. Let me be plain:
If I should speak as much as I should speak,
I should talk of a thousand things at once,
And all of thee; of thee, my child, of thee!
My tears, like ruffling winds lock'd up in caves,

Do bustle for a vent;—on t'other side,
To fly out into mirth were not so comely.
Come hither, let me kiss thee. [*To Ero.*] With a pride,
Strength, courage, and fresh blood, which now thy
    presence
Hath stor'd me with, I kneel before their altars,
Whose sovereignty kept guard about thy safety.
Ask, ask thy sister, prithee, she will tell thee
How I have been much mad.
    Cleo.   Much discontented,
Shunning all means that might procure him comfort.
    Ero. Heaven has at last been gracious.
    Mel.   So say I:
But wherefore drop thy words in such a sloth,
As if thou wert afraid to mingle truth
With thy misfortunes? Understand me throughly;
I would not have thee to report at large,
From point to point, a journal of thy absence,
'Twill take up too much time; I would securely
Engross the little remnant of my life,
That thou mightst every day be telling somewhat,
Which might convey me to my rest with comfort.
Let me bethink me: how we parted first,
Puzzles my faint remembrance—but soft—
Cleophila, thou told'st me that the prince
Sent me this present.
    Cleo.   From his own fair hands
I did receive my sister.
    Mel.   To requite him,
We will not dig his father's grave anew,
Although the mention of him much concerns
The business we inquire of:—as I said,
We parted in a hurry at the court;
I to this castle, after made my jail.—
But whither thou, dear heart?

Rhe.   Now they fall to't;
I look'd for this.
   Ero.   I, by my uncle's care,
Sophronos, my good uncle, suddenly
Was like a sailor's boy convey'd a-shipboard
That very night.
   Mel.   A policy quick and strange.
   Ero. The ship was bound for Corinth; whither first,
Attended only with your servant Rhetias
And all fit necessaries, we arriv'd:
From thence, in habit of a youth, we journey'd
To Athens, where, till our return of late,
Have we liv'd safe.
   Mel.   O, what a thing is man,
To bandy factions of distemper'd passions
Against the sacred Providence above him!
Here, in the legend of thy two years' exile,
Rare pity and delight are sweetly mix'd.—
And still thou wert a boy?
   Ero.   So I obey'd
My uncle's wise command.
   Mel.   'Twas safely carried:
I humbly thank thy fate.
   Ero.   If earthly treasures
Are pour'd in plenty down from heaven on mortals,
They rain[14] amongst those oracles that flow
In schools of sacred knowledge; such is Athens;
Yet Athens was to me but a fair prison:
The thoughts of you, my sister, country, fortunes,
And something of the prince, barr'd all contents,
Which else might ravish sense; for had not Rhetias
Been always comfortable to me, certainly
Things had gone worse.

   [14] *rain*] The 4to has "reigne."—Gifford printed "reign." D

Mel.   Speak low, Eroclea,
That "something of the prince" bears danger in it:
Yet thou hast travell'd, wench, for such endowments
As might create a prince a wife fit for him,
Had he the world to guide: but touch not there.
How cam'st thou home?
          Rhe.   Sir, with your noble favour,
Kissing your hand first, that point I can answer.
          Mel. Honest, right honest Rhetias!
          Rhe.   Your grave brother
Perceiv'd with what a hopeless love his son,
Lord Menaphon, too eagerly pursu'd
Thamasta, cousin to our present prince;
And, to remove the violence of affection,
Sent him to Athens, where, for twelve months' space,
Your daughter, my young lady, and her cousin,
Enjoy'd each other's griefs; till by his father,
The Lord Sophronos, we were all call'd home.
          Mel. Enough, enough: the world shall henceforth
                    witness
My thankfulness to heaven and those people
Who have been pitiful to me and mine.—
Lend me a looking-glass.—How now! how came I
So courtly, in fresh raiments?
          Rhe.   Here's the glass, sir.
          [*Hands a glass to Mel.*
          Mel. I'm in the trim too.—O Cleophila,
This was the goodness of thy care and cunning.—
                    [*Loud music.*
Whence comes this noise?[15]
          Rhe.   The prince, my lord, in person.
                    [*They kneel.*

---

[15] *noise?*] i. e. music; in which sense the word was formerly not uncommon. D.

Re-enter PALADOR, SOPHRONOS, ARETUS, AMETHUS,
MENAPHON, CORAX, THAMASTA, *with* KALA.

Pal. Ye shall not kneel to us; rise all, I charge
 ye.— [*They rise.*
Father, you wrong your age; henceforth my arms
 [*Embracing Mel.*
And heart shall be your guard: we have o'erheard
All passages of your united loves.
Be young again, Meleander; live to number
A happy generation, and die old
In comforts as in years! The offices
And honours which I late on thee conferr'd
Are not fantastic bounties, but thy merit:
Enjoy them liberally.
 Mel. My tears must thank ye,
For my tongue cannot.
 Cor. I have kept my promise,
And given you a sure cordial.
 Mel. O, a rare one!
 Pal. Good man, we both have shar'd enough of
 sadness,
Though thine has tasted deeper of th' extreme:
Let us forget it henceforth. Where's the picture
I sent ye? Keep it; 'tis a counterfeit;
And, in exchange of that, I seize on this,
 [*Takes Ero. by the hand.*
The real substance. With this other hand
I give away, before her father's face,
His younger joy, Cleophila, to thee,
Cousin Amethus: take her, and be to her
More than a father, a deserving husband.
Thus, robb'd of both thy children in a minute,
Thy cares are taken off.
 Mel. My brains are dull'd;

I am entranc'd, and know not what you mean.
Great, gracious sir, alas, why do you mock me?
I am a weak old man, so poor and feeble,
That my untoward joints can scarcely creep
Unto the grave, where I must seek my rest.

 Pal. Eroclea was, you know, contracted mine;
Cleophila my cousin's, by consent
Of both their hearts; we both now claim our own:
It only rests in you to give a blessing,
For confirmation.

 Rhe.   Sir, 'tis truth and justice.

 Mel. The gods, that lent ye to me, bless your vows!
O, children, children, pay your prayers to heaven,
For they[16] have show'd much mercy.—But, Sophronos,
Thou art my brother—I can say no more—
A good, good brother!

 Pal.   Leave the rest to time.—
Cousin Thamasta, I must give you too.—
She's thy wife, Menaphon.—Rhetias, for thee,
And Corax, I have more than common thanks.—
On to the temple! there all solemn rites
Perform'd, a general feast shall be proclaim'd.
The LOVER'S MELANCHOLY hath found cure;[17]
Sorrows are chang'd to bride-songs. So they thrive
Whom fate in spite of storms hath kept alive. [*Exeunt.*

---

[16]   *heaven,*
 For they, &c.] Here, as frequently in our old writers, "*heaven*" is used as a plural. D.

 [17] This line alludes to the last couplet of the Prologue. The concluding scene of this drama is wrought up with singular art and beauty. If the *Very Woman* of Massinger preceded the *Lover's Melancholy* (as I believe it did), Ford is indebted to it for no inconsiderable part of his plot.

EPILOGUE.

To be too confident is as unjust
In any work as too much to distrust:
Who from the laws of study have not swerv'd
Know begg'd applauses never were deserv'd.
We must submit to censure: so doth he
Whose hours begot this issue; yet, being free,
For his part, if he have not pleas'd you, then
In this kind he'll not trouble you agen.[18]

[18] This Epilogue does not appear in all the copies. Mr. Heber's has it not. I can hardly believe it to have been really spoken on the stage; for there is an expression in it which, in that case, would bear an air of insult to the poet's poorer brethren, as well as to the audience. By "*being free*" he means that he was not compelled by necessity to have recourse to the stage; indeed, he appears from his Dedications to have been much engaged in professional business; and he had besides, I believe, some hereditary property.

'TIS PITY SHE'S A WHORE.

This tragedy, in the dedication to the Earl of Peterborough, is styled "the first fruits of the author's leisure." How long it had been written, or what was the date of its first appearance, is nowhere mentioned; but it was given to the press in 1633, with the following title: "'Tis Pity Shee's a Whore. Acted by the Queenes Maiesties Seruants, at The Phœnix, in Drury-Lane. London. Printed by Nicholas Okes for Richard Collins, and are to be sold at his shop in Pauls Church-yard, at the signe of the three Kings. 1633." 4to. It was one of the plays appropriated by the Lord Chamberlain to the Cockpit or Phœnix Theatre, in 1639.[1]

[1] This tragedy was selected for publication by Mr. Dodsley. The choice was not very judicious; for, though the language of it is eminently beautiful, the plot is repulsive: and the *Lover's Melancholy* or the *Broken Heart* would have been fully as characteristic of the author's manner. It owes little to the taste, and nothing to the judgment, of the former editors. Dodsley merely copied the 4to, and Reed republished the transcript with a few childish "illustrations," *worth a sponge.*

TO

THE TRULY NOBLE

JOHN,

EARL OF PETERBOROUGH, LORD MORDAUNT, BARON OF TURVEY.[2]

———◆———

MY LORD,

WHERE a truth of merit hath a general warrant, there love is but a debt, acknowledgment a justice. Greatness cannot often claim virtue by inheritance; yet, in this, yours appears most eminent, for that you are not more rightly heir to your fortunes than glory shall be to your memory. Sweetness of disposition ennobles a freedom of birth; in both your lawful interest adds honour to your own name, and mercy to my presumption. Your noble allowance of these first fruits of my leisure in the action emboldens my confidence of

---

[2] John, first Earl of Peterborough, Collins informs us, "obtained that dignity in the year 1627-8. He was brought up in the Romish religion, but was converted by a disputation at his own house between the learned Bishop Usher (then only Dr. Usher) and a Papist, who confessed himself silenced by the just hand of God, for presuming to dispute without leave from his superiors." vol. iii. p. 317. No miraculous event appears to have confirmed his *loyalty* (whatever may be said of his *faith*), for "he joined the Parliamentary Army in 1642, and was made General of the Ordnance and Colonel of a regiment of foot, under Essex." His military career was of short duration, as "he departed this life June 18th the same year."

your as noble construction in this presentment; especially since my service must ever owe particular duty to your favours, by a particular engagement.³ The gravity of the subject may easily excuse the lightness of the title, otherwise I had been a severe judge against mine own guilt. Princes have vouchsafed grace to trifles offered from a purity of devotion; your lordship may likewise please to admit into your good opinion, with these weak endeavours, the constancy of affection from the sincere lover of your deserts in honour,

JOHN FORD.

³ So little of Ford's personal history is known, that no allusion to any circumstance peculiar to himself can be explained. He seems here (and all is but seeming) to speak of some legal business in which he was engaged under this nobleman; but of what nature it would be useless to inquire.

DRAMATIS PERSONÆ.

BONAVENTURA, a friar.
A CARDINAL, nuncio to the Pope.
SORANZO, a nobleman.
FLORIO, }
DONADO, } citizens of Parma.
GRIMALDI, a Roman gentleman.
GIOVANNI, son to Florio.
BERGETTO, nephew to Donado.
RICHARDETTO, a supposed physician.
VASQUES, servant to Soranzo.
POGGIO, servant to Bergetto.
Banditti.

ANNABELLA, daughter to Florio.
HIPPOLITA, wife to Richardetto.
PHILOTIS, his niece.
PUTANA, tutoress to Annabella. != putain! quelle dommage

Officers, Attendants, Servants, &c.

SCENE—*Parma*.

'TIS PITY SHE'S A WHORE.

ACT I.

SCENE I. *Friar* BONAVENTURA'S *cell.*

Enter FRIAR *and* GIOVANNI.

Friar. Dispute no more in this; for know, young man,
These are no school-points; nice philosophy
May tolerate unlikely arguments,
But Heaven admits no jest: wits that presum'd
On wit too much, by striving how to prove
There was no God with foolish grounds of art,
Discover'd first the nearest way to hell,
And fill'd the world with devilish atheism.
Such questions, youth, are fond:[1] far better 'tis[2]
To bless the sun than reason why it shines;
Yet He thou talk'st of is above the sun.
No more! I may not hear it.
   Gio.   Gentle father,
To you I have unclasp'd my burden'd soul,
Emptied the storehouse of my thoughts and heart,
Made myself poor of secrets; have not left

---

[1] *fond:*] i.e. idle, unprofitable.
[2] *far better 'tis*] The 4to reads "*for.*" Reed.

Another word untold, which hath not spoke
All what I ever durst or think or know;
And yet is here the comfort I shall have?
Must I not do what all men else may,—love?
    Friar. Yes, you may love, fair son.
    Gio.   Must I not praise
That beauty which, if fram'd anew, the gods
Would make a god of, if they had it there,
And kneel to it, as I do kneel to them?
    Friar. Why, foolish madman,—
    Gio.   Shall a peevish[3] sound,
A customary form, from man to man,
Of brother and of sister, be a bar
'Twixt my perpetual happiness and me?
Say that we had one father; say one womb—
Curse to my joys!—gave both us life and birth;
Are we not therefore each to other bound
So much the more by nature? by the links
Of blood, of reason? nay, if you will have't,
Even of religion, to be ever one,
One soul, one flesh, one love, one heart, one all?.
    Friar. Have done, unhappy youth! for thou art
        lost.
    Gio. Shall, then, for that I am her brother born,
My joys be ever banish'd from her bed?
No, father; in your eyes I see the change
Of pity and compassion; from your age,
As from a sacred oracle, distils
The life of counsel: tell me, holy man,
What cure shall give me ease in these extremes?
    Friar. Repentance, son, and sorrow for this sin:
For thou hast mov'd a Majesty above
With thy unrangèd almost blasphemy.

---

[3] *peevish*] Weak, trifling, unimportant. See *Mass.* vol. i. p. 71.

Gio. O, do not speak of that, dear confessor!
Friar. Art thou, my son, that miracle of wit
Who once, within these three months, wert esteem'd
A wonder of thine age throughout Bononia?
How did the University applaud
Thy government, behaviour, learning, speech,
Sweetness, and all that could make up a man!
I was proud of my tutelage, and chose
Rather to leave my books than part with thee;
I did so:—but the fruits of all my hopes
Are lost in thee, as thou art in thyself.
O, Giovanni![4] hast thou left the schools
Of knowledge to converse with lust and death?
For death waits on thy lust. Look through the world,
And thou shalt see a thousand faces shine
More glorious than this idol thou ador'st:
Leave her, and take thy choice, 'tis much less sin;
Though in such games as those they lose that win.
 Gio. It were more ease to stop the ocean
From floats and ebbs than to dissuade my vows.
 Friar. Then I have done, and in thy wilful flames
Already see thy ruin; Heaven is just.
Yet hear my counsel.
 Gio.   As a voice of life.
 Friar. Hie to thy father's house; there lock thee fast
Alone within thy chamber; then fall down
On both thy knees, and grovel on the ground;
Cry to thy heart; wash every word thou utter'st
In tears—and if't be possible—of blood:
Beg Heaven to cleanse the leprosy of lust

---

[4] *O, Giovanni!*]. Our old dramatists appear to have learned Italian entirely from books; few, if any, of them pronounce it correctly. Giovanni is here used by Ford as a quadrisyllable, as it was by Massinger and others of his contemporaries.

That rots thy soul; acknowledge what thou art,
A wretch, a worm, a nothing; weep, sigh, pray
Three times a-day and three times every night:
For seven days' space do this; then, if thou find'st
No change in thy desires, return to me:
I'll think on remedy. Pray for thyself
At home, whilst I pray for thee here.—Away!
My blessing with thee! we have need to pray.
    Gio. All this I'll do, to free me from the rod
Of vengeance; else I'll swear my fate's my god.
                                    [*Exeunt.*[5]

SCENE II. *The street before* FLORIO'S *house.*

Enter GRIMALDI *and* VASQUES, *with their swords drawn.*

Vas. Come, sir, stand to your tackling; if you prove craven, I'll make you run quickly.

Grim. Thou art no equal match for me.

Vas. Indeed, I never went to the wars to bring home news; nor cannot[6] play the mountebank for a meal's meat, and swear I got my wounds in the field. See you these gray hairs? they'll not flinch for a bloody nose. Wilt thou to this gear?

---

[5] It is observed by Langbaine that the loves of Giovanni and Annabella are painted in too beautiful colours · this, though it may impeach the writer's taste in selecting such a subject, is yet complimentary to his judgment in treating it. What but the most glowing diction, the most exquisite harmony of versification, could hope to allure the reader through the dreadful display of vice and misery which lay before him! With respect to the scene which has just passed, it is replete with excellence as a composition; it may be doubted, however, whether it does not let us somewhat too abruptly into the plot, which, from its revolting nature, should have been more gradually opened. The character of the Friar is artfully drawn; pious, but gentle, irresolute, and, to speak tenderly, strangely indulgent; and thus we are prepared for his subsequent conduct, which involves the fate of his young charge.

[6] *nor cannot*] Gifford printed "*nor* I *cannot.*" D.

Grim. Why, slave, thinkest thou I'll balance my reputation with a cast-suit? Call thy master; he shall know that I dare—

Vas. Scold like a cot-quean;[7]—that's your profession. Thou poor shadow of a soldier, I will make thee know my master keeps servants thy betters in quality and performance. Comest thou to fight or prate?

Grim. Neither, with thee. I am a Roman and a gentleman; one that have got mine honour with expense of blood.

Vas. You are a lying coward and a fool. Fight, or, by these hilts, I'll kill thee :—brave my lord!— you'll fight?

Grim. Provoke me not, for if thou dost—

Vas.   Have at you!
        [*They fight; Grimaldi is worsted.*

Enter FLORIO, DONADO, *and* SORANZO, *from opposite sides.*

Flo. What mean[8] these sudden broils so near my doors?
Have you not other places but my house
To vent the spleen of your disorder'd bloods?
Must I be haunted still with such unrest
As not to eat or sleep in peace at home?
Is this your love, Grimaldi? Fie! 'tis naught.

Don. And, Vasques, I may tell thee; 'tis not well
To broach these quarrels; you are ever forward
In seconding contentions.

---

[7] *Scold like a* cot-quean;] A contemptuous term for one who cerns himself with female affairs; an effeminate meddler.

[8] *mean*] The 4to has "meaned." D.

Enter above[9] ANNABELLA *and* PUTANA.

Flo. What's the ground?
Sor. That, with your patience, signiors, I'll resolve :
This gentleman, whom fame reports a soldier,—
For else I know not,—rivals me in love
To Signior Florio's daughter ; to whose ears
He still prefers his suit, to my disgrace ;
Thinking the way to recommend himself
Is to disparage me in his report :—
But know, Grimaldi, though, may be, thou art
My equal in thy blood, yet this bewrays
A lowness in thy mind, which, wert thou noble,
Thou wouldst as much disdain as I do thee
For this unworthiness :—and on this ground
I will'd my servant to correct his[10] tongue,
Holding a man so base no match for me.

Vas. And had [not] your sudden coming prevented us, I had let my gentleman blood under the gills :—I should have wormed you, sir, for running mad.[11]

Grim. I'll be reveng'd, Soranzo.

Vas. On a dish of warm broth to stay your stomach—do, honest innocence, do ! spoon-meat is a wholesomer diet than a Spanish blade.

Grim. Remember this !
Sor.   I fear thee not, Grimaldi.
                              [*Exit Grim.*

---

[9] *Enter* above] i. e. on the raised platform which stood on the old stage, and which served for a balcony to the street, and a gallery to the rooms within doors.
[10] *his*] The 4to has "this." D.
[11] *I should have* wormed *you, sir,* for running mad.] i. e. to prevent you from running mad. *Jonson*, vol. iv. p. 181. The allusion is to the practice of cutting what is called the *worm* from under a dog's tongue, as a *preventive* of madness.

Flo. My Lord Soranzo, this is strange to me,
Why you should storm, having my word engag'd;
Owing her heart,[12] what need you doubt her ear?
Losers may talk by law of any game.

Vas. Yet the villany of words, Signior Florio, may be such as would make any unspleened dove choleric. Blame not my lord in this.

Flo. Be you more silent:
I would not for my wealth, my daughter's love
Should cause the spilling of one drop of blood.
Vasques, put up: let's end this fray in wine. [*Exeunt.*

Put. How like you this, child? here's threatening, challenging, quarrelling, and fighting on every side; and all is for your sake: you had need look to yourself, charge; you'll be stolen away sleeping else shortly.

Ann. But, tutoress, such a life gives no content
To me; my thoughts are fix'd on other ends.
Would you would leave me!

Put. Leave you! no marvel else; leave me no leaving, charge; this is love outright. Indeed, I blame you not; you have choice fit for the best lady in Italy.

Ann. Pray do not talk so much.

Put. Take the worst with the best, there's Grimaldi the soldier, a very well-timbered fellow. They say he is a Roman, nephew to the Duke Montferrato; they say he did good service in the wars against the Milanese; but, 'faith, charge, I do not like him, an't be for nothing but for being a soldier: [not] one amongst twenty of your skirmishing captains but have some privy maim or other that mars their standing

---

[12] Owing *her heart,*] i.e. *possessing, owning:* in this sense the word is used by all our old dramatists. Florio's reasoning, however, is far from correct. It does not follow that, because Soranzo had his *word*, he *owed* his daughter's heart: in short, Annabella seems to have thought nothing of him.

upright. I like him the worse, he crinkles so much in the hams : though he might serve if there were no more men, yet he's not the man I would choose.

Ann. Fie, how thou pratest!

Put. As I am a very woman, I like Signior Soranzo well; he is wise, and what is more, rich; and what is more than that, kind; and what is more than all this, a nobleman : such a one, were I the fair Annabella myself, I would wish and pray for. Then he is bountiful; besides, he is handsome, and, by my troth, I think, wholesome,—and that's news in a gallant of three-and-twenty; liberal, that I know; loving, that you know; and a man sure, else he could never ha' purchased such a good name with Hippolita, the lusty widow, in her husband's lifetime : an 'twere but for that report, sweetheart, would 'a were thine! Commend a man for his qualities, but take a husband as he is a plain, sufficient, naked man : such a one is for your bed, and such a one is Signior Soranzo, my life for't.

Ann. Sure the woman took her morning's draught too soon.

Enter BERGETTO *and* POGGIO.

Put. But look, sweetheart, look what thing comes now! Here's another of your ciphers to fill up the number: O, brave old ape in a silken coat! Observe.

Berg. Didst thou think, Poggio, that I would spoil my new clothes, and leave my dinner, to fight?

Pog. No, sir, I did not take you for so arrant a baby.

Berg. I am wiser than so : for I hope, Poggio, thou never heardst of an elder brother that was a coxcomb; didst, Poggio?

Pog. Never, indeed, sir, as long as they had either land or money left them to inherit.

Berg. Is it possible, Poggio? O, monstrous! Why, I'll undertake with a handful of silver to buy a headful of wit at any time: but, sirrah, I have another purchase in hand; I shall have the wench, mine uncle says. I will but wash my face and shift socks, and then have at her, i'faith!—Mark my pace, Poggio!
[*Passes over the stage, and exit.*

Pog. Sir,—I have seen an ass and a mule trot the Spanish pavin[13] with a better grace, I know not how often. [*Aside, and follows him.*

Ann. This idiot haunts me too.

Put. Ay, ay, he needs no description. The rich magnifico that is below with your father, charge, Signior Donado his uncle, for that he means to make this, his cousin,[14] a golden calf, thinks that you will be a right Israelite, and fall down to him presently: but I hope I have tutored you better. They say a fool's bauble is a lady's playfellow; yet you, having wealth enough, you need not cast upon the dearth of flesh, at any rate. Hang him, innocent![15]

GIOVANNI *passes over the stage.*

Ann. But see, Putana, see! what blessèd shape

---

[13] *the Spanish* pavin] "The pavan, from *pavo*, a peacock, is a grave and majestic dance; the method of performing it was anciently by gentlemen dressed with a cap and sword; by those of the long robe, in their gowns; by princes, in their mantles; and by ladies, in gowns with long trains, the motion whereof in the dance resembled that of a peacock's tail." *Sir John Hawkins.* [The derivation of the word *pavin* is disputed. D.]

[14] *cousin,*] i.e. nephew. D.

[15] *innocent!*] A natural fool. Thus, in the *Two Noble Kinsmen*, act iv. sc. 1;

"but this very day
I ask'd her questions, and she answer'd me
So far from what she was, so childishly,
So sillily, as if she were a fool,
An *innocent;* and I was very angry." *Reed.*

Of some celestial creature now appears!—
What man is he, that with such sad aspéct
Walks careless of himself?
  Put.   Where?
  Ann.   Look below.
  Put. O, 'tis your brother, sweet.
  Ann.   Ha!
  Put.   'Tis your brother.
  Ann. Sure, 'tis not he; this is some woful thing
Wrapp'd up in grief, some shadow of a man.
Alas, he beats his breast and wipes his eyes,
Drown'd all in tears: methinks I hear him sigh:
Let's down, Putana, and partake the cause.
I know my brother, in the love he bears me,
Will not deny me partage in his sadness.—
My soul is full of heaviness and fear.   [*Aside.*
                                  [*Exit above with Put.*

SCENE III. *A hall in* FLORIO'S *house.*

  Gio. Lost! I am lost! my fates have doom'd my
        death:
The more I strive, I love; the more I love,
The less I hope: I see my ruin certain.
What judgment or endeavours could apply
To my incurable and restless wounds,
I throughly have examin'd, but in vain.
O, that it were not in religion sin
To make our love a god, and worship it!
I have even wearied heaven with prayers, dried up
The spring of my continual tears, even starv'd
My veins with daily fasts: what wit or art
Could counsel, I have practis'd; but, alas,
I find all these but dreams, and old men's tales,

To fright unsteady youth; I'm still the same:
Or I must speak, or burst. 'Tis not, I know,
My lust, but 'tis my fate that leads me on.[16]
Keep fear and low faint-hearted shame with slaves!
I'll tell her that I love her, though my heart
Were rated at the price of that attempt.—
O me! she comes.

Enter ANNABELLA *and* PUTANA.

Ann. Brother!
Gio. [*aside*] If such a thing
As courage dwell in men, ye heavenly powers,
Now double all that virtue in my tongue!
  Ann. Why, brother,
Will you not speak to me?
  Gio. Yes: how d'ye, sister?
  Ann. Howe'er I am, methinks you are not well.
  Put. Bless us! why are you so sad, sir?
  Gio. Let me entreat you, leave us a while, Putana.—
Sister, I would be private with you.
  Ann. Withdraw, Putana.
  Put. I will.—If this were any other company for her, I should think my absence an office of some credit: but I will leave them together.
  [*Aside, and exit.*
  Gio. Come, sister, lend your hand: let's walk together;

---

[16] This is a repetition of the sentiment with which he had taken leave of the Friar—*My fate's my god*. I would not detain the reader in these scenes, on which Ford has lavished all the charms of his eloquence; but it may be cursorily observed, that characters like Giovanni, desperately abandoned to vice, endeavour to cheat their conscience by setting up a deity of their own, and pretending to be swayed by his resistless influence. This is the last stage of human depravation, and in Scripture language is called "hardening the heart." See *Mass.* vol. i. p. 217.

I hope you need not blush to walk with me;
Here's none but you and I.
 Ann.   How's this?
 Gio.   [I'] faith,
I mean no harm.
 Ann.   Harm?
 Gio.   No, good faith.
How is't with ye?
 Ann. [*aside*] I trust he be not frantic.—
I am very well, brother.
 Gio. Trust me, but I am sick; I· fear so sick
'Twill cost my life.
 Ann. Mercy forbid it! 'tis not so, I hope.
 Gio. I think you love me, sister.
 Ann.   Yes, you know
I do.
 Gio. I know't, indeed.—You're very fair.
 Ann. Nay, then I see you have a merry sickness.
 Gio. That's as it proves. The poets feign, I read,
That Juno for her forehead did exceed
All other goddesses; but I durst swear
Your forehead exceeds hers, as hers did their.[17]
 Ann. 'Troth, this is pretty!
 Gio.   Such a pair of stars
As are thine eyes would, like Promethean fire,
If gently glanc'd, give life to senseless stones.
 Ann. Fie upon ye!
 Gio. The lily and the rose, most sweetly strange,
Upon your dimpled cheeks do strive for change:
Such lips would tempt a saint; such hands as those
Would make an anchorite lascivious.
 Ann. D'ye mock me or flatter me?
 Gio. If you would see a beauty more exact
Than art can counterfeit or nature frame,

 [17] *their.*] The 4to has "theirs;" which Gifford retained. D.

Look in your glass, and there behold your own.
 Ann. O, you are a trim youth !
 Gio. Here !   [*Offers his dagger to her.*
 Ann.   What to do ?
 Gio.   And here's my breast ; strike home !
Rip up my bosom ; there thou shalt behold
A heart in which is writ the truth I speak.
Why stand ye ?
 Ann.   Are you earnest ?
 Gio.   Yes, most earnest.
You cannot love ?
 Ann.   Whom ?
 Gio.   Me. My tortur'd soul
Hath felt affliction in the heat of death.
O, Annabella, I am quite undone !
The love of thee, my sister, and the view
Of thy immortal beauty have untun'd
All harmony both of my rest and life.
Why d'ye not strike ?
 Ann.   Forbid it, my just fears !
If this be true, 'twere fitter I were dead.
 Gio. True, Annabella ! 'tis no time to jest.
I have too long suppress'd the[18] hidden flames
That almost have consum'd me : I have spent
Many a silent night in sighs and groans ;
Ran over all my thoughts, despis'd my fate,
Reason'd against the reasons of my love,
Done all that smooth-cheek'd[19] virtue could advise ;
But found all bootless : 'tis my destiny
That you must either love, or I must die.
 Ann. Comes this in sadness[20] from you ?

---

  [18] *the*] Gifford printed " my." D.

  [19] *smooth-cheek'd*] The 4to has " smooth'd-cheeke ;" which perhaps (though altered here by Gifford) is what Ford wrote. D.

  [20] *Comes this in* sadness] i. e. in seriousness.

Gio.   Let some mischief
Befall me soon, if I dissemble aught.
   Ann. You are my brother Giovanni.
   Gio.   You
My sister Annabella ; I know this,
And could afford you instance why to love
So much the more for this ; to which intent
Wise nature first in your creation meant
To make you mine ; else't had been sin and foul
To share one beauty to a double soul.
Nearness in birth and[21] blood doth but persuade
A nearer nearness in affection.
I have ask'd counsel of the holy church,
Who tells me I may love you ; and 'tis just
That, since I may, I should ; and will, yes, will.
Must I now live or die ?
   Ann.   Live ; thou hast won
The field, and never fought : what thou hast urg'd
My captive heart had long ago resolv'd.
I blush to tell thee,—but I'll tell thee now,—
For every sigh that thou hast spent for me
I have sigh'd ten ; for every tear shed twenty :
And not so much for that I lov'd, as that
I durst not say I lov'd, nor scarcely think it.
   Gio. Let not this music be a dream, ye gods,
For pity's sake, I beg ye !
   Ann.   On my knees, [*She kneels.*
Brother, even by our mother's dust, I charge you,
Do not betray me to your mirth or hate :
Love me or kill me, brother.
   Gio.   On my knees, [*He kneels.*
Sister, even by my mother's dust, I charge you,
Do not betray me to your mirth or hate :

---

[21] *and*] The 4to has "or." D.

Love me or kill me, sister.

Ann. You mean good sooth, then?

Gio.   In good troth, I do;
And so do you, I hope: say, I'm in earnest.

Ann. I'll swear it, I.[22]

Gio.   And I; and by this kiss,—
                                    [*Kisses her.*
Once more, yet once more: now let's rise [*they rise*],
        —by this,
I would not change this minute for Elysium.
What must we now do?

Ann.   What you will.

Gio.   Come, then;
After so many tears as we have wept,
Let's learn to court in smiles, to kiss, and sleep.
                                    [*Exeunt.*

SCENE IV. *A street.*

Enter FLORIO *and* DONADO.

Flo. Signior Donado, you have said enough,
I understand you; but would have you know
I will not force my daughter 'gainst her will.
You see I have but two, a son and her;
And he is so devoted to his book,
As I must tell you true, I doubt his health:
Should he miscarry, all my hopes rely
Upon my girl.[23] As for worldly fortune,
I am, I thank my stars, bless'd with enough.

---

[22] *I'll swear it, I.*] The old copy has "*and*" before "I;" evidently an oversight of the press.

[23] *Upon my* girl.] *Girl* is here, and almost everywhere else in these plays, a dissyllable. See pp. 18 and 134. The practice is not peculiar to our poet; f* Fanshaw, and others of that age, have numerous examples of it — ford.

My care is, how to match her to her liking:
I would not have her marry wealth, but love;
And if she like your nephew, let him have her.
Here's all that I can say.
　　Don.　　　　　　Sir, you say well,
Like a true father; and, for my part, I,
If the young folks can like,—'twixt you and me,—
Will promise to assure my nephew presently
Three thousand florins yearly during life,
And after I am dead my whole estate.
　　Flo. 'Tis a fair proffer, sir; meantime your nephew
Shall have free passage to commence his suit:
If he can thrive, he shall have my consent.
So for this time I'll leave you, signior.　　[*Exit.*
　　Don.　　　　　　　　　　　　　Well,
Here's hope yet, if my nephew would have wit;
But he is such another dunce, I fear
He'll never win the wench. When I was young,
I could have done't, i'faith; and so shall he,
If he will learn of me; and, in good time,
He comes himself.

　　　　　　Enter BERGETTO *and* POGGIO.

How now, Bergetto, whither away so fast?
　　Berg. O, uncle, I have heard the strangest news that ever came out of the mint!—Have I not, Poggio?
　　Pog. Yes, indeed, sir.
　　Don. What news, Bergetto?
　　Berg. Why, look ye, uncle, my barber told me just now that there is a fellow come to town who undertakes to make a mill go without the mortal help of any water or wind, only with sand-bags: and this fellow hath a strange horse, a most excellent beast, I'll assure you, uncle, my barber says; whose head, to

the wonder of all Christian people, stands just behind where his tail is.—Is't not true, Poggio?

Pog. So the barber swore, forsooth.

Don. And you are running [t]hither?

Berg. Ay, forsooth, uncle.

Don. Wilt thou be a fool still? Come, sir, you shall not go: you have more mind of a puppet-play than on the business I told ye. Why, thou great baby, wilt never have wit? wilt make thyself a May-game[24] to all the world?

Pog. Answer for yourself, master.

Berg. Why, uncle, should I sit at home still, and not go abroad to see fashions like other gallants?

Don. To see hobby-horses! What wise talk, I pray, had you with Annabella, when you were at Signior Florio's house?

Berg. O, the wench,—Ud's sa'me, uncle, I tickled her with a rare speech, that I made her almost burst her belly with laughing.

Don. Nay, I think so; and what speech was't?

Berg. What did I say, Poggio?

Pog. Forsooth, my master said, that he loved her almost as well as he loved parmasent;[25] and swore— I'll be sworn for him—that she wanted but such a nose as his was, to be as pretty a young woman as any was in Parma.

Don. O, gross!

Berg. Nay, uncle:—then she asked me whether my father had any[26] more children than myself? and

---

[24] *a May-game*] See note, p. 17. D.

[25] *parmasent;*] i.e. parmesan, the cheese of Parma, where the scene is laid.—Reed suggests that this word may mean a trick in drinking so called; but poor Bergetto had no tricks of any kind: the allusion is evidently to the cheese, which is sufficiently strong to affect the breath, and therefore ridiculously put in competition with the lady.

[26] *any*] Omitted by Gifford. D.

I said "No; 'twere better he should have had his brains knocked out first."

Don. This is intolerable.

Berg. Then said she, "Will Signior Donado, your uncle, leave you all his wealth?"

Don. Ha! that was good; did she harp upon that string?

Berg. Did she harp upon that string! ay, that she did. I answered, "Leave me all his wealth! why, woman, he hath no other wit; if he had, he should hear on't to his everlasting glory and confusion: I know," quoth I, "I am his white-boy,[27] and will not be gulled:" and with that she fell into a great smile, and went away. Nay, I did fit her.

Don. Ah, sirrah, then I see there is no changing of nature. Well, Bergetto, I fear thou wilt be a very ass still.

Berg. I should be sorry for that, uncle.

Don. Come, come you home with me: since you are no better a speaker, I'll have you write to her after some courtly manner, and enclose some rich jewel in the letter.

Berg. Ay, marry, that will be excellent.

Don. Peace, innocent![28]
Once in my time I'll set my wits to school:
If all fail, 'tis but the fortune of a fool.

Berg. Poggio, 'twill do, Poggio. [*Exeunt.*

---

[27] *white-boy,*] A childish term of endearment. Warton says that Dr. Busby used to call his favourite scholars his *white-boys*. The word occurs in Massinger and most of our old poets.

[28] *innocent!*] See note, p. 121. D.

ACT II.

SCENE I. *An apartment in* FLORIO'S *house.*

Enter GIOVANNI *and* ANNABELLA.

Gio. Come, Annabella,—no more sister now,
But love, a name more gracious,—do not blush,
Beauty's sweet wonder, but be proud to know
That yielding thou hast conquer'd, and inflam'd
A heart whose tribute is thy brother's life.
  Ann. And mine is his. O, how these stol'n con-
     tents
Would print a modest crimson on my cheeks,
Had any but my heart's delight prevail'd!
  Gio. I marvel why the chaster of your sex
Should think this pretty toy call'd maidenhead
So strange a loss, when, being lost, 'tis nothing,
And you are still the same.
  Ann.   'Tis well for you;
Now you can talk.
  Gio.   Music as well consists
In th' ear as in the playing.
  Ann.   O, you're wanton!
Tell on't, you're[1] best; do.
  Gio.   Thou wilt chide me, then.
Kiss me :—so! Thus hung Jove on Leda's neck,
And suck'd divine ambrosia from her lips.
I envy not the mightiest man alive;
But hold myself, in being king of thee,
More great than were I king of all the world.
But I shall lose you, sweetheart.

---

[1] *you're*] Gifford printed "you were:" but the contraction has the same meaning; so in Shakespeare's *Cymbeline*, act iii. sc. 2, "Madam, *you're* best consider." D.

Ann. But you shall not.
Gio. You must be married, mistress.
Ann. Yes! to whom?
Gio. Some one must have you.
Ann. You must.
Gio. Nay, some other.
Ann. Now, prithee do not speak so; without jesting
You'll make me weep in earnest.
Gio. What, you will not!
But tell me, sweet, canst thou be dar'd to swear
That thou wilt live to me, and to no other?
Ann. By both our loves I dare; for didst thou know,
My Giovanni, how all suitors seem
To my eyes hateful, thou wouldst trust me then.
Gio. Enough, I take thy word: sweet, we must part:
Remember what thou vow'st; keep well my heart.
Ann. Will you be gone?
Gio. I must.
Ann. When to return?
Gio. Soon.
Ann. Look you do.
Gio. Farewell.
Ann. Go where thou wilt, in mind I'll keep thee here,
And where thou art, I know I shall be there. [*Exit Gio.*
Guardian!

Enter PUTANA.

Put. Child, how is't, child? well, thank heaven, ha!
Ann. O guardian, what a paradise of joy
Have I pass'd over!

SCENE I.   'TIS PITY SHE'S A WHORE.   133

  Put. Nay, what a paradise of joy have you passed under! Why, now I commend thee, charge. Fear nothing, sweetheart : what though he be your brother? your brother's a man, I hope; and I say still, if a young wench feel the fit upon her, let her take any body, father or brother, all is one.
  Ann. I would not have it known for all the world.
  Put. Nor I, indeed; for the speech of the people : else 'twere nothing.
  Flo. [*within*] Daughter Annabella!
  Ann. O me, my father!—Here, sir!—Reach my work.
  Flo. [*within*] What are you doing?
  Ann.   So : let him come now.

Enter FLORIO, *followed by* RICHARDETTO *as a Doctor of Physic, and* PHILOTIS *with a lute.*

  Flo. So hard at work! that's well; you lose no time.
Look, I have brought you company ; here's one,
A learnèd doctor lately come from Padua,
Much skill'd in physic ; and, for that I see
You have of late been sickly, I entreated
This reverend man to visit you some time.
  Ann. You're very welcome, sir.
  Rich.   I thank you, mistress.
Loud fame in large report hath spoke your praise
As well for virtue as perfection ;[2]
For which I have been bold to bring with me
A kinswoman of mine, a maid, for song
And music one perhaps will give content :
Please you to know her.

---

  [2] *As well for virtue as* perfection ;] For *perfect* beauty, or fulness of accomplishments.

Ann. They are parts I love,
And she for them most welcome.
Phi. Thank you, lady.
Flo. Sir, now you know my house, pray make not strange;
And if you find my daughter need your art,
I'll be your pay-master.
Rich. Sir, what I am
She shall command.
Flo. [Sir], you shall bind me to you.—
Daughter, I must have conference with you
About some matters that concern us both.—
Good Master Doctor, please you but walk in,
We'll crave a little of your cousin's cunning :[3]
I think my girl[4] hath not quite forgot
To touch an instrument; she could have done't:
We'll hear them both.
Rich. I'll wait upon you, sir. [*Exeunt.*

SCENE II. *A room in* SORANZO'S *house.*

Enter SORANZO *with a book.*

[*Reads*]
*Love's measure is extreme, the comfort pain,
The life unrest, and the reward disdain.*
What's here? look't o'er again.—'Tis so; so writes
This smooth licentious poet in his rhymes:
But, Sannazar, thou liest; for, had thy bosom
Felt such oppression as is laid on mine,
Thou wouldst have kiss'd the rod that made the[e] smart.—

---

[3] *cunning;*] i.e. skill: the word is used in this sense by all our old writers.
[4] *I think my* girl] See pp. 18 and 127.

SCENE II.   'TIS PITY SHE'S A WHORE.   135

To work, then, happy Muse, and contradict
What Sannazar hath in his envy writ.   [*Writes.*
Love's measure is the mean, sweet his annoys,
His pleasures life, and his reward all joys.
Had Annabella liv'd when Sannazar
Did, in his brief Encomium,[5] celebrate
Venice, that queen of cities, he had left
That verse which gain'd him such a sum of gold,
And for one only look from Annabel
Had writ of her and her diviner cheeks.
O, how my thoughts are—
    Vas. [*within*] Pray, forbear; in rules of civility, let me give notice on't : I shall be taxed of my neglect of duty and service.
    Sor. What rude intrusion interrupts my peace? Can I be no where private?
    Vas. [*within*] Troth, you wrong your modesty.
    Sor. What's the matter, Vasques? who is't?

    Enter HIPPOLITA *and* VASQUES.

    Hip.   'Tis I ;
Do you know me now? Look, perjur'd man, on her
Whom thou and thy distracted lust have wrong'd.

---

[5]   *when Sannazar Did, in his brief Encomium,* &c.] This is the well-known Epigram, beginning

      "Viderat Hadriacis Venetam Neptunus in undis
      Stare urbem, &c."

It is given by Coryat, who thus speaks of it: "I heard in Venice that a certaine Italian poet, called Jacobus Sannazarius, had a hundred crownes bestowed upon him by the Senate of Venice for each of these verses following. I would to God my poeticall friend Master Benjamin Johnson were so well rewarded for his poems here in England, seeing he hath made many as good verses (in my opinion) as these of Sannazarius." Tom is right. The verses have nothing very extraordinary in them; but they flattered the vanity of the republic: and, after all, there is no great evil in overpaying a poet once in fifteen centuries, for so long it is between the times of Virgil and Sannazarius.

Thy sensual rage of blood hath made my youth
A scorn to men and angels; and shall I
Be now a foil to thy unsated change?
Thou know'st, false wanton, when my modest fame
Stood free from stain or scandal, all the charms
Of hell or sorcery could not prevail
Against the honour of my chaster bosom.
Thine eyes did plead in tears, thy tongue in oaths,
Such and so many, that a heart of steel
Would have been wrought to pity, as was mine:
And shall the conquest of my lawful bed,
My husband's death, urg'd on by his disgrace,
My loss of womanhood, be ill-rewarded
With hatred and contempt? No; know, Soranzo,
I have a spirit doth as much distaste
The slavery of fearing thee, as thou
Dost loathe the memory of what hath pass'd.
    Sor. Nay, dear Hippolita,—
    Hip.   Call me not dear,
Nor think with supple words to smooth the grossness
Of my abuses: 'tis not your new mistress,
Your goodly madam-merchant, shall triúmph
On my dejection; tell her thus from me,
My birth was nobler and by much more free.
    Sor. You are too violent.
    Hip.   You are too double
In your dissimulation. Seest thou this,
This habit, these black mourning weeds of care?
'Tis thou art cause of this; and hast divorc'd
My husband from his life, and me from him,
And made me widow in my widowhood.
    Sor. Will you yet hear?
    Hip.   More of thy[6] perjuries?

---

[6] *thy*] The 4to has " the." D.

Thy soul is drown'd too deeply in those sins;
Thou need'st not add to th' number.

Sor.   Then I'll leave you;
You're past all rules of sense.

Hip.   And thou of grace.

Vas. Fie, mistress, you are not near the limits of reason: if my lord had a resolution as noble as virtue itself, you take the course to unedge it all.—Sir, I beseech you do not perplex her; griefs, alas, will have a vent: I dare undertake Madam Hippolita will now freely hear you.

Sor. Talk to a woman frantic!—Are these the fruits of your love?

Hip. They are the fruits of thy untruth, false man!
Didst thou not swear, whilst yet my husband liv'd,
That thou wouldst wish no happiness on earth
More than to call me wife? didst thou not vow,
When he should die, to marry me? for which
The devil in my blood, and thy protests,
Caus'd me to counsel him to undertake
A voyage to Ligorne, for that we heard
His brother there was dead, and left a daughter
Young and unfriended, who,[7] with much ado,
I wish'd him to bring hither: he did so,
And went; and, as thou know'st, died on the way.
Unhappy man, to buy his death so dear,
With my advice! yet thou, for whom I did it,
Forgett'st thy vows, and leav'st me to my shame.

Sor. Who could help this?

Hip.   Who! perjur'd man, thou couldst,
If thou hadst faith or love.

Sor.   You are deceiv'd:

---

[7] *who,*] Gifford printed "whom:" but see Shakespeare and our old poets passim. D.

The vows I made, if you remember well,
Were wicked and unlawful; 'twere more sin
To keep them than to break them : as for me,
I cannot mask my penitence. Think thou
How much thou hast digress'd from honest shame
In bringing of a gentleman to death
Who was thy husband ; such a one as he,
So noble in his quality, condition,
Learning, behaviour, entertainment, love,
As Parma could not show a braver man.

Vas. You do not well; this was not your promise.

Sor. I care not; let her know her monstrous life.
Ere I'll be servile to so black a sin,
I'll be a curse.—Woman, come here no more ;
Learn to repent, and die ; for, by my honour,
I hate thee and thy lust: you've been too foul. [*Exit.*

Vas. [*aside*] This part has been scurvily played.

Hip. How foolishly this beast contemns his fate,
And shuns the use of that which I more scorn
Than I once lov'd, his love ! But let him go ;
My vengeance shall give comfort to his woe.[8] [*Going.*

Vas. Mistress, mistress, Madam Hippolita ! pray, a word or two.

Hip. With me, sir ?

Vas. With you, if you please.

Hip. What is't ?

Vas. I know you are infinitely moved now, and you think you have cause : some I confess you have, but sure not so much as you imagine.

Hip. Indeed!

Vas. O, you were miserably bitter, which you followed even to the last syllable; 'faith, you were some-

---

[8] *to his woe.*] i. e. to the woe occasioned by his falsehood. She recurs to this idea in the concluding speech of this scene.

what too shrewd: by my life, you could not have took my lord in a worse time since I first knew him; tomorrow you shall find him a new man.

Hip. Well, I shall wait his leisure.

Vas. Fie, this is not a hearty patience; it comes sourly from you: 'troth, let me persuade you for once.

Hip. [*aside*] I have it, and it shall be so; thanks, opportunity!—Persuade me! to what?

Vas. Visit him in some milder temper. O, if you could but master a little your female spleen, how might you win him!

Hip. He will never love me. Vasques, thou hast been a too trusty servant to such a master, and I believe thy reward in the end will fall out like mine.

Vas. So perhaps too.

Hip. Resolve thyself it will.[9] Had I one so true, so truly honest, so secret to my counsels, as thou hast been to him and his, I should think it a slight acquittance, not only to make him master of all I have, but even of myself.

Vas. O, you are a noble gentlewoman!

Hip. Wilt thou feed always upon hopes? well, I know thou art wise, and seest the reward of an old servant daily, what it is.

Vas. Beggary and neglect.

Hip. True; but, Vasques, wert thou mine, and wouldst be private to me and my designs, I here protest, myself and all what I can else call mine should be at thy dispose.

Vas. [*aside*] Work you that way, old mole? then I have the wind of you.—I were not worthy of it by any desert that could lie within my compass: if I could—

---

[9] Resolve *thyself it will.*] i. e. *assure, convince* thyself. The word occurs before and after in the same sense.

Hip. What then?

Vas. I should then hope to live in these my old years with rest and security.

Hip. Give me thy hand : now promise but thy silence,
And help to bring to pass a plot I have,
And here, in sight of heaven, that being done,
I make thee lord of me and mine estate.

Vas. Come, you are merry; this is such a happiness that I can neither think or believe.

Hip. Promise thy secrecy, and 'tis confirm'd.

Vas. Then here I call our good genii for witnesses,[10] whatsoever your designs are, or against whomsoever, I will not only be a special actor therein, but never disclose it till it be effected.

Hip. I take thy word, and, with that, thee for mine ;
Come, then, let's more confer of this anon.—
On this delicious bane my thoughts[11] shall banquet;
Revenge shall sweeten what my griefs have tasted.
      [*Aside, and exit with Vas.*

SCENE III. *The street.*

Enter RICHARDETTO *and* PHILOTIS.

Rich. Thou seest, my lovely niece, these strange mishaps,
How all my fortunes turn to my disgrace ;
Wherein I am but as a looker-on,
Whiles others act my shame, and I am silent.

Phi. But, uncle, wherein can this borrow'd shape

---

[10] *for witnesses,*] The 4to has "foe-*witnesses.*" D.
[11] *thoughts*] Gifford printed "thought." D.

Give you content?
  Rich.   I'll tell thee, gentle niece:
Thy wanton aunt in her lascivious riots
Lives now secure, thinks I am surely dead
In my late journey to Ligorne for you,—
As I have caus'd it to be rumour'd out.
Now would I see with what an impudence
She gives scope to her loose adultery,
And how the common voice allows hereof:
Thus far I have prevail'd.
  Phi.   Alas, I fear
You mean some strange revenge.
  Rich.   O, be not troubled;
Your ignorance shall plead for you in all:
But to our business.—What! you learn'd for certain
How Signior Florio means to give his daughter
In marriage to Soranzo?
  Phi.   Yes, for certain.
  Rich. But how find you young Annabella's love
Inclin'd to him?
  Phi.   For aught I could perceive,
She neither fancies him or any else.
  Rich. There's mystery in that, which time must
    show.
She us'd you kindly?
  Phi.   Yes.
  Rich.   And crav'd your company?
  Phi. Often.
  Rich.   'Tis well; it goes as I could wish.
I am the doctor now; and as for you,
None knows you: if all fail not, we shall thrive.—
But who comes here? I know him; 'tis Grimaldi,
A Roman and a soldier, near allied
Unto the Duke of Montferrato, one
Attending on the nuncio of the pope

That now resides in Parma; by which means
He hopes to get the love of Annabella.

Enter GRIMALDI.

Grim. Save you, sir.
Rich. And you, sir.
Grim. I have heard
Of your approvèd skill, which through the city
Is freely talk'd of, and would crave your aid.
Rich. For what, sir?
Grim. Marry, sir, for this—
But I would speak in private.
Rich. Leave us, cousin.[12] [*Exit Phi.*
Grim. I love fair Annabella, and would know
Whether in art[13] there may not be receipts
To move affection.
Rich. Sir, perhaps there may;
But these will nothing profit you.
Grim. Not me?
Rich. Unless I be mistook, you are a man
Greatly in favour with the cardinal.
Grim. What of that?
Rich. In duty to his grace,
I will be bold to tell you, if you seek
To marry Florio's daughter, you must first
Remove a bar 'twixt you and her.
Grim. Who's that?
Rich. Soranzo is the man that hath her heart;
And while he lives, be sure you cannot speed.
Grim. Soranzo! what, mine enemy![14] is't he?

[12] *cousin.*] i.e. niece. D. [13] *art*] The 4to "arts;" so Gifford. D.
[14] Grim. *Soranzo! what, mine enemy!*] It is strange that this should appear a new discovery to Grimaldi, when he had been fully apprised of it in the rencontre with Vasques in the first act. It is not often, however, that Ford thus wholly forgets himself. In Grimaldi's next speech there is apparently some slight error: "I'll *tell* him straight," should probably be, "I'll *to* him straight."

SCENE IV.   'TIS PITY SHE'S A WHORE.   143

Rich. Is he your enemy?
Grim.   The man I hate
Worse than confusion; I will tell him straight.
Rich. Nay, then, take mine[15] advice,
Even for his grace's sake the cardinal:
I'll find a time when he and she do meet,
Of which I'll give you notice; and, to be sure
He shall not scape you, I'll provide a poison
To dip your rapier's point in: if he had
As many heads as Hydra had, he dies.
Grim. But shall I trust thee, doctor?
Rich.   As yourself;
Doubt not in aught. [*Exit Grim.*]—Thus shall the fates decree
By me Soranzo falls, that ruin'd me.[16]   [*Exit.*

SCENE IV. *Another part of the street.*

Enter DONADO *with a letter,* BERGETTO, *and* POGGIO.

Don. Well, sir, I must be content to be both your secretary and your messenger myself. I cannot tell what this letter may work; but, as sure as I am alive, if thou come once to talk with her, I fear thou wilt mar whatsoever I make.

Ber. You make, uncle! why, am not I big enough to carry mine own letter, I pray?

Don. Ay, ay, carry a fool's head o' thy own! why, thou dunce, wouldst thou write a letter, and carry it thyself?

[15] *mine*] Gifford printed "my." D.
[16] *that* ruin'd *me.*] The old copy reads "that *min'd* me." What a detestable set of characters has Ford here sharked-up for the exercise of his fine talents! With the exception of poor Bergetto and his uncle, most of the rest seem contending which of them shall prove worthiest of the wheel and the gibbet.

Ber. Yes, that I would, and read it to her with my own mouth; for you must think, if she will not believe me myself when she hears me speak, she will not believe another's handwriting. O, you think I am a blockhead, uncle. No, sir, Poggio knows I have indited a letter myself; so I have.

Pog. Yes, truly, sir; I have it in my pocket.

Don. A sweet one, no doubt; pray let's see't.

Ber. I cannot read my own hand very well, Poggio; read it, Poggio.

Don. Begin.

Pog. [*reads*] " Most dainty and honey-sweet mistress; I could call you fair, and lie as fast as any that loves you; but my uncle being the elder man, I leave it to him, as more fit for his age and the colour of his beard. I am wise enough to tell you I can bourd where I see occasion;[17] or if you like my uncle's wit better than mine, you shall marry me; if you like mine better than his, I will marry you, in spite of your teeth. So, commending my best parts to you, I rest

  Yours upwards and downwards, or you may
   choose,   Bergetto."

Ber. Ah, ha! here's stuff, uncle!

Don. Here's stuff indeed—to shame us all. Pray, whose advice did you take in this learned letter?

Pog. None, upon my word, but mine own.

Ber. And mine, uncle, believe it, nobody's else; 'twas mine own brain, I thank a good wit for't.

Don. Get you home, sir, and look you keep within doors till I return.

---

[17] *I can* bourd *where I see occasion;*] i.e. jest; see *Jonson*, vol. iv. p. 222. In the old spelling, this word is frequently confounded with *board*, which as Sir Toby truly says, means to *accost*. The words in the text are borrowed from Nic. Bottom, confessedly a very facetious personage.

Ber. How! that were a jest indeed! I scorn it, i'faith.

Don. What! you do not?

Ber. Judge me, but I do now.

Pog. Indeed, sir, 'tis very unhealthy.

Don. Well, sir, if I hear any of your apish running to motions[18] and fopperies, till I come back, you were as good no;[19] look to't. [*Exit.*

Ber. Poggio, shall's steal to see this horse with the head in's tail?

Pog. Ay, but you must take heed of whipping.

Ber. Dost take me for a child, Poggio? Come, honest Poggio. [*Exeunt.*

SCENE V. *Friar* BONAVENTURA'S *cell.*

Enter Friar *and* GIOVANNI.

Friar. Peace! thou hast told a tale whose every word
Threatens eternal slaughter to the soul;
I'm sorry I have heard it: would mine ears
Had been one minute deaf, before the hour
That thou cam'st to me! O young man, castaway,
By the religious number of mine order,[20]
I day and night have wak'd my agèd eyes
Above my[21] strength, to weep on thy behalf;
But Heaven is angry, and be thou resolv'd
Thou art a man remark'd to taste a mischief.[22]

---

[18] *if I hear of your running to* motions] i.e. to puppet-shows; see *Jonson*, vol. ii. p. 7.
[19] *no;*] Gifford printed "not." D.
[20] *By the religious* number *of mine order,*] A misprint probably for *founder;* but I have changed nothing.
[21] *my*] The 4to has "thy." D.
[22] *Thou art a man* remark'd *to taste a* mischief.] i.e. *marked out* to experience some *fearful evil:* in this sense the word 'mischief' is sometimes used by our old writers.

Look for't; though it come late, it will come sure.
   Gio. Father, in this you are uncharitable ;
What I have done I'll prove both fit and good.
It is a principle which you have taught,
When I was yet your scholar, that the frame[23]
And composition of the mind doth follow
The frame and composition of [the] body :
So, where the body's furniture is *beauty*,
The mind's must needs be *virtue;* which allow'd,
Virtue itself is reason but refin'd,
And love the quintessence of that : this proves,
My sister's beauty being rarely fair
Is rarely virtuous ; chiefly in her love,
And chiefly in that love, her love to me :
If hers to me, then so is mine to her ;
Since in like causes are effects alike.
   Friar. O ignorance in knowledge ! Long ago,
How often have I warn'd thee this before !
Indeed, if we were sure there were no Deity,
Nor Heaven nor Hell, then to be led alone
By Nature's light—as were philosophers
Of elder times—might instance some defence.
But 'tis not so : then, madman, thou wilt find
That Nature is in Heaven's positions blind.
   Gio. Your age o'errules you ; had you youth like mine,
You'd make her love your heaven, and her divine.
   Friar. Nay, then I see thou'rt too far sold to hell:
It lies not in the compass of my prayers
To call thee back, yet let me counsel thee ;
Persuade thy sister to some marriage.
   Gio. Marriage ! why, that's to damn her ; that's to prove
Her greedy of variety of lust.

---

[23] *frame*] The 4to has "fame." D.

Friar. O, fearful! if thou wilt not, give me leave
To shrive her, lest she should die unabsolv'd.
    Gio. At your best leisure, father: then she'll tell
        you
How dearly she doth prize my matchless love;
Then you will know what pity 'twere we two
Should have been sunder'd from each other's arms.
View well her face, and in that little round
You may observe a world's variety;
For colour, lips;[24] for sweet perfumes, her breath;
For jewels, eyes; for threads of purest gold,
Hair; for delicious choice of flowers, cheeks;
Wonder in every portion of that throne.
Hear her but speak, and you will swear the spheres
Make music to the citizens in heaven.
But, father, what is else for pleasure fram'd,
Lest I offend your ears, shall go unnam'd.
    Friar. The more I hear, I pity thee the more,
That one so excellent should give those parts
All to a second death. What I can do
Is but to pray; and yet—I could advise thee,
Wouldst thou be rul'd.
    Gio. "   In what?
    Friar.   Why, leave her yet:

   [24] *For* colour, *lips;*] Dodsley reads "for *coral*, lips;" but the old copy is right; colour is placed in apposition to perfume. Just below he has "*form*" for "*throne.*" In the extravagance of Giovanni's praise, it is scarcely possible to know what terms he would adopt; but "*form*" appears too tame to be genuine, and "*fram'd*" occurs in the next verse but two. It is not quite clear to me that a line has not been dropped after "*throne.*" [I suspect that Dodsley rightly substituted "form." D.]
   For "*world's variety*" the old copy reads "world of variety," which spoils the metre. I suppose the printer mistook the '*s* for *o*', the old abridgment of *of*. It would be unjust to say that the Friar has anything in him of "the old squire of Troy;" yet he certainly betrays his duty both to God and man in the feeble resistance which he offers to the commencement and continuance of this fatal intercourse. [I by no means share in Gifford's confident belief that Ford did not write "a world of variety." D.]

The throne of mercy is above your trespass;
Yet time is left you both—
   Gio.   To embrace each other,
Else let all time be struck quite out of number:
She is like me, and I like her, resolv'd.
   Friar. No more! I'll visit her.—This grieves me most,
Things being thus, a pair of souls are lost.   *[Exeunt.*

SCENE VI. *A room in* FLORIO'S *house.*

Enter FLORIO, DONADO, ANNABELLA, *and* PUTANA.

   Flo. Where's Giovanni?
   Ann.   Newly walk'd abroad,
And, as I heard him say, gone to the friar,
His reverend tutor.
   Flo.   That's a blessèd man,
A man made up of holiness: I hope
He'll teach him how to gain another world.
   Don. Fair gentlewoman, here's a letter sent
To you from my young cousin;[25] I dare swear
He loves you in his soul: would you could hear
Sometimes what I see daily, sighs and tears,
As if his breast were prison to his heart!
   Flo. Receive it, Annabella.
   Ann. Alas, good man!   *[Takes the letter.*
   Don. What's that she said?
   Put. An't please you, sir, she said, "Alas, good man!" Truly I do commend him to her every night before her first sleep, because I would have her dream of him; and she hearkens to that most religiously.

---

[25] *from my young* cousin;] Our author, like all the writers of his day, commonly uses *cousin* for *nephew* and *niece.*

Don. Sayest so? God-a'-mercy, Putana! there's something for thee [*Gives her money*]: and prithee do what thou canst on his behalf; 'shall not be lost labour, take my word for't.

Put. Thank you most heartily, sir: now I have a feeling of your mind, let me alone to work.

Ann. Guardian,—

Put. Did you call?

Ann. Keep this letter.

Don. Signior Florio, in any case bid her read it instantly.

Flo. Keep it! for what? pray, read it me here-right.

Ann. I shall, sir. [*She reads the letter.*

Don. How d'ye find her inclined, signior?

Flo. Troth, sir, I know not how; not all so well As I could wish.

Ann. Sir, I am bound to rest your cousin's debtor. The jewel I'll return; for if he love, I'll count that love a jewel.

Don. Mark you that?— Nay, keep them both, sweet maid.

Ann. You must excuse me, Indeed I will not keep it.

Flo. Where's the ring, That which your mother, in her will, bequeath'd, And charg'd you on her blessing not to give 't To any but your husband? send back that.[26]

Ann. I have it not.

Flo. Ha! have it not! where is't?

Ann. My brother in the morning took it from me,

---

[26] *send back that.*] Florio juggles strangely with his daughter's suitors. He tells Soranzo in act i. that he had "his word engaged;" and yet he here endeavours to force her upon another! His subsequent conduct is not calculated to increase our respect for his character, or our sympathy for his overwhelming afflictions.

Said he would wear't to-day.
　Flo. 　　　　　　　Well, what do you say
To young Bergetto's love? are you content to
Match with him? speak.
　Don. 　　　　　There is the point, indeed.
　Ann. [*aside*] What shall I do? I must say something now.
　Flo. What say? why d'ye not speak?
　Ann. 　　　　　　　Sir, with your leave—
Please you to give me freedom?
　Flo. 　　　　　　　　Yes, you have [it].
　Ann. Signior Donado, if your nephew mean
To raise his better fortunes in his match,
The hope of me will hinder such a hope:
Sir, if you love him, as I know you do,
Find one more worthy of his choice than me:
In short, I'm sure I shall not be his wife.
　Don. Why, here's plain dealing; I commend thee for't;
And all the worst I wish thee is, heaven bless thee!
Your father yet and I will still be friends :—
Shall we not, Signior Florio?
　Flo. 　　　　　　　Yes; why not?
Look, here your cousin[27] comes.

　　　　　Enter BERGETTO *and* POGGIO.

　Don. [*aside*] O, coxcomb! what doth he make here?
　Ber. Where's my uncle, sirs?
　Don. What's the news now?
　Ber. Save you, uncle, save you!—You must not think I come for nothing, masters.—And how, and how is't? what, you have read my letter? ah, there I —tickled you, i' faith.

[27] *cousin*] i. e. nephew. D.

Pog. [*aside to Ber.*] But 'twere better you had tickled her in another place.

Ber. Sirrah sweetheart, I'll tell thee a good jest; and riddle what 'tis.

Ann. You say you'll[28] tell me.

Ber. As I was walking just now in the street, I met a swaggering fellow would needs take the wall of me; and because he did thrust me, I very valiantly called him rogue. He hereupon bade me draw; I told him I had more wit than so: but when he saw that I would not, he did so maul me with the hilts of his rapier, that my head sung whilst my feet capered in the kennel.

Don. [*aside*] Was ever the like ass seen!

Ann. And what did you all this while?

Ber. Laugh at him for a gull, till I saw[29] the blood run about mine ears, and then I could not choose but find in my heart to cry; till a fellow with a broad beard—they say he is a new-come doctor—called me into his[30] house, and gave me a plaster, look you, here 'tis:—and, sir, there was a young wench washed my face and hands most excellently; i' faith, I shall love her as long as I live for't.—Did she not, Poggio?

Pog. Yes, and kissed him too.

Ber. Why, la, now, you think I tell a lie, uncle, I warrant.

Don. Would he that beat thy blood out of thy head had beaten some wit into it! for I fear thou never wilt have any.

Ber. O, uncle, but there was a wench would have done a man's heart good to have looked on her.—By this light, she had a face methinks worth twenty of you, Mistress Annabella.

[28] *you'll*] The 4to has "you'd." D.
[29] *saw*] The 4to has "see." D.
[30] *his*] The 4to has "this." D.

Don. [*aside*] Was ever such a fool born!

Ann. I am glad she liked you,[31] sir.

Ber. Are you so? by my troth, I thank you, forsooth.

Flo. Sure, 'twas the doctor's niece, that was last day with us here.

Ber. 'Twas she, 'twas she.

Don. How do you know that, simplicity?

Ber. Why, does not he[32] say so? if I should have said no, I should have given him the lie, uncle, and so have deserved a dry beating again: I'll none of that.

Flo. A very modest well-behav'd young maid
As I have seen.

Don. Is she indeed?

Flo. Indeed she is, if I have any judgment.

Don. Well, sir, now you are free: you need not care for sending letters now; you are dismissed, your mistress here will none of you.

Ber. No! why, what care I for that? I can have wenches enough in Parma for half-a-crown a-piece:—cannot I, Poggio?

Pog. I'll warrant you, sir.

Don. Signior Florio,
I thank you for your free recourse you gave
For my admittance:—and to you, fair maid,
That jewel I will give you 'gainst your marriage.—
Come, will you go, sir?

Ber. Ay, marry, will I.—Mistress, farewell, mistress; I'll come again to-morrow; farewell, mistress.

[*Exeunt Don., Ber., and Pog.*

---

[31] *I am glad she* liked *you,*] i.e. pleased you. So in *Lear*, "His face *likes* me not." *Maid's Tragedy*, act ii., "What look *likes* you best." *Reed.*

[32] *does not he*] Gifford printed "does he not." D.

Enter GIOVANNI.

Flo. Son, where have you been? what, alone, alone still?[33]
I would not have it so; you must forsake
This over-bookish humour. Well, your sister
Hath shook the fool off.
  Gio.   'Twas no match for her.
  Flo. 'Twas not indeed; I meant it nothing less;
Soranzo is the man I only like :—
Look on him, Annabella.—Come, 'tis supper-time,
And it grows late.   [*Exit.*
  Gio. Whose jewel's that?
  Ann. Some sweetheart's.
  Gio.   So I think.
  Ann.   A lusty youth,
Signior Donado, gave it me to wear
Against my marriage.
  Gio.   But you shall not wear it:
Send it him back again.
  Ann.   What, you are jealous?
  Gio. That you shall know anon, at better leisure.
Welcome sweet night! the evening crowns the day.
                                       [*Exeunt.*

[33] *still?*] The 4to has "*still*, still?" D.

ACT III.

SCENE I. *A room in* DONADO'S *house.*

Enter BERGETTO *and* POGGIO.

Ber. Does my uncle think to make me a baby still? No, Poggio; he shall know I have a sconce now.

Pog. Ay, let him not bob you off like an ape with an apple.

Ber. 'Sfoot, I will have the wench, if he were ten uncles, in despite of his nose, Poggio.

Pog. Hold him to the grindstone, and give not a jot of ground: she hath in a manner promised you already.

Ber. True, Poggio; and her uncle, the doctor, swore I should marry her.

Pog. He swore; I remember.

Ber. And I will have her, that's more: didst see the codpiece-point she gave me and the box of marmalade?

Pog. Very well; and kissed you, that my chops watered at the sight on't. There's no way but to clap-up a marriage in hugger-mugger.

Ber. I will do't; for I tell thee, Poggio, I begin to grow valiant methinks, and my courage begins to rise.

Pog. Should you be afraid of your uncle?

Ber. Hang him, old doting rascal! no: I say I will have her.

Pog. Lose no time, then.

Ber. I will beget a race of wise men and constables that shall cart whores at their own charges;

SCENE II.   'TIS PITY SHE'S A WHORE.   155

and break the duke's peace ere I have done myself.
Come away.   [*Exeunt.*

SCENE II. *A room in* FLORIO'S *house.*

Enter FLORIO, GIOVANNI, SORANZO, ANNABELLA, PUTANA,
and VASQUES.

Flo. My Lord Soranzo, though I must confess
The proffers that are made me have been great
In marriage of my daughter, yet the hope
Of your still rising honours have prevail'd[1]
Above all other jointures : here she is ;
She knows my mind ; speak for yourself to her,—
And hear you, daughter, see you use him nobly :
For any private speech I'll give you time.—
Come, son, and you the rest ; let them alone ;
Agree [they] as they may.
    Sor.   I thank you, sir.
    Gio. [*aside to Ann.*] Sister, be not all woman; think
        on me.
    Sor. Vasques,—
    Vas.   My lord ?
    Sor.   Attend me without.
        [*Exeunt all but Sor. and Ann.*
    Ann. Sir, what's your will with me ?
    Sor.   Do you not know
What I should tell you ?
    Ann.   Yes; you'll say you love me.
    Sor. And I will swear it too ; will you believe it ?
    Ann. 'Tis no[2] point of faith.

---

[1]   *the hope*
  Of your still rising honours have prevail'd] See note, p. 85. D.
[2] *no*] The 4to has "not." D.

Enter GIOVANNI *in the gallery above.*

Sor. Have you not will to love?
Ann. Not you.
Sor. Whom then?
Ann. That's as the fates infer.
Gio. [*aside*] Of those I'm regent now.
Sor. What mean you, sweet?
Ann. To live and die a maid.
Sor. O, that's unfit.
Gio. [*aside*] Here's one can say that's but a woman's note.
Sor. Did you but see my heart, then would you swear—
Ann. That you were dead.
Gio. [*aside*] That's true, or somewhat near it.
Sor. See you these true love's tears?
Ann. No.
Gio. [*aside*] Now she winks.
Sor. They plead to you for grace.
Ann. Yet nothing speak.
Sor. O, grant my suit!
Ann. What is't?
Sor. To let me live—
Ann. Take it.
Sor. Still yours.
Ann. That is not mine to give.
Gio. [*aside*] One such another word would kill his hopes.
Sor. Mistress, to leave those fruitless strifes of wit,
Know I have lov'd you long and lov'd you truly:
Not hope of what you have, but what you are,
Hath drawn me on; then let me not in vain
Still feel the rigour of your chaste disdain:
I'm sick, and sick to the heart.

Ann.   Help, aqua-vitæ!
Sor. What mean you?
Ann.   Why, I thought you had been sick.
Sor. Do you mock my love?
Gio. [*aside*]   There, sir, she was too nimble.
Sor. [*aside*] 'Tis plain she laughs at me.—These scornful taunts
Neither become your modesty or years.
    Ann. You are no looking-glass; or if you were,
I'd dress my language by you.
    Gio. [*aside*]   I'm confirm'd.
    Ann. To put you out of doubt, my lord, methinks
Your common sense should make you understand
That if I lov'd you, or desir'd your love,
Some way I should have given you better taste:
But since you are a nobleman, and one
I would not wish should spend his youth in hopes,
Let me advise you to[3] forbear your suit,
And think I wish you well, I tell you this.
    Sor. Is't you speak this?
    Ann.   Yes, I myself; yet know,—
Thus far I give you comfort,—if mine eyes
Could have pick'd out a man amongst all those
That su'd to me to make a husband of,
You should have been that man: let this suffice;
Be noble in your secrecy and wise.
    Gio. [*aside*] Why, now I see she loves me.
    Ann.   One word more.
As ever virtue liv'd within your mind,
As ever noble courses were your guide,
As ever you would have me know you lov'd me,
Let not my father know hereof by you:
If I hereafter find that I must marry,

---

[3] *advise you to*] The 4to has "*aduise you* here, *to.*" D.

It shall be you or none.
Sor.   I take that promise.
Ann. O, O my head!
Sor. What's the matter? not well?
Ann. O, I begin to sicken!
Gio.   Heaven forbid!
         [*Aside, and exit from above.*
Sor. Help, help, within there, ho!

  Re-enter FLORIO, GIOVANNI, *and* PUTANA.

Look to your daughter,[4] Signior Florio.
Flo. Hold her up, she swoons.
Gio. Sister, how d'ye?
Ann.   Sick,—brother, are you there?
Flo. Convey her to her[5] bed instantly, whilst I send for a physician; quickly, I say.
Put. Alas, poor child!   [*Exeunt all but Sor.*

    Re-enter VASQUES.

Vas. My lord,—
Sor. O, Vasques, now I doubly am undone
Both in my present and my future hopes!
She plainly told me that she could not love,
And thereupon soon sicken'd; and I fear
Her life's in danger.
 Vas. [*aside*] By'r lady, sir, and so is yours, if you knew all.—'Las, sir, I am sorry for that: may be 'tis but the maid's-sickness, an over-flux of youth; and then, sir, there is no such present remedy as present marriage. But hath she given you an absolute denial?
 Sor. She hath, and she hath not; I'm full of grief: But what she said I'll tell thee as we go. [*Exeunt.*

---

[4] *Look to your daughter,*] The old copy gives this speech to the brother. It is evidently a continuation of Soranzo's call for assistance.
[5] *her*] Omitted by Gifford. D.

SCENE III. *Another room in the same.*

Enter GIOVANNI *and* PUTANA.

Put. O, sir, we are all undone, quite undone, utterly undone, and shamed for ever! your sister, O, your sister!

Gio. What of her? for heaven's sake, speak; how does she?

Put. O, that ever I was born to see this day!

Gio. She is not dead, ha? is she?

Put. Dead! no, she is quick; 'tis worse, she is with child. You know what you have done; heaven forgive ye! 'tis too late to repent now, heaven help us!

Gio. With child? how dost thou know't?

Put. How do I know't! am I at these years ignorant what the meanings of qualms and water-pangs be? of changing of colours, queasiness of stomachs, pukings, and another thing that I could name? Do not, for her and your credit's sake, spend the time in asking how, and which way, 'tis so: she is quick, upon my word: if you let a physician see her water, you're undone.

Gio. But in what case is she?

Put. Prettily amended: 'twas but a fit, which I soon espied, and she must look for often henceforward.

Gio. Commend me to her, bid her take no care;[6]
Let not the doctor visit her, I charge you;
Make some excuse, till I return.—O, me!
I have a world of business in my head.—
Do not discomfort her.—

---

[6] *bid her* take no care;] i.e. bid her not to be too anxious or apprehensive.

How do these news perplex me!—If my father
Come to her, tell him she's recover'd well;
Say 'twas but some ill diet—d'ye hear, woman?
Look you to't.
 Put. I will, sir.   [*Exeunt.*

   SCENE IV. *Another room in the same.*

    Enter FLORIO *and* RICHARDETTO.

 Flo. And how d'ye find her, sir?
 Rich.   Indifferent well;
I see no danger, scarce perceive she's sick,
But that she told me she had lately eaten
Melons, and, as she thought, those disagreed
With her young stomach.
 Flo.   Did you give her aught?
 Rich. An easy surfeit-water, nothing else.
You need not doubt her health: I rather think
Her sickness is a fulness of her blood,—
You understand me?
 Flo.   I do; you counsel well;
And once, within these few days, will so order 't
She shall be married ere she know the time.
 Rich. Yet let not haste, sir, make unworthy choice;
That were dishonour.
 Flo.   Master Doctor, no;
I will not do so neither: in plain words,
My Lord Soranzo is the man I mean.
 Rich. A noble and a virtuous gentleman.
 Flo. As any is in Parma. Not far hence
Dwells Father Bonaventure, a grave friar,
Once tutor to my son: now at his cell
I'll have 'em married.

Rich. You have plotted wisely.
Flo. I'll send one straight to speak with him tonight.
Rich. Soranzo's wise; he will delay no time.
Flo. It shall be so.

Enter Friar *and* GIOVANNI.

Friar. Good peace be here and love!
Flo. Welcome, religious friar; you are one
That still bring blessing to the place you come to.
Gio. Sir, with what speed I could, I did my best
To draw this holy man from forth his cell
To visit my sick sister; that with words
Of ghostly comfort, in this time of need,
He might absolve her, whether she live or die.
Flo. 'Twas well done, Giovanni; thou herein
Hast show'd a Christian's care, a brother's love.—
Come, father, I'll conduct you to her chamber,
And one thing would entreat you.
Friar. Say on, sir.
Flo. I have a father's dear impression
And wish, before I fall into my grave,
That I might see her married, as 'tis fit:
A word from you, grave man, will win her more
Than all our best persuasions.
Friar. Gentle sir,
All this I'll say, that Heaven may prosper her.
[*Exeunt.*

SCENE V. *A room in* RICHARDETTO'S *house.*

Enter GRIMALDI.

Grim. Now if the doctor keep his word, Soranzo,
Twenty to one you miss your bride. I know
'Tis an unnoble act, and not becomes

A soldier's valour; but in terms of love,
Where merit cannot sway, policy must:
I am resolv'd, if this physician
Play not on both hands, then Soranzo falls.

Enter RICHARDETTO.

Rich. You're come as I could wish; this very
night
Soranzo, 'tis ordain'd, must be affied
To Annabella, and, for aught I know,
Married.
Grim. How!
Rich. Yet your patience:—
The place, 'tis Friar Bonaventure's cell.
Now I would wish you to bestow this night
In watching thereabouts; 'tis but a night:
If you miss now, to-morrow I'll know all.[7]
Grim. Have you the poison?
Rich. Here 'tis, in this box:
Doubt nothing, this will do't; in any case,
As you respect your life, be quick and sure.
Grim. I'll speed him.
Rich. Do.—Away; for 'tis not safe
You should be seen much here. Ever my love!
Grim. And mine to you. [*Exit.*
Rich. So! if this hit, I'll laugh and hug revenge;
And they that now dream of a wedding-feast
May chance to mourn the lusty bridegroom's ruin.
But to my other business.—Niece Philotis!

Enter PHILOTIS.

Phi. Uncle?

---

[7] *'tis but a night:*
If you miss now, to-morrow I'll know all.] i.e. It is but a night lost; for if you miss now, I shall have the whole to-morrow, and shall then be enabled to give you fresh instructions.

Rich. My lovely niece!
You have bethought ye?
Phi. Yes,—and, as you counsell'd,
Fashion'd my heart to love him: but he swears
He will to-night be married: for he fears
His uncle else, if he should know the drift,
Will hinder all, and call his coz[8] to shrift.
Rich. To-night! why, best of all: but, let me see—
Ay—ha! yes, so it shall be—in disguise
We'll early to the friar's; I have thought on't.
Phi. Uncle, he comes.

Enter BERGETTO *and* POGGIO.

Rich. Welcome, my worthy coz.
Ber. Lass, pretty lass, come buss, lass!—A-ha, Poggio! [*Kisses her.*
Rich. [*aside*] There's hope of this yet.[9]—
You shall have time enough; withdraw a little;
We must confer at large.
Ber. Have you not sweetmeats or dainty devices for me?
Phi. You shall [have] enough, sweetheart.
Ber. Sweetheart! mark that, Poggio.—By my troth, I cannot choose but kiss thee once more for that word, *sweetheart.*—Poggio, I have a monstrous swelling about my stomach, whatsoever the matter be.
Pog. You shall have physic for't, sir.
Rich. Time runs apace.
Ber. Time's a blockhead.
Rich. Be rul'd: when we have done what's fit to do, Then you may kiss your fill, and bed her too. [*Exeunt.*

[8] *coz*] i.e. nephew. D.
[9] *There's hope of this yet.*] The 4to erroneously gives this hemistich to Philotis. If it be not a side-speech of the uncle, it must be considered as a continuation of poor Bergetto's rapture at the condescension of his mistress.

SCENE VI. FLORIO'S *house.*

ANNABELLA'S *chamber. A table with wax lights;* ANNABELLA *at confession before the* Friar; *she weeps and wrings her hands.*

Friar. I'm glad to see this penance; for, believe me,
You have unripp'd a soul so foul and guilty,
As, I must tell you true, I marvel how
The earth hath borne you up : but weep, weep on,
These tears may do you good; weep faster yet,
Whiles I do read a lecture.
   Ann.   Wretched creature !
   Friar. Ay, you are wretched, miserably wretched,
Almost condemn'd alive. There is a place,—
List, daughter !—in a black and hollow vault,
Where day is never seen ; there shines no sun,
But flaming horror of consuming fires,
A lightless sulphur, chok'd with smoky fogs
Of an infected darkness : in this place
Dwell many thousand thousand sundry sorts
Of never-dying deaths: there damnèd souls
Roar without pity ; there are gluttons fed
With toads and adders; there is burning oil
Pour'd down the drunkard's throat ; the usurer
Is forc'd to sup whole draughts of molten gold ;
There is the murderer for ever stabb'd,
Yet can he never die ; there lies the wanton
On racks of burning steel, whiles in his soul
He feels the torment of his raging lust.
   Ann. Mercy! O, mercy !
   Friar.   There stand these wretched things
Who have dream'd out whole years in lawless sheets
And secret incests, cursing one another.
Then you will wish each kiss your brother gave

Had been a dagger's point; then you shall hear
How he will cry, " O, would my wicked sister
Had first been damn'd, when she did yield to lust!"—
But soft, methinks I see repentance work
New motions in your heart: say, how is't with you?
    Ann. Is there no way left to redeem my miseries?
    Friar. There is, despair not; Heaven is merciful,
And offers grace even now. 'Tis thus agreed:
First, for your honour's safety, that you marry
My Lord Soranzo; next, to save your soul,
Leave off this life, and henceforth live to him.
    Ann. Ay me![10]
    Friar.   Sigh not; I know the baits of sin
Are hard to leave; O, 'tis a death to do't:
Remember what must come. Are you content?
    Ann. I am.
    Friar.   I like it well; we'll take the time.—
Who's near us there?

          Enter FLORIO *and* GIOVANNI.

    Flo.   Did you call, father?
    Friar. Is Lord Soranzo come?
    Flo.   He stays below.
    Friar. Have you acquainted him at full?
    Flo.   I have,
And he is overjoy'd.
    Friar.   And so are we.
Bid him come near.
    Gio. [*aside*]   My sister weeping! Ha!
I fear this friar's falsehood.—I will call him.
                                             [*Exit.*
    Flo. Daughter, are you resolv'd?
    Ann.   Father, I am.

---

[10] *Ay me!*] The Italian *aimè*.—Gifford printed "Ah me!" D.

Re-enter GIOVANNI *with* SORANZO *and* VASQUES.

Flo. My Lord Soranzo, here
Give me your hand; for that I give you this.
            [*Joins their hands.*
Sor. Lady, say you so too?
Ann.   I do, and vow
To live with you and yours.
Friar.   Timely resolv'd:
My blessing rest on both! More to be done,
You may perform it on the morning sun. [*Exeunt.*

SCENE VII. *The street before the monastery.*

Enter GRIMALDI *with his rapier drawn and a dark lantern.*

Grim. 'Tis early night as yet, and yet too soon
To finish such a work; here I will lie
To listen who comes next.   [*He lies down.*

Enter BERGETTO *and* PHILOTIS *disguised, and followed at a short distance by* RICHARDETTO *and* POGGIO.

Ber. We are almost at the place, I hope, sweetheart.

Grim. [*aside*] I hear them near, and heard one say
  sweetheart.
'Tis he; now guide my hand, some angry justice,
Home to his bosom!—Now have at you, sir!
           [*Stabs Ber. and exit.*

Ber. O, help, help! here's a stitch fallen in my guts: O for a flesh-tailor quickly!—Poggio!

Phi. What ails my love?

Ber. I am sure I cannot piss forward and backward, and yet I am wet before and behind.—Lights! lights! ho, lights!

Phi. Alas, some villain here has slain my love!

Rich. O, Heaven forbid it!— Raise up the next neighbours
Instantly, Poggio, and bring lights. [*Exit Pog.*
How is't, Bergetto? slain! It cannot be;
Are you sure you're hurt?

Ber. O, my belly seethes like a porridge-pot! Some cold water, I shall boil over else: my whole body is in a sweat, that you may wring my shirt; feel here— Why, Poggio!

Re-enter POGGIO *with* Officers *and lights.*

Pog. Here. Alas, how do you?

Rich. Give me a light.—What's here? all blood!
—O, sirs,
Signior Donado's nephew now is slain.
Follow the murderer with all the haste
Up to the city, he cannot be far hence:
Follow, I beseech you.

Officers. Follow, follow, follow! [*Exeunt.*

Rich. Tear off thy linen, coz, to stop his wounds.—
Be of good comfort, man.

Ber. Is all this mine own blood? nay, then, good night with me.—Poggio, commend me to my uncle, dost hear? bid him, for my sake, make much of this wench.—O, I am going the wrong way sure, my belly aches so.—O, farewell, Poggio!—O, O! [*Dies.*

Phi. O, he is dead!

Pog. How! dead!

Rich. He's dead indeed;
'Tis now too late to weep: let's have him home,
And with what speed we may find out the murderer.

Pog. O, my master! my master! my master!
[*Exeunt.*

SCENE VIII. *A room in* HIPPOLITA'S *house.*

Enter VASQUES *and* HIPPOLITA.

Hip. Betroth'd?
Vas. I saw it.
Hip. And when's the marriage-day?
Vas.   Some two days hence.
Hip. Two days! why, man, I would but wish two
    hours
To send him to his last and lasting sleep;
And, Vasques, thou shalt see I'll do it bravely.
    Vas. I do not doubt your wisdom, nor, I trust,
you my secrecy; I am infinitely yours.
    Hip. I will be thine in spite of my disgrace.—
So soon? O wicked man, I durst be sworn
He'd laugh to see me weep.
    Vas. And that's a villanous fault in him.
    Hip. No, let him laugh; I'm arm'd in my resolves:
Be thou still true.
    Vas. I should get little by treachery against so
hopeful a preferment as I am like to climb to.
    Hip. Even to—my bosom, Vasques. Let my youth
Revel in these new pleasures: if we thrive,
He now hath but a pair of days to live.   [*Exeunt.*

SCENE IX. *The street before the* Cardinal's *gates.*

Enter FLORIO, DONADO, RICHARDETTO, POGGIO, *and* Officers.

    Flo. 'Tis bootless now to show yourself a child,
Signior Donado; what is done, is done:
Spend not the time in tears, but seek for justice.
    Rich. I must confess somewhat I was in fault
That had not first acquainted you what love

Pass'd 'twixt him and my niece; but, as I live,
His fortune grieves me as it were mine own.

Don. Alas, poor creature! he meant no man harm,
That I am sure of.

Flo. I believe that too.
But stay, my masters: are you sure you saw
The murderer pass here?

First Officer. An it please you, sir, we are sure we saw a ruffian, with a naked weapon in his hand all bloody, get into my Lord Cardinal's Grace's gate; that we are sure of; but for fear of his grace—bless us!—we durst go no farther.

Don. Know you what manner of man he was?

First Officer. Yes, sure, I know the man; they say he is a soldier; he that loved your daughter, sir, an't please ye; 'twas he for certain.

Flo. Grimaldi, on my life!

First Officer. Ay, ay, the same.

Rich. The Cardinal is noble; he no doubt
Will give true justice.

Don. Knock some one at the gate.

Pog. I'll knock, sir. [*Knocks.*

Serv. [*within*] What would ye?

Flo. We require speech with the Lord Cardinal
About some present business: pray inform
His grace that we are here.

Enter Cardinal, *followed by* GRIMALDI.

Car. Why, how now, friends! what saucy mates
 are you
That know nor duty nor civility?
Are we a person fit to be your host;
Or is our house become your common inn,
To beat our doors at pleasure? What such haste
Is yours, as that it cannot wait fit times?

Are you the masters of this commonwealth,
And know no more discretion? O, your news
Is here before you; you have lost a nephew,
Donado, last night by Grimaldi slain :
Is that your business? well, sir, we have knowledge
   on't;
Let that suffice.
 Grim. In presence of your grace,
In thought I never meant Bergetto harm :
But, Florio, you can tell with how much scorn
Soranzo, back'd with his confederates,
Hath often wrong'd me; I to be reveng'd,—
For that I could not win him else to fight,—
Had thought by way of ambush to have kill'd him,
But was unluckily therein mistook ;
Else he had felt what late Bergetto did :
And though my fault to him were merely chance,
Yet humbly I submit me to your grace, [*Kneeling.*
To do with me as you please.
 Car.   Rise up, Grimaldi.— [*He rises.*
You citizens of Parma, if you seek
For justice, know, as nuncio from the Pope,
For this offence I here receive Grimaldi
Into his holiness' protection :
He is no common man, but nobly born,
Of princes' blood, though you, Sir Florio,
Thought him too mean a husband for your daughter.
If more you seek for, you must go to Rome,
For he shall thither : learn more wit, for shame.—
Bury your dead.—Away, Grimaldi ; leave 'em !
    [*Exeunt Cardinal and Grimaldi.*
 Don. Is this a churchman's voice? dwells justice
  here?
 Flo. Justice is fled to heaven, and comes no nearer.
Soranzo !—was't for him? O, impudence !

Had he the face to speak it, and not blush?
Come, come, Donado, there's no help in this,
When cardinals think murder's not amiss.
Great men may do their wills, we must obey;
But Heaven will judge them for't another day.
[*Exeunt.*

ACT IV.

SCENE I.[1] *A room in* FLORIO'S *house. A banquet set out; hautboys.*

Enter the Friar, GIOVANNI, ANNABELLA, PHILOTIS, SORANZO, DONADO, FLORIO, RICHARDETTO, PUTANA, *and* VASQUES.

Friar. These holy rites perform'd, now take your times
To spend the remnant of the day in feast:
Such fit repasts are pleasing to the saints,
Who are your guests, though not with mortal eyes
To be beheld.—Long prosper in this day,
You happy couple, to each other's joy!

Sor. Father, your prayer is heard; the hand of goodness
Hath been a shield for me against my death:
And, more to bless me, hath enrich'd my life
With this most precious jewel; such a prize
As earth hath not another like to this.—

---

[1] I have reluctantly followed the 4to (which has no division of scenes), and begun the fourth act here. The reader will see, as he proceeds, the impropriety of this arrangement. After all, there is but a choice of evils; for as some time must necessarily have elapsed (two days according to Vasques) since the death of Bergetto, sufficient would hardly be gained on the score of probability to justify disturbing the author's distribution of the story; though it might be wished that this scene had concluded the third act.

Cheer up, my love :—and, gentlemen my friends,
Rejoice with me in mirth : this day we'll crown
With lusty cups to Annabella's health.
  Gio. [*aside*] O, torture ! were the marriage yet undone,
Ere I'd endure this sight, to see my love
Clipt² by another, I would dare confusion,
And stand the horror of ten thousand deaths.
  Vas. Are you not well, sir?
  Gio.   Prithee, fellow, wait;
I need not thy officious diligence.
  Flo. Signior Donado, come, you must forget
Your late mishaps, and drown your cares in wine.
  Sor. Vasques!
  Vas.   My lord?
  Sor.   Reach me that weighty bowl.—
Here, brother Giovanni, here's to you ;
Your turn comes next, though now a bachelor;
Here's to your sister's happiness and mine !
            [*Drinks, and offers him the bowl.*
  Gio. I cannot drink.
  Sor.   What !
  Gio.   'Twill indeed offend me.
  Ann. Pray, do not urge him, if he be not willing.
                                [*Hautboys.*
  Flo. How now ! what noise³ is this?
  Vas. O, sir, I had forgot to tell you; certain young maidens of Parma, in honour to Madam Annabella's marriage, have sent their loves to her in a Masque, for which they humbly crave your patience and silence.
  Sor. We are much bound to them ; so much the more
As it comes unexpected : guide them in.

---

² *Clipt*] i. e. Embraced. D.
³ *noise*] See note, p. 103. D.

SCENE I.   'TIS PITY SHE'S A WHORE.   173

Enter HIPPOLITA, *followed by* Ladies *in white robes
with garlands of willows, all masked.*

MUSIC AND A DANCE.

Thanks, lovely virgins! now might we but know
To whom we've been beholding for this[4] love,
We shall acknowledge it.
    Hip.   Yes, you shall know. [*Unmasks.*
What think you now?
    Omnes.   Hippolita!
    Hip.   'Tis she;
Be not amaz'd; nor blush, young lovely bride;
I come not to defraud you of your man:
'Tis now no time to reckon-up the talk
What Parma long hath rumour'd of us both:
Let rash report run on; the breath that vents it
Will, like a bubble, break itself at last.
But now to you, sweet creature;—lend's[5] your hand;—
Perhaps it hath been said that I would claim
Some interest in Soranzo, now your lord;
What I have right to do, his soul knows best:
But in my duty to your noble worth,
Sweet Annabella, and my care of you,—
Here, take, Soranzo, take this hand from me;
I'll once more join what by the holy church
Is finish'd and allow'd.—Have I done well?
    Sor. You have too much engag'd us.
    Hip.   One thing more.
That you may know my single charity,[6]
Freely I here remit all interest

    [4] *this*] So the 4to in the Brit. Museum.—My copy has "thy." See note p. 34. D.
    [5] *lend's*] Gifford printed "lend." D.
    [6] *my* single *charity,*] i.e. pure, genuine, disinterested charity.

174   'TIS PITY SHE'S A WHORE.   ACT IV.

I e'er could claim, and give you back your vows;
And to confirm't,—reach me a cup of wine,—
     [*Vas. gives her a poisoned cup.*
My Lord Soranzo, in this draught I drink
Long rest t' ye! [*She drinks*].—[*Aside to Vas.*] Look
     to it, Vasques.
  Vas. [*aside to Hip.*] Fear nothing.
  Sor. Hippolita, I thank you; and will pledge
This happy union as another life.—
Wine, there!
  Vas. You shall have none; neither shall you
pledge her.
  Hip. How!
  Vas. Know now, Mistress She-devil, your own
mischievous treachery hath killed you; I must not
marry you.
  Hip. Villain!
  Omnes. What's the matter?
  Vas. Foolish woman, thou art now like a fire-
brand that hath kindled others and burnt thyself:—
troppo sperar, inganna,—thy vain hope hath deceived
thee; thou art but dead; if thou hast any grace, pray.
  Hip. Monster!
  Vas. Die in charity, for shame.—This thing of
malice, this woman, had[7] privately corrupted me with
promise of marriage,[8] under this politic reconciliation,
to poison my lord, whiles she might laugh at his confusion on his marriage-day. I promised her fair; but
I knew what my reward should have been, and would
willingly have spared her life, but that I was acquainted
with the danger of her disposition; and now have fitted
her a just payment in her own coin: there she is, she

---

[7] *had*] Gifford printed "hath." D.
[8] *marriage*,] The 4to has "malice." D.

SCENE I.   'TIS PITY SHE'S A WHORE.   175

hath yet⁹ —— and end thy days in peace, vile woman;
as for life, there's no hope; think not on't.
    Omnes. Wonderful justice!
    Rich. Heaven, thou art righteous.
    Hip.   O, 'tis true;
I feel my minute coming. Had that slave
Kept promise,—O, my torment!—thou this hour
Hadst died, Soranzo;—heat above hell-fire!—
Yet, ere I pass away,—cruel, cruel flames!—
Take here my curse amongst you: may thy bed
Of marriage be a rack unto thy heart,
Burn blood, and boil in vengeance;—O, my heart,
My flame's intolerable!—mayst thou live
To father bastards; may her womb bring forth
Monsters,—and die together in your sins,
Hated, scorn'd, and unpitied!—O, O!   [*Dies.*
    Flo. Was e'er so vile a creature!
    Rich.   Here's the end
Of lust and pride.
    Ann.   It is a fearful sight.
    Sor. Vasques, I know thee now a trusty servant,
And never will forget thee.—Come, my love,
We'll home, and thank the heavens for this escape.—
Father and friends, we must break-up this mirth;
It is too sad a feast.
    Don.   Bear hence the body.
    Friar [*aside to Gio.*]. Here's an ominous change!
Mark this, my Giovanni, and take heed!—
I fear th' event: that marriage seldom's good
Where the bride-banquet so begins in blood. [*Exeunt.*

    ⁹ *she hath yet*] The old copy has a considerable double break here, probably from some defect in the Ms.

SCENE II.[10] *A room in* RICHARDETTO'S *house.*

Enter RICHARDETTO *and* PHILOTIS.

Rich. My wretched wife, more wretched in her shame
Than in her wrongs to me, hath paid too soon
The forfeit of her modesty and life.
And I am sure, my niece, though vengeance hover,
Keeping aloof yet from Soranzo's fall,
Yet he will fall, and sink with his own weight.
I need not now—my heart persuades me so—
To further his confusion; there is One
Above begins to work: for, as I hear,
Debates already 'twixt his wife and him
Thicken and run to head; she, as 'tis said,
Slightens his love, and he abandons hers :
Much talk I hear. Since things go thus, my niece,
In tender love and pity of your youth,
My counsel is, that you should free your years
From hazard of these woes by flying hence
To fair Cremona, there to vow your soul
In holiness, a holy votaress :
Leave me to see the end of these extremes.
All human worldly courses are uneven;
No life is blessèd but the way to heaven.

[10] *Scene II.*] As the play is now divided, this conversation takes place on the way home from the marriage-feast, or immediately after it, and in either case before Richardetto could have heard a word of what he informs his niece;

"*Debates* already '*twixt his wife and him
Thicken and run to head; she,* as 'tis said,
Slightens his love, and he abandons hers:
Much talk *I hear.*"

Enough, and more than enough, of improbability would perhaps remain, were even the arrangement recommended in a former page [171] to take place; but the most glaring part of it would certainly be removed or weakened by the change.

Phi. Uncle, shall I resolve to be a nun?
Rich. Ay, gentle niece; and in your hourly prayers
Remember me, your poor unhappy uncle.
Hie to Cremona now, as fortune leads,
Your home your cloister, your best friends your beads:
Your chaste and single life shall crown your birth :
Who dies a virgin live[s] a saint on earth.
 Phi. Then farewell, world, and worldly thoughts,
  adieu!
Welcome, chaste vows; myself I yield to you.
          [*Exeunt.*

SCENE III. *A chamber in* SORANZO'S *house.*

Enter SORANZO *unbraced, and dragging in* ANNABELLA.

Sor. Come, strumpet, famous whore! were every
  drop
Of blood that runs in thy adulterous veins
A life, this sword—dost see't?—should in one blow
Confound them all. Harlot, rare, notable harlot,
That with thy brazen face maintain'st thy sin,
Was there no man in Parma to be bawd
To your loose cunning whoredom else but I?
Must your hot itch and plurisy of lust,
The heyday of your luxury,[11] be fed
Up to a surfeit, and could none but I
Be pick'd out to be cloak to your close tricks,
Your belly-sports? Now I must be the dad
To all that gallimaufry that is stuff'd

---

[11] *The heyday of your* luxury,] i.e. the height of your wantonness. *Reed. Luxury,* about which the commentators on Shakespeare have drivelled out so much indecency, is simply the French *luxure,* the old word for *lust,* and common to every writer of the poet's age. Luxury in the present sense of the word is their *luxe.*

In thy corrupted bastard-bearing womb!
Say, must I?
   Ann.   Beastly man! why, 'tis thy fate.[12]
I su'd not to thee; for, but that I thought
Your over-loving lordship would have run
Mad on denial, had ye lent me time,
I would have told ye in what case I was:
But you would needs be doing.
   Sor.   Whore of whores!
Darest thou tell me this?
   Ann.   O, yes; why not?
You were deceiv'd in me; 'twas not for love
I chose you, but for honour: yet know this,
Would you be patient yet, and hide your shame,
I'd see whether I could love you.
   Sor.   Excellent quean!
Why, art thou not with child?
   Ann.   What needs all this,
When 'tis superfluous? I confess I am.
   Sor. Tell me by whom.
   Ann.   Soft![13] 'twas not in my bargain.
Yet somewhat, sir, to stay your longing stomach,
I am content t' acquaint you with; THE man,
The more than man, that got this sprightly boy,—
For 'tis a boy, [and] therefore glory, sir,[14]

---

[12] *Say, must I?*
    Ann.   *Beastly man! why, 'tis thy fate.*] Gifford printed
"Why, *must I?*
    Ann.   *Beastly man! Why — 'tis thy fate;*"
and he observed; "The 4to is corrupt in this place, and reads '*Shey,
must I?*' Dodsley has corrected it into '*Say*;' but I prefer the expression in the text, as it seems borne out by Annabella's answer."
It must have escaped Gifford's notice, that, though in the first of these words, which stand at the top of the page, the 4to has "Shey," yet the catch-word at the bottom of the preceding page is "*Say.*" D.

[13] *Soft*, sir,] I have omitted "*sir,*" which spoils the verse, and appears to have crept in from the line immediately below it.

[14] therefore *glory, sir,*] This is made out by Dodsley from the old copy, which reads "For 'tis a boy *that for* glory, sir;" and has

Your heir shall be a son—
Sor.   Damnable monster!
Ann. Nay, an you will not hear, I'll speak no more.
Sor. Yes, speak, and speak thy last.
Ann.   A match, a match!—
This noble creature was in every part
So angel-like, so glorious, that a woman,
Who had not been but human, as was I,
Would have kneel'd to him, and have begg'd for love.—
You! why, you are not worthy once to name
His name without true worship, or, indeed,
Unless you kneel'd, to hear another name him.
  Sor. What was he call'd?
  Ann.   We are not come to that;
Let it suffice that you shall have the glory
To father what so brave a father got.
In brief, had not this chance fall'n out as 't doth,
I never had been troubled with a thought
That you had been a creature:—but for marriage,
I scarce dream yet of that.
  Sor.   Tell me his name.
  Ann. Alas, alas, there's all! will you believe?
  Sor. What?
  Ann.   You shall never know.
  Sor.   How!
  Ann.   Never: if
You do, let me be[15] curs'd!
  Sor. Not know it, strumpet! I'll rip up thy heart,
And find it there.

---

all the appearance of being genuine. The insulting and profligate language of this wretched woman, if not assumed, like that of Bianca in *Love's Sacrifice*, to provoke her husband to destroy her on the spot, is perfectly loathsome and detestable. Well sung the poet,
          " nihil est audacius illis
     Deprensis: iram atque animos a crimine sumunt."

[15] *be*] Omitted by Gifford. D.

Ann.   Do, do.
Sor.   And with my teeth
Tear the prodigious lecher joint by joint.
    Ann. Ha, ha, ha ! the man's merry.
    Sor.   Dost thou laugh ?
Come, whore, tell me your lover, or, by truth,
I'll hew thy flesh to shreds; who is't ?
    Ann. [*sings*] *Che morte più dolce che morire per
        amore ?*
    Sor. Thus will I pull thy hair, and thus I'll drag
Thy lust-be-leper'd body through the dust.
                                 [*Hales her up and down.*
Yet tell his name.
    Ann. [*sings*] *Morendo in grazia*[16] *dee morire senza
        dolore.*
    Sor. Dost thou triúmph ? The treasure of the
        earth
Shall not redeem thee ; were there kneeling kings
Did beg thy life, or angels did come down
To plead in tears, yet should not all prevail
Against my rage : dost thou not tremble yet ?
    Ann. At what ? to die ! no, be a gallant hang-
        man ;[17]
I dare thee to the worst : strike, and strike home ;
I leave revenge behind, and thou shalt feel 't.
    Sor. Yet tell me ere thou diest, and tell me truly,
Knows thy old father this ?
    Ann.   No, by my life.

    [16] *Morendo in grazia,* &c.] This quotation is incorrectly given in the 4to. It has been *amended* into impiety, for which there is little occasion. We have already seen more than enough to prove that when a woman loses the sense of religion (and Annabella, like her brother, is a *fatalist*), modesty, self-respect, every virtuous and every amiable feeling speedily follow.
    [17] *hangman ;*] This passage might be added to the passages which I have cited in my *Glossary to Shakespeare* as proofs that our old writers frequently used "hangman" in the general sense of "executioner." D.

Sor. Wilt thou confess, and I will spare thy life?
Ann. My life! I will not buy my life so dear.
Sor. I will not slack my vengeance.
[*Draws his sword.*

Enter VASQUES.

Vas. What d'ye mean, sir?
Sor. Forbear, Vasques; such a damnèd whore deserves no pity.
Vas. Now the gods forfend! And would you be her executioner, and kill her in your rage too? O, 'twere most unmanlike. She is your wife: what faults have been done by her before she married you were not against you: alas, poor lady, what hath she committed, which any lady in Italy, in the like case, would not? Sir, you must be ruled by your reason, and not by your fury; that were unhuman and beastly.
Sor. She shall not live.
Vas. Come, she must. You would have her confess the author[18] of her present misfortunes, I warrant ye; 'tis an unconscionable demand, and she should lose the estimation that I, for my part, hold of her worth, if she had done it: why, sir, you ought not, of all men living, to know it. Good sir, be reconciled: alas, good gentlewoman!
Ann. Pish, do not beg for me; I prize my life
As nothing; if the man will needs be mad,
Why, let him take it.
Sor. Vasques, hear'st thou this?
Vas. Yes, and commend her for it;[19] in this she

---

[18] *author*] The 4to has "Authors;" and so Gifford. D.

[19] This odious wretch has no variety in his bloody tricks: here is a repetition of the paltry artifice by which Hippolita was deceived; and Putana is subsequently wrought upon much in the same manner. Vasques is fortunate in finding such easy gulls.

shows the nobleness of a gallant spirit, and beshrew
my heart, but it becomes her rarely.—[*Aside to Sor.*]
Sir, in any case, smother your revenge; leave the
scenting-out your wrongs to me : be ruled, as you
respect your honour, or you mar all.—[*Aloud*] Sir, if
ever my service were of any credit with you, be not
so violent in your distractions: you are married now;
what a triumph might the report of this give to other
neglected suitors! 'Tis as manlike to bear extremities
as godlike to forgive.

Sor. O, Vasques, Vasques, in this piece of flesh,
This faithless face of hers, had I laid up
The treasure of my heart!—Hadst thou been virtuous,
Fair, wicked woman, not the matchless joys
Of life itself had made me wish to live
With any saint but thee : deceitful creature,
How hast thou mock'd my hopes, and in the shame
Of thy lewd womb even buried me alive !
I did too dearly love thee.

Vas. [*aside to Sor.*] This is well; follow this temper with some passion : be brief and moving; 'tis for
the purpose.

Sor. Be witness to my words thy soul and thoughts;
And tell me, didst not think that in my heart
I did too superstitiously adore thee ?

Ann. I must confess I know you lov'd me well.

Sor. And wouldst thou use me thus ! O Anna-
bella,
Be thou assur'd, whoe'er[20] the villain was
That thus hath tempted thee to this disgrace,
Well he might lust, but never lov'd like me :
He doted on the picture that hung out
Upon thy cheeks to please his humorous eye;

---

[20] *Be thou assur'd, whoe'er*] The 4to has "*Bee* thus *assur'd*, what-
soe're." D.

Not on the part I lov'd, which was thy heart,
And, as I thought, thy virtues.
Ann. O, my lord!
These words wound deeper than your sword could do.
Vas. Let me not ever take comfort, but I begin to weep myself, so much I pity him: why, madam, I knew, when his rage was over-past, what it would come to.
Sor. Forgive me, Annabella. Though thy youth
Hath tempted thee above thy strength to folly,
Yet will not I[21] forget what I should be,
And what I am—a husband; in that name
Is hid divinity: if I do find
That thou wilt yet be true, here I remit
All former faults, and take thee to my bosom.
Vas. By my troth, and that's a point of noble charity.
Ann. Sir, on my knees,—
Sor. Rise up, you shall not kneel.
Get you to your chamber; see you make no show
Of alteration; I'll be with you straight:
My reason tells me now that " 'tis as common
To err in frailty as to be a woman."
Go to your chamber. [*Exit Ann.*
Vas. So! this was somewhat to the matter: what do you think of your heaven of happiness now, sir?
Sor. I carry hell about me; all my blood
Is fir'd in swift revenge.
Vas. That may be; but know you how, or on whom? Alas, to marry a great woman, being made great in the stock to your hand, is a usual sport in

---

[21] *will not I*] Gifford printed "will I not." D.

these days; but to know what ferret it was[22] that hunted your cony-berry,[23]—there's the cunning.

Sor. I'll make her tell herself, or—

Vas. Or what? you must not do so; let me yet persuade your sufferance a little while: go to her, use her mildly; win her, if it be possible, to a voluntary, to a weeping tune: for the rest, if all hit, I will not miss my mark. Pray, sir, go in: the next news I tell you shall be wonders.

Sor. Delay in vengeance gives a heavier blow.

[*Exit.*

Vas. Ah, sirrah, here's work for the nonce! I had a suspicion of a bad matter in my head a pretty whiles ago; but after my madam's scurvy looks here at home, her waspish perverseness and loud fault-finding, then I remembered the proverb, that "where hens crow, and cocks hold their peace, there are sorry houses." 'Sfoot, if the lower parts of a she-tailor's cunning can cover such a swelling in the stomach, I'll never blame a false stitch in a shoe whiles I live again. Up, and up so quick? and so quickly too? 'twere a fine policy to learn by whom: this must be known; and I have thought on't:—

Enter PUTANA *in tears.*

Here's the way, or none.—What, crying, old mistress! alas, alas, I cannot blame ye; we have a lord, Heaven help us, is so mad as the devil himself, the more shame for him.

[22] *to know what* ferret *it was*] This is the ingenious emendation of Dodsley. The 4to reads "*secret;*" and it may be conjectured that the substantive which probably followed it has been lost. The present reading, however, leaves nothing to regret.

[23] *cony-berry,*] Gifford printed "*coney*-burrow,"—a most unnecessary alteration. Coles gives "A cunny berry, *cuniculorum latibulum.*" *Lat. and Engl. Dict.* D.

Put. O, Vasques, that ever I was born to see this day! Doth he use thee so too sometimes, Vasques?

Vas. Me? why, he makes a dog of me: but if some were of my mind, I know what we would do. As sure as I am an honest man, he will go near to kill my lady with unkindness: say she be with child, is that such a matter for a young woman of her years to be blamed for?

Put. Alas, good heart, it is against her will full sore.

Vas. I durst be sworn all his madness is for that she will not confess whose 'tis, which he will know; and when he doth know it, I am so well acquainted with his humour, that he will forget all straight. Well, I could wish she would in plain terms tell all, for that's the way, indeed.

Put. Do you think so?

Vas. Foh, I know't; provided that he did not win her to 't by force. He was once in a mind that you could tell, and meant to have wrung it out of you; but I somewhat pacified him for[24] that: yet, sure, you know a great deal.

Put. Heaven forgive us all! I know a little, Vasques.

Vas. Why should you not? who else should? Upon my conscience, she loves you dearly; and you would not betray her to any affliction for the world.

Put. Not for all the world, by my faith and troth, Vasques.

Vas. 'Twere pity of your life if you should; but in this you should both relieve her present discomforts, pacify my lord, and gain yourself everlasting love and preferment.

[24] *for*] Gifford printed "from." D.

Put. Dost think so, Vasques?

Vas. Nay, I know 't; sure 'twas some near and entire friend.

Put. 'Twas a dear friend indeed; but—

Vas. But what? fear not to name him; my life between you and danger: 'faith, I think 'twas no base fellow.

Put. Thou wilt stand between me and harm?

Vas. Ud's pity, what else? you shall be rewarded too, trust me.

Put. 'Twas even no worse than her own brother.

Vas. Her brother Giovanni, I warrant ye!

Put. Even he, Vasques; as brave a gentleman as ever kissed fair lady. O, they love most perpetually.

Vas. A brave gentleman indeed! why, therein I commend her choice.—[*Aside*] Better and better.—You are sure 'twas he?

Put. Sure; and you shall see he will not be long from her too.

Vas. He were to blame if he would: but may I believe thee?

Put. Believe me! why, dost think I am a Turk or a Jew? No, Vasques, I have known their dealings too long to belie them now.

Vas. Where are you there? within, sirs!

Enter Banditti.[25]

Put. How now! what are these?

Vas. You shall know presently.—Come, sirs, take me this old damnable hag, gag her instantly, and put out her eyes, quickly, quickly!

---

[25] Enter *Banditti.*] It may appear singular that Vasques should have a body of assassins awaiting his call, before he had any assurance that they would be needed; the circumstance serves, however, to illustrate the savage nature of this revengeful villain.

Put. Vasques! Vasques!—

Vas. Gag her, I say; 'sfoot, d'ye suffer her to prate? what d'ye fumble about? let me come to her. I'll help your old gums, you toad-bellied bitch! [*They gag her.*] Sirs, carry her closely into the coal-house, and put out her eyes instantly; if she roars, slit her nose: d'ye hear, be speedy and sure. [*Exeunt Ban. with Put.*] Why, this is excellent, and above expectation—her own brother! O, horrible! to what a height of liberty in damnation hath the devil trained our age! her brother, well! there's yet but a beginning; I must to my lord, and tutor him better in his points of vengeance: now I see how a smooth tale goes beyond a smooth tail.—But soft! what thing comes next? Giovanni! as I would[26] wish: my belief is strengthened, 'tis as firm as winter and summer.

Enter GIOVANNI.

Gio. Where's my sister?

Vas. Troubled with a new sickness, my lord; she's somewhat ill.

Gio. Took too much of the flesh, I believe.

Vas. Troth, sir, and you, I think, have e'en hit it: but my virtuous lady—

Gio. Where's she?

Vas. In her chamber; please you visit her; she is alone. [*Gio. gives him money.*] Your liberality hath doubly made me your servant, and ever shall, ever.

[*Exit Gio.*

Re-enter SORANZO.

Sir, I am made a man; I have plied my cue with cunning and success: I beseech you let's be private.

---

[26] *would*] Gifford printed "could." D.

Sor. My lady's brother's come; now he'll know all.

Vas. Let him know't; I have made some of them fast enough. How have you dealt with my lady?

Sor. Gently, as thou hast counsell'd ; O, my soul Runs circular in sorrow for revenge :
But, Vasques, thou shalt know—

Vas. Nay, I will know no more, for now comes your turn to know : I would not talk so openly with you.—[*Aside*] Let my young master take time enough, and go at pleasure; he is sold to death, and the devil shall not ransom him.—Sir, I beseech you, your privacy.

Sor. No conquest can gain glory of my fear.

[*Exeunt.*

ACT V.

SCENE I. *The street before* SORANZO'S *house.*

ANNABELLA *appears at a window above.*

Ann. Pleasures, farewell, and all ye thriftless minutes
Wherein false joys have spun a weary life!
To these my fortunes now I take my leave.
Thou, precious Time, that swiftly rid'st in post
Over the world, to finish-up the race
Of my last fate, here stay thy restless course,
And bear to ages that are yet unborn
A wretched, woful woman's tragedy !
My conscience now stands up against my lust
With depositions[1] character'd in guilt,

[1] *depositions*] The 4to has " dispositions." D.

SCENE I. "TIS PITY SHE'S A WHORE.

Enter Friar *below*.

And tells me I am lost: now I confess
Beauty that clothes the outside of the face
Is cursèd if it be not cloth'd with grace.
Here like a turtle mew'd-up in a cage,
Unmated, I converse with air and walls,
And descant on my vile unhappiness.
O, Giovanni, that hast had the spoil
Of thine own virtues and my modest fame,
Would thou hadst been less subject to those stars
That luckless reign'd at my nativity!
O, would the scourge due to my black offence
Might pass from thee, that I alone might feel
The torment of an uncontrollèd flame!
   Friar [*aside*]. What's this I hear?
   Ann.   That man, that blessèd friar,
Who join'd in ceremonial knot my hand
To him whose wife I now am, told me oft
I trod the path to death, and show'd me how.
But they who sleep in lethargies of lust
Hug their confusion, making Heaven unjust;
And so did I.
   Friar [*aside*]. Here's music to the soul!
   Ann. Forgive me, my good Genius, and this once
Be helpful to my ends: let some good man
Pass this way, to whose trust I may commit
This paper, double-lin'd with tears and blood;
Which being granted, here I sadly vow
Repentance, and a leaving-of that life
I long have died in.
   Friar.   Lady, Heaven hath heard you,
And hath by providence ordain'd that I
Should be his minister for your behoof.
   Ann. Ha, what are you?

Friar. Your brother's friend, the Friar;
Glad in my soul that I have liv'd to hear
This free confession 'twixt your peace and you.
What would you, or to whom? fear not to speak.
 Ann. Is Heaven so bountiful? then I have found
More favour than I hop'd. Here, holy man:
        [*Throws down a letter.*
Commend me to my brother; give him that,
That letter; bid him read it, and repent.
Tell him that I, imprison'd in my chamber,
Barr'd of all company, even of my guardian,—
Who[2] gives me cause of much suspect,—have time
To blush at what hath pass'd; bid him be wise,
And not believe the friendship of my lord:
I fear much more than I can speak: good father,
The place is dangerous, and spies are busy.
I must break off. You'll do't?
 Friar.   Be sure I will,
And fly with speed. My blessing ever rest
With thee, my daughter; live, to die more blest!
           [*Exit.*
 Ann. Thanks to the heavens, who have prolong'd
  my breath
To this good use! now I can welcome death.
      [*Withdraws from the window.*

SCENE II. *A room in* SORANZO'S *house.*

Enter SORANZO *and* VASQUES.

 Vas. Am I to be believed now? first marry a strumpet, that cast herself away upon you but to laugh at your horns, to feast on your disgrace, riot in your

---

[2] *Who*] Gifford printed "Which." D.

vexations, cuckold you in your bride-bed, waste your estate upon panders and bawds!—

Sor. No more, I say, no more!

Vas. A cuckold is a goodly tame beast, my lord.

Sor. I am resolv'd; urge not another word;
My thoughts are great, and all as resolute
As thunder: in mean time I'll cause our lady
To deck herself in all her bridal robes;
Kiss her, and fold her gently in my arms.
Begone,—yet, hear you, are the banditti ready
To wait in ambush?

Vas. Good sir, trouble not yourself about other business than your own resolution: remember that time lost cannot be recalled.

Sor. With all the cunning words thou canst, invite
The states[3] of Parma to my birthday's feast:
Haste to my brother-rival and his father,
Entreat them gently, bid them not to fail.
Be speedy, and return.

Vas. Let not your pity betray you till my coming back; think upon incest and cuckoldry.

Sor. Revenge is all th' ambition I aspire;
To that I'll climb or fall: my blood's on fire. [*Exeunt.*

SCENE III. *A room in* FLORIO'S *house.*

Enter GIOVANNI.

Gio. Busy opinion is an idle fool,
That, as a school-rod keeps a child in awe,
Frights th' unexperienc'd temper of the mind:
So did it me, who, ere my precious sister
Was married, thought all taste of love would die

---

[3] *states*] i.e. persons of high rank, nobles. D.

In such a contract; but I find no change
Of pleasure in this formal law of sports.
She is still one to me, and every kiss
As sweet and as delicious as the first
I reap'd, when yet the privilege of youth
Entitled her a virgin. O, the glory
Of two united hearts like hers and mine!
Let poring book-men dream of other worlds;
My world and all of happiness is here,
And I'd not change it for the best to come:
A life of pleasure is Elysium.

Enter Friar.

Father, you enter on the jubilee
Of my retir'd delights: now I can tell you,
The hell you oft have prompted is nought else
But slavish and fond superstitious fear;
And I could prove it too—
    Friar.   Thy blindness slays thee:
Look there, 'tis writ to thee.   [*Gives him the letter.*
    Gio. From whom?
    Friar. Unrip the seals and see;
The blood's yet seething hot, that will anon
Be frozen harder than congealèd coral.—
Why d'ye change colour, son?
    Gio.   'Fore heaven, you make
Some petty devil factor 'twixt my love
And your religion-maskèd sorceries.
Where had you this?
    Friar.   Thy conscience, youth, is sear'd,
Else thou wouldst stoop to warning.
    Gio.   'Tis her hand,
I know't; and 'tis all written in her blood.
She writes I know not what. *Death!* I'll not fear
An armèd thunderbolt aim'd at my heart.

SCENE III.   'TIS PITY SHE'S A WHORE.   193

She writes, we are discover'd :—Pox on dreams
Of low faint-hearted cowardice !—discover'd ?
The devil we are ! which way is't possible ?
Are we grown traitors to our own delights ?
Confusion take such dotage ! 'tis but forg'd :
This is your peevish chattering, weak old man !

Enter VASQUES.

Now, sir, what news bring you ?

Vas. My lord, according to his yearly custom, keeping this day a feast in honour of his birthday, by me invites you thither. Your worthy father, with the pope's reverend nuncio, and other magnificoes of Parma, have promised their presence : will't please you to be of the number ?

Gio. Yes, tell him[4] I *dare* come.

Vas. Dare come !

Gio. So I said ; and tell him more, I *will* come.

Vas. These words are strange to me.

Gio. Say, I will come.

Vas. You will not miss ?

Gio. Yet more ! I'll come, sir. Are you answered ?

Vas. So I'll say.—My service to you.   [*Exit.*

Friar. You will not go, I trust.

Gio.   Not go ! for what ?

Friar. O, do not go : this feast, I'll gage my life,
Is but a plot to train you to your ruin.
Be rul'd, you shall not go.

Gio.   Not go ! stood Death
Threatening his armies of confounding plagues,
With hosts of dangers hot as blazing stars,
I would be there : not go ! yes, and resolve

[4] *him*] The 4to has "them." D.

VOL. I.   O

To strike as deep in slaughter as they all;
For I will go.
    Friar.   Go where thou wilt : I see
The wildness of thy fate draws to an end,
To a bad fearful end. I must not stay
To know thy fall : back to Bononia I
With speed will haste, and shun this coming blow.—
Parma, farewell; would I had never known thee,
Or aught of thine !—Well, young man, since no prayer
Can make thee safe, I leave thee to despair.   [*Exit.*
    Gio. Despair, or tortures of a thousand hells ;
All's one to me : I have set up my rest.[5]
Now, now, work serious thoughts on baneful plots ;
Be all a man, my soul ; let not the curse
Of old prescription rent[6] from me the gall
Of courage, which enrols a glorious death :
If I must totter like a well-grown oak,
Some under-shrubs shall in my weighty fall
Be crush'd to splits ; with me they all shall perish !
                                                    [*Exit.*

SCENE IV. *A hall in* SORANZO'S *house.*

Enter SORANZO, VASQUES *with masks, and* Banditti.

    Sor. You will not fail, or shrink in the attempt?
    Vas. I will undertake for their parts.—Be sure, my masters, to be bloody enough, and as unmerciful as if you were preying upon a rich booty on the very mountains of Liguria : for your pardons trust to my

[5] *I have* set up my rest.] i.e. I have made my determination, taken my fixed and final resolution.—See *Jonson,* vol. ii. p. 142. [Here Gifford ought rather to have referred to his note on Massinger's *Works,* vol. ii. p. 21, ed. 1813. D.]

[6] *rent*] Gifford printed "rend:" but the other form was common enough in our author's days. D.

lord; but for reward you shall trust none but your own pockets.

Banditti. We'll make a murder.

Sor. Here's gold [*Gives them money*]; here's more; want nothing; what you do
Is noble, and an act of brave revenge:
I'll make ye rich, banditti, and all free.

Banditti. Liberty! liberty!

Vas. Hold, take every man a vizard [*Gives them masks*]: when ye are withdrawn, keep as much silence as you can possibly. You know the watch-word;[7] till which be spoken, move not; but when you hear that, rush in like a stormy flood: I need not instruct ye in your own profession.

Banditti. No, no, no.

Vas. In, then: your ends are profit and preferment: away! [*Exeunt Ban.*

Sor. The guests will all come, Vasques?

Vas. Yes, sir. And now let me a little edge your resolution: you see nothing is unready to this great work, but a great mind in you; call to your remembrance your disgraces, your loss of honour, Hippolita's blood, and arm your courage in your own wrongs; so shall you best right those wrongs in vengeance, which you may truly call your own.

Sor. 'Tis well: the less I speak, the more I burn,
And blood shall quench that flame.

Vas. Now you begin to turn Italian. This beside:—when my young incest-monger comes, he will be sharp set on his old bit: give him time enough, let him have your chamber and bed at liberty; let my hot hare have law ere he be hunted to his death,

---

[7] *You know the* watch-word;] It appears from a subsequent passage (p. 204) that this was "VENGEANCE."

that, if it be possible, he may[8] post to hell in the very
act of his damnation.[9]

Sor. It shall be so; and see, as we would wish,
He comes himself first.

Enter GIOVANNI.

Welcome, my much-lov'd brother:
Now I perceive you honour me; you're welcome.
But where's my father?

Gio.   With the other states,[10]
Attending on the nuncio of the pope,
To wait upon him hither. How's my sister?

Sor. Like a good housewife, scarcely ready yet;
You're[11] best walk to her chamber.

Gio.   If you will.

Sor. I must expect my honourable friends;
Good brother, get her forth.

Gio.   You're busy, sir. [*Exit.*

Vas. Even as the great devil himself would havé
it! let him go and glut himself in his own destruction.—[*Flourish.*] Hark, the nuncio is at hand: good
sir, be ready to receive him.

Enter Cardinal, FLORIO, DONADO, RICHARDETTO, *and*
Attendants.

Sor. Most reverend lord, this grace hath made me
    proud,
That you vouchsafe my house; I ever rest

---

[8] *may*] Omitted by Gifford. D.

[9] *that, if it be possible, he may post to hell in the very act of his damnation.*] This infernal sentiment has been copied from Shakespeare [*Hamlet*, act iii. sc. 3] by several writers who were nearly his contemporaries. *Reed.* It is not, however, ill placed in the mouth of such an incarnate fiend as Vasques.

[10] *states,*] See note, p. 191. D.

[11] *You're*] Gifford printed "You were."—See note, p. 131. D.

Your humble servant for this noble favour.
 Car. You are our friend, my lord : his Holiness
Shall understand how zealously you honour
Saint Peter's vicar in his substitute :
Our special love to you.
 Sor.   Signiors, to you
My welcome, and my ever best of thanks
For this so memorable courtesy.—
Pleaseth your grace walk[12] near ?
 Car.   My lord, we come
To celebrate your feast with civil mirth,
As ancient custom teacheth : we will go.
 Sor. Attend his grace there!—Signiors, keep your
   way.   [*Exeunt.*

SCENE V. ANNABELLA'S *bed-chamber in the same.*

ANNABELLA *richly dressed*[13] *and* GIOVANNI [*discovered*].
 Gio. What, chang'd so soon ! hath your new
   sprightly lord
Found out a trick in night-games more than we
Could know in our simplicity ? Ha ! is't so ?
Or does the fit come on you, to prove treacherous
To your past vows and oaths ?
 Ann.   Why should you jest
At my calamity, without all sense
Of the approaching dangers you are in ?
 Gio. What danger's half so great as thy revolt ?
Thou art a faithless sister, else thou know'st,
Malice, or any treachery beside,

---

[12] *grace walk*] The 4to has "*Grace to walke.*" D.
[13] *Annabella* richly dressed, &c.] The 4to, with the usual absurdity of stage-directions from the prompter's book, has "Enter Giouanni and Annabella lying on a bed." D.

Would stoop to my bent brows : why, I hold fate
Clasp'd in my fist, and could command the course
Of time's eternal motion, hadst thou been
One thought more steady than an ebbing sea.
And what? you'll now be honest, that's resolv'd?
    Ann. Brother, dear brother, know what I have been,
And know that now there's but a dining-time[14]
'Twixt us and our confusion : let's not waste
These precious hours in vain and useless speech.
Alas, these gay attires were not put on
But to some end ; this sudden solemn feast
Was not ordain'd to riot in expense ;
I, that have now been chamber'd here alone,
Barr'd of my guardian or of any else,
Am not for nothing at an instant freed
To fresh access. Be not deceiv'd, my brother ;
This banquet is an harbinger of death
To you and me ; resolve yourself it is,
And be prepar'd to welcome it.
    Gio.   Well, then ;
The schoolmen teach that all this globe of earth
Shall be consum'd to ashes in a minute.
    Ann. So I have read too.
    Gio.   But 'twere somewhat strange
To see the waters burn : could I believe
This might be true, I could believe as well
There might be hell or heaven.
    Ann.   That's most certain.
    Gio. A dream, a dream! else in this other world
We should know one another.
    Ann.   So we shall.
    Gio. Have you heard so?

---

[14] *dining-time*] So the 4to in my possession.—A 4to in the King's Library, British Museum, has " dying *time.*"—See note, p. 34. D.

SCENE V.   'TIS PITY SHE'S A WHORE.   199

 Ann.   For certain.
 Gio.   But d'ye think
That I shall see you there?—You look on me.[15]—
May we kiss one another, prate or laugh,
Or do as we do here?
 Ann.   I know not that.
But, brother, for the present, what d'ye mean[16]
To free yourself from danger? some way think
How to escape : I'm sure the guests are come.
  Gio. Look up, look here; what see you in my
    face?
 Ann. Distraction and a troubled conscience.[17]
  Gio. Death, and a swift repining wrath :—yet
    look;
What see you in mine eyes?
 Ann.   Methinks you weep.
 Gio. I do indeed: these are the funeral tears
Shed on your grave; these furrow'd-up my cheeks
When first I lov'd and knew not how to woo.
Fair Annabella, should I here repeat
The story of my life, we might lose time.
Be record all the spirits of the air,
And all things else that are, that day and night,
Early and late, the tribute which my heart
Hath paid to Annabella's sacred love
Hath been these tears, which are her mourners now!
Never till now did Nature do her best
To show a matchless beauty to the world,

  [15] *You* look *on me.*] i. e. You look with *surprise* or *astonishment* on me. Such is the force of this expression.—See *Jonson*, vol. iv. p. 180.
  [16] *But,* brother, *for the present, what d'ye mean*] The 4to, which is imperfect in this place, reads "But *good* for the present." The word adopted is certainly not the author's; but it is safe, at least; and I prefer it to inserting a monosyllable at random.
  [17] *Distraction and a troubled* conscience.] The old copy reads "a troubled *countenance*;" well corrected by Dodsley.

Which in an instant, ere it scarce was seen,
The jealous Destinies requir'd[18] again.
Pray, Annabella, pray! Since we must part,
Go thou, white in thy soul, to fill a throne
Of innocence and sanctity in heaven.
Pray, pray, my sister!
   Ann.   Then I see your drift.—
Ye blessèd angels, guard me!
   Gio.   So say I.
Kiss me. If ever after-times should hear
Of our fast-knit affections, though perhaps
The laws of conscience and of civil use
May justly blame us, yet when they but know
Our loves, that love will wipe away that rigour
Which would in other incests be abhorr'd.
Give me your hand: how sweetly life doth run
In these well-colour'd veins! how constantly
These palms do promise health! but I could chide
With Nature for this cunning flattery.
Kiss me again:—forgive me.
   Ann.   With my heart.
   Gio. Farewell!
   Ann.   Will you be gone?
   Gio.   Be dark, bright sun,
And make this mid-day night, that thy gilt rays
May not behold a deed will turn their splendour
More sooty than the poets feign their Styx!—
One other kiss, my sister.
   Ann.   What means this?
   Gio. To save thy fame, and kill thee in a kiss.
                                          [*Stabs her.*
Thus die, and die by me, and by my hand!
Revenge is mine; honour doth love command.
   Ann. O, brother, by your hand!

---

[18] *requir'd*] The 4to has "require." D.

Gio.   When thou art dead
I'll give my reasons for't; for to dispute
With thy—even in thy death—most lovely beauty,
Would make me stagger to perform this act,
Which I most glory in.
    Ann. Forgive him, Heaven—and me my sins!
        Farewell,
Brother unkind, unkind—Mercy, great Heaven!
O, O!   [*Dies.*
    Gio. She's dead, alas, good soul! The hapless fruit
That in her womb receiv'd its life from me
Hath had from me a cradle and a grave.
I must not dally. This sad marriage-bed,
In all her best, bore her alive and dead.
Soranzo, thou hast miss'd thy aim in this:
I have prevented now thy reaching plots,
And kill'd a love, for whose each drop of blood
I would have pawn'd my heart.—Fair Annabella,
How over-glorious art thou in thy wounds,
Triúmphing over infamy and hate!—
Shrink not, courageous hand, stand up, my heart,
And boldly act my last and greater part!
                            [*The scene closes.*

SCENE VI. *A banqueting-room*[19] *in the same.*

A banquet set out. Enter the Cardinal, FLORIO, DONADO, SORANZO, RICHARDETTO, VASQUES, *and* Attendants.

    Vas. [*aside to Sor.*] Remember, sir, what you have to do; be wise and resolute.
    Sor. [*aside to Vas.*] Enough: my heart is fix'd.—
        Pleaseth your grace

[19] A banqueting-room] They had dined in another room, and, according to the usual practice, repaired to the apartment in which the confectionery was set out.

To taste these coarse confections: though the use
Of such set entertainments more consists
In custom than in cause, yet, reverend sir,
I am still made your servant by your presence.
   Car. And we your friend.
   Sor. But where's my brother Giovanni?

   Enter GIOVANNI *with a heart upon his dagger.*
   Gio. Here, here, Soranzo! trimm'd in reeking blood,
That triumphs over death, proud in the spoil
Of love and vengeance! Fate, or all the powers
That guide the motions of immortal souls,
Could not prevent me.
   Car. What means this?
   Flo. Son Giovanni!
   Sor. [*aside*] Shall I be forestall'd?
   Gio. Be not amaz'd: if your misgiving hearts
Shrink at an idle sight, what bloodless fear
Of coward passion would have seiz'd your senses,
Had you beheld the rape of life and beauty
Which I have acted!—My sister, O, my sister!
   Flo. Ha! what of her?
   Gio.   The glory of my deed
Darken'd the mid-day sun, made noon as night.
You came to feast, my lords, with dainty fare:
I came to feast too; but I digg'd for food
In a much richer mine than gold or stone
Of any value balanc'd; 'tis a heart,
A heart, my lords, in which is mine entomb'd:
Look well upon't; d'ye know't?
   Vas. [*aside*] What strange riddle's this?
   Gio. 'Tis Annabella's heart, 'tis:— why d'ye startle?—
I vow 'tis hers: this dagger's point plough'd up

Her fruitful womb, and left to me the fame
Of a most glorious executioner.
 Flo. Why, madman, art thyself?
 Gio. Yes, father; and, that times to come may
    know
How, as my fate, I honour'd my revenge,
List, father; to your ears I will yield up
How much I have deserv'd to be your son.
 Flo. What is't thou say'st?
 Gio.   Nine moons have had their changes
Since I first throughly view'd and truly lov'd
Your daughter and my sister.
 Flo.   How!—Alas, my lords,
He is a frantic madman!
 Gio.   Father, no.
For nine months' space in secret I enjoy'd
Sweet Annabella's sheets; nine months I liv'd
A happy monarch of her heart and her.—
Soranzo, thou know'st this: thy paler cheek
Bears the confounding print of thy disgrace;
For her too-fruitful womb too soon bewray'd
The happy passage of our stol'n delights,
And made her mother to a child unborn.
 Car. Incestuous villain!
 Flo.   O, his rage belies him.
 Gio. It does not, 'tis the oracle of truth;
I vow it is so.
 Sor. I shall burst with fury.—
Bring the strumpet forth!
 Vas. I shall, sir.   [*Exit.*
 Gio.   Do, sir.—Have you all no faith
To credit yet my triumphs? Here I swear
By all that you call sacred, by the love
I bore my Annabella whilst she liv'd,
These hands have from her bosom ripp'd this heart.

Re-enter VASQUES.

Is't true, or no, sir?
Vas.   'Tis most strangely true.
Flo. Cursèd man!—Have I liv'd to—   [*Dies.*
Car.   Hold up, Florio.—
Monster of children! see what thou hast done,
Broke thy old father's heart.—Is none of you
Dares venture on him?
Gio.   Let 'em!—O, my father,
How well his death becomes him in his griefs!
Why, this was done with courage : now survives
None of our house but I, gilt in the blood
Of a fair sister and a hapless father.
   Sor. Inhuman scorn of men, hast thou a thought
T' outlive thy murders?   .   [*Draws.*
Gio.   Yes, I tell thee, yes;
For in my fists I bear the twists of life.
Soranzo, see this heart, which was thy wife's;
Thus I exchange it royally for thine,   [*They fight.*
And thus, and thus!   [*Soranzo falls.*
           Now brave revenge is mine.
   Vas. I cannot hold any longer.—You, sir, are you grown insolent in your butcheries? have at you!
   Gio. Come, I am arm'd to meet thee. [*They fight.*
   Vas. No! will it not be yet? if this will not, another shall. Not yet? I shall fit you anon.—VENGEANCE![20]
        The Banditti *rush in.*
   Gio. Welcome! come more of you; whate'er you be,
I dare your worst.   [*They surround and wound him.*
O, I can stand no longer! feeble arms,

---

[20] VENGEANCE!] This, as was observed p. 195, was the *watchword*, or preconcerted signal for assistance.

Have you so soon lost strength? [*Falls.*

Vas. Now you are *welcome*, sir!—[*Aside to Band.*]
Away, my masters, all is done; shift for yourselves,
your reward is your own; shift for yourselves.

Banditti. Away, away! [*Exeunt.*

Vas. How d'ye, my lord?—See you this? [*pointing to Gio.*] How is't?

Sor. Dead; but in death well pleas'd that I have
 liv'd
To see my wrongs reveng'd on that black devil.
O, Vasques, to thy bosom let me give
My last of breath; let not that lecher live.
O! [*Dies.*

Vas. The reward of peace and rest be with him,[21]
my ever dearest lord and master!

Gio. Whose hand gave me this wound?

Vas. Mine, sir; I was your first man: have you
enough?

Gio. I thank thee;[22] thou hast done for me
But what I would have else done on myself.
Art sure thy lord is dead?

Vas. O, impudent slave!
As sure as I am sure to see thee die.

Car. Think on thy life and end, and call for
 mercy.

Gio. Mercy! why, I have found it in this justice.

Car. Strive yet to cry to Heaven.

Gio. O, I bleed fast!
Death, thou'rt a guest long look'd for; I embrace
Thee and thy wounds: O, my last minute comes!
Where'er I go, let me enjoy this grace,
Freely to view my Annabella's face. [*Dies.*

Don. Strange miracle of justice!

---

[21] *with him,*] Gifford printed "*with* [you]." D.
[22] *I thank thee;*] Qy. "*I thank thee,* Vasques"? D.

Car. Raise up the city; we shall be murder'd all !

Vas. You need not fear, you shall not: this strange task being ended, I have paid the duty to the son which I have vowed to the father.

Car. Speak, wretched villain, what incarnate fiend Hath led thee on to this ?

Vas. Honesty, and pity of my master's wrongs : for know, my lord, I am by birth a Spaniard, brought forth my country in my youth by Lord Soranzo's father, whom whilst he lived I served faithfully; since whose death I have been to this man as I was to him. What I have done was duty, and I repent nothing, but that the loss of my life had not ransomed his.

Car. Say, fellow, know'st thou any yet unnam'd Of counsel in this incest ?

Vas. Yes, an old woman, sometimes[23] guardian to this murdered lady.

Car. And what's become of her ?

Vas. Within this room she is; whose eyes, after her confession, I caused to be put out, but kept alive, to confirm what from Giovanni's own mouth you have heard. Now, my lord, what I have done you may judge of; and let your own wisdom be a judge in your own reason.

Car. Peace !—First this woman,[24] chief in these effects,
My sentence is, that forthwith she be ta'en
Out of the city, for example's sake,
There to be burnt to ashes.

[23] *sometimes*] i.e. formerly, in other times (see my *Glossary to Shakespeare*).—Gifford printed "sometime." D.

[24] *First this woman*, &c.] What! without hearing her? It is well, however, that some one was at hand to satisfy the Cardinal's fierce love of justice. The sacrifice, it must be confessed, is somewhat like that of *the poor bed-rid weaver* in *Hudibras;* and if, of the four who now remain alive upon the stage, three, including his Eminence, had been sentenced to the hurdle with her, few would have thought them too hardly dealt with.

Don.   'Tis most just.
Car. Be it your charge, Donado, see it done.
Don. I shall.
Vas. What for me? if death, 'tis welcome: I have been honest to the son, as I was to the father.
 Car. Fellow, for thee, since what thou didst was done
Not for thyself, being no Italian,
We banish thee for ever; to depart
Within three days: in this we do dispense
With grounds of reason, not of thine offence.
 Vas. 'Tis well: this conquest is mine, and I rejoice that a Spaniard outwent an Italian in revenge. [*Exit.*
 Car. Take up these slaughter'd bodies, see them buried;
And all the gold and jewels, or whatsoever,
Confiscate by the canons of the church,
We seize upon to the pope's proper use.
 Rich. [*discovers himself*] Your grace's pardon: thus long I liv'd disguis'd,
To see th' effect of pride and lust at once
Brought both to shameful ends.
 Car. What! Richardetto, whom we thought for dead?
 Don. Sir, was it you—
 Rich.   Your friend.
 Car.   We shall have time
To talk at large of all: but never yet
Incest and murder have so strangely met.
Of one so young, so rich in nature's store,
Who could not say, 'TIS PITY SHE'S A WHORE?
              [*Exeunt.*

Here, instead of an epilogue, we have, in the old copy, an apology for the errors of the press. It forms, as the learned Partridge says, a strange *non sequitur*, and is, in truth, more captious than logical. As a just compliment, however, to the skill of the performers and the good taste of Lord Peterborough, it merits preservation. "The general commendation deserved by the actors in their[25] presentment of this tragedy may easily excuse such few[26] faults as are escaped in the printing. A common charity may allow him the ability of spelling, whom a secure confidence assures that he cannot ignorantly err in the application of sense."

The remarks on this dreadful story cannot be more appositely terminated, perhaps, than by the following passage from the concluding chapter of Sir Thomas Browne's *Vulgar Errors*. It is, as Mr. Lamb observes, "solemn and fine." "As there are many relations," he begins, "whereto we cannot assent, and make some doubt thereof, so there are divers others whose verities we fear, and heartily wish there were no truth therein."—" For of sins heteroclital, and such as want either name or precedent, there is ofttimes a sin even in their histories. We desire no records of such enormities; sins should be accounted new, that so they may be esteemed monstrous. They amit of monstrosity, as they fall from their rarity; for men count it venial to err with their forefathers, and foolishly conceive they divide a sin in its society. The pens of men may sufficiently expatiate without these singularities of villany; for as they increase the hatred of vice in some, so do they enlarge the theory of wickedness in all. And this is one thing that may make latter ages worse than were the former: for the vicious examples of ages past poison the curiosity of these present, affording a hint of sin unto seducible spirits, and soliciting those unto the imitation of them whose heads were never so perversely principled as to invent them. . . . . In things of this nature silence commendeth history; 'tis the veniable part of things lost, wherein there must never rise a Pancirollus, nor remain any register but that of hell." *Works*, vol. iii. pp. 370, 372, 373.

[25] *their*] Gifford printed "the." D.
[26] *few*] Omitted by Gifford. D.

THE BROKEN HEART.

There is no account to be found of the first appearance of this tragedy, or of its success on the stage; but it was given to the public in 1633. In the title it is said to have been "acted by the King's Majestie's servants, at the Private House in the Black Friers." Ford has prefixed as a motto the words FIDE HONOR, an anagram of his own name, which therefore should perhaps be written, as he sometimes wrote it himself, JOHN FORDE. It would appear from the Prologue, that the story, which is admitted to be of ancient date, had some foundation in fact. It may one day perhaps be met with. [The full title of the 4to is, *The Broken Heart. A Tragedy. Acted By the Kings Majesties Seruants at the priuate House in the Black-Friers. Fide Honor. London: Printed by I. B. for Hvgh Beeston, and are to be sold at his Shop, neere the Castle in Corne-hill.* 1633. D.]

TO THE

MOST WORTHY DESERVER OF THE NOBLEST TITLES IN HONOUR,

WILLIAM,

LORD CRAVEN, BARON OF HAMPSTED-MARSHALL.[1]

MY LORD,

THE glory of a great name, acquired by a greater glory of action, hath in all ages lived the truest chronicle to his own memory. In the practice of which argument your growth to perfection, even in youth, hath appeared so sincere, so unflattering a penman, that posterity cannot with more delight read the merit of noble endea-

[1] The following extract from Collins's *Peerage* will sufficiently explain the allusions in the Dedication to the active life of this eminent person. "William, first Baron and Earl Craven, the eldest son of Sir W. Craven, Lord Mayor, was much affected with military exercises from his youth, and signalised himself in Germany and in the Netherlands under Henry, Prince of Orange. In which valiant adventures he gained such honour, that on his return he was first knighted at Newmarket, March 4, 1626, and in the year after deservedly raised to the dignity of Lord Craven of Hampsted-Marshall. In 1631 he was one of the commanders of those forces sent to the assistance of the great Gustavus Adolphus, and was wounded in the assault upon the strong fortress of Kreutznach; after the surrender of which, he was told by the Swedish monarch, 'he adventured so desperately, he bid his younger brother fair play for his estate.' Subsequently he was advanced to the dignities of Viscount and Earl, and served Charles I. and II. and James II. faithfully; and died, after a very active and chequered life, April 9, 1697, at the advanced age of 88. He is now chiefly remembered for his romantic attachment to the Queen of Bohemia, daughter of James I., to whom it is generally supposed he was privately married."

vours than noble endeavours merit thanks from posterity to be read with delight. Many nations, many eyes have been witnesses of your deserts, and loved them: be pleased, then, with the freedom of your own name, to admit *one* amongst all, particularly into the list of such as honour a fair example of nobility. There is a kind of humble ambition, not uncommendable, when the silence of study breaks forth into discourse, coveting rather encouragement than applause; yet herein censure commonly is too severe an auditor, without the moderation of an able patronage. I have ever been slow in courtship of greatness, not ignorant of such defects as are frequent to opinion : but the justice of your inclination to industry emboldens my weakness of confidence to relish an experience of your mercy, as many brave dangers have tasted of your courage. Your Lordship strove to be known to the world, when the world knew you least, by voluntary but excellent attempts : like allowance I plead of being known to your Lordship (in this low presumption), by tendering, to a favourable entertainment, a devotion offered from a heart that can be as truly sensible of any least respect as ever profess the owner in my best, my readiest services, a lover of your natural love to virtue,

JOHN FORD.

DRAMATIS PERSONÆ.

AMYCLAS, king of Laconia.
ITHOCLES, a favourite.
ORGILUS, son to Crotolon.
BASSANES, a jealous nobleman.
ARMOSTES, a counsellor of state.
CROTOLON, another counsellor.
PROPHILUS, friend to Ithocles.
NEARCHUS, prince of Argos.
TECNICUS, a philosopher.
HEMOPHIL, } courtiers.
GRONEAS,
AMELUS, friend to Nearchus.
PHULAS, servant to Bassanes.

CALANTHA, the King's daughter.
PENTHEA, sister to Ithocles.
EUPHRANEA, daughter to Crotolon, a maid of honour.
CHRISTALLA, } maids of honour.
PHILEMA,
GRAUSIS, overseer of Penthea.

Courtiers, Officers, Attendants, &c.

SCENE—*Sparta.*

Here Ford gives what he calls "the names of the speakers fitted to their qualities." If he found them elsewhere, it is well; if not, he has not been very successful in his appropriation of some of them.

ITHOCLES, Honour of Loveliness.
ORGILUS, Angry.
BASSANES, Vexation.
ARMOSTES, an Appeaser.
CROTOLON, Noise.
PROPHILUS, Dear.
NEARCHUS, Young Prince.
TECNICUS, Artist.
HEMOPHIL, Glutton.
GRONEAS, Tavern-haunter.
AMELUS, Trusty.
PHULAS, Watchful.

CALANTHA, Flower of Beauty.
PENTHEA, Complaint.
EUPHRANEA, Joy.
CHRISTALLA, Crystal.
PHILEMA, a Kiss.
GRAUSIS, Old Beldam.

Persons included.

THRASUS, Fierceness.
APLOTES, Simplicity.

PROLOGUE.

Our scene is Sparta. He whose best of art
Hath drawn this piece calls it The Broken Heart.
The title lends no expectation here
Of apish laughter, or of some lame jeer
At place or persons; no pretended clause
Of jests fit for a brothel courts applause
From vulgar admiration: such low songs,
Tun'd to unchaste ears, suit not modest tongues.
The virgin-sisters then deserv'd fresh bays
When innocence and sweetness crown'd their lays;
Then vices gasp'd for breath, whose whole commérce
Was whipp'd to exile by unblushing verse.
This law we keep in our presentment now,
Not to take freedom more than we allow;
What may be here thought fiction,[2] when time's youth
Wanted some riper years, was known a truth:
In which, if words have cloth'd the subject right,
You may partake a pity with delight.

[2] *fiction,*] The 4to has "a fiction." D.

This Prologue has been hitherto most strangely printed. It is in the author's best manner, and, whether considered in a moral or poetical light, entitled to considerable praise.

THE BROKEN HEART.

ACT I.

SCENE I. *A room in* CROTOLON'S *house.*

Enter CROTOLON *and* ORGILUS.

   Crot. Dally not further; I will know the reason
That speeds thee to this journey.
   Org.   Reason! good sir,
I can yield many.
   Crot.   Give me one, a good one;
Such I expect, and ere we part must have:
Athens! pray, why to Athens? you intend not
To kick against the world, turn cynic, stoic,
Or read the logic-lecture, or become
An Areopagite, and judge in cases
Touching the commonwealth; for, as I take it,
The budding of your chin cannot prognosticate
So grave an honour.
   Org.   All this I acknowledge.
   Crot. You do! then, son, if books and love of
            knowledge
Inflame you to this travel, here in Sparta
You may as freely study.
   Org.   'Tis not that, sir.

Crot. Not that, sir! As a father, I command thee
T' acquaint me with the truth.
  Org.   Thus I obey ye.
After so many quarrels as dissension,
Fury, and rage had broach'd in blood, and sometimes
With death to such confederates as sided
With now-dead Thrasus and yourself, my lord;
Our present king, Amyclas, reconcil'd
Your eager swords and seal'd a gentle peace:
Friends you profess'd yourselves; which to confirm,
A resolution for a lasting league
Betwixt your families was entertain'd,
By joining in a Hymenean bond
Me and the fair Penthea, only daughter
To Thrasus.
  Crot.   What of this?
  Org.   Much, much, dear sir.
A freedom of convérse, an interchange
Of holy and chaste love, so fix'd our souls
In a firm growth of union,[1] that no time
Can eat into the pledge: we had enjoy'd
The sweets our vows expected, had not cruelty
Prevented all those triumphs we prepar'd for,
By Thrasus his untimely death.
  Crot.   Most certain.
  Org. From this time sprouted-up that poisonous stalk
Of aconite, whose ripen'd fruit hath ravish'd
All health, all comfort of a happy life;
For Ithocles, her brother, proud of youth,
And prouder in his power, nourish'd closely

---

[1] *In a firm growth of union,*] I have omitted "*holy*" before "*union*," which had evidently crept in from the preceding line, and wholly destroys the metre. [But, though "holy" is found in one copy of the 4to in my possession, yet it is omitted in another copy I possess, as also in the copy in the King's Library, British Museum.— See note, p. 34. D.]

The memory of former discontents,
To glory in revenge. By cunning partly,
Partly by threats, he woos at once and forces
His virtuous sister to admit a marriage
With Bassanes, a nobleman, in honour
And riches, I confess, beyond my fortunes.
 Crot. All this is no sound reason to impórtune
My leave for thy departure.
 Org.   Now it follows.
Beauteous Penthea, wedded to this torture
By an insulting brother, being secretly
Compell'd to yield her virgin freedom up
To him, who never can usurp her heart,
Before contracted mine, is now so yok'd
To a most barbarous thraldom, misery,
Affliction, that he savours not humanity,
Whose sorrow melts not into more than pity
In hearing but her name.
 Crot.   As how, pray?
 Org.   Bassanes,
The man that calls her wife, considers truly
What heaven of perfections he is lord of
By thinking fair Penthea his : this thought
Begets a kind of monster-love, which love
Is nurse unto a fear so strong and servile
As brands all dotage with a jealousy :
All eyes who gaze upon that shrine of beauty
He doth resolve[2] do homage to the miracle ;
Some one, he is assur'd, may now or then,
If opportunity but sort, prevail :
So much, out of a self-unworthiness,
His fears transport him ; not that he finds cause
In her obedience, but his own distrust.

[2] *He doth* resolve] i.e. he doth *satisfy, convince himself.*

Crot. You spin-out your discourse.
Org.   My griefs are violent :
For, knowing how the maid was heretofore
Courted by me, his jealousies grow wild
That I should steal again into her favours,
And undermine her virtues ; which the gods
Know I nor dare nor dream of. Hence, from hence,
I undertake a voluntary exile ;
First, by my absence to take off the cares
Of jealous Bassanes ; but chiefly, sir,
To free Penthea from a hell on earth ;
Lastly, to lose the memory of something
Her presence makes to live in me afresh.
Crot. Enough, my Orgilus, enough. To Athens,
I give a full consent.—Alas, good lady !—
We shall hear from thee often ?
Org.   Often.
Crot.   See,
Thy sister comes to give a farewell.

Enter EUPHRANEA.

Euph.   Brother !—
Org. Euphranea, thus upon thy cheeks I print
A brother's kiss ; more careful of thine honour,
Thy health, and thy well-doing, than my life.
Before we part, in presence of our father,
I must prefer a suit t' ye.
Euph.   You may style it,
My brother, a command.
Org.   That you will promise[3]

---

[3] *That you will promise*, &c.] Orgilus seems to entertain some suspicion of Ithocles ; but the exaction of such a promise appears not altogether consistent in one who had just been describing the misery of his own sufferings from the power and influence of a brother. This, however, is an admirable introductory scene ; and in

Never to pass[4] to any man, however
Worthy, your faith, till, with our father's leave,
I give a free consent.
    Crot.   An easy motion!
I'll promise for her, Orgilus.
    Org.   Your pardon;
Euphranea's oath must yield me satisfaction.
    Euph. By Vesta's sacred fires I swear.
    Crot.   And I,
By great Apollo's beams, join in the vow,
Not without thy allowance to bestow her
On any living.
    Org.   Dear Euphranea,
Mistake me not: far, far 'tis from my thought,
As far from any wish of mine, to hinder
Preferment to an honourable bed
Or fitting fortune; thou art young and handsome;
And 'twere injustice,—more, a tyranny,—
Not to advance thy merit: trust me, sister,
It shall be my first care to see thee match'd
As may become thy choice and our contents.
I have your oath.
    Euph.   You have. But mean you, brother,
To leave us, as you say?
    Crot.   Ay, ay, Euphranea:
He has just grounds direct him. I will prove
A father and a brother to thee.
    Euph.   Heaven
Does look into the secrets of all hearts:
Gods, you have mercy with ye, else—
    Crot.   Doubt nothing;

---

justice to the author it should be observed, that few of his contemporaries open the plot of their drama so happily as he occasionally does.

    [4] *Never to pass*] The 4to has "To passe neuer." D.

Thy brother will return in safety to us.
  Org. Souls sunk in sorrows never are without 'em;
They change fresh airs, but bear their griefs about 'em.
                                           [*Exeunt.*

SCENE II. *A room in the palace.*

Flourish. Enter AMYCLAS, ARMOSTES, PROPHILUS, Courtiers,
          and Attendants.

  Amyc. The Spartan gods are gracious; our humility
Shall bend before their altars, and perfume
Their temples with abundant sacrifice.
See, lords, Amyclas, your old king, is entering
Into his youth again ! I shall shake off
This silver badge of age, and change this snow
For hairs as gay as are Apollo's locks;
Our heart leaps in new vigour.
  Arm.   May old time
Run back to double your long life, great sir !
  Amyc. It will, it must, Armostes : thy bold nephew,
Death-braving Ithocles, brings to our gates
Triumphs and peace upon his conquering sword.
Laconia is a monarchy at length ;
Hath in this latter war trod under foot
Messene's pride ; Messene bows her neck
To Lacedæmon's royalty. O, 'twas
A glorious victory, and doth deserve
More than a chronicle—a temple, lords,
A temple to the name of Ithocles.—
Where didst thou leave him, Prophilus ?
  Pro.   At Pephon,
Most gracious sovereign ; twenty of the noblest
Of the Messenians there attend your pleasure,
For such conditions as you shall propose
In settling peace, and liberty of life.

Amyc. When comes your friend the general?
Pro. He promis'd
To follow with all speed convenient.

Enter CALANTHA, EUPHRANEA; CHRISTALLA *and*
PHILEMA *with a garland; and* CROTOLON.

Amyc. Our daughter!—Dear Calantha, the happy news,
The conquest of Messene, hath already
Enrich'd thy knowledge.
Cal. With the circumstance
And manner of the fight, related faithfully
By Prophilus himself.—But, pray, sir, tell me
How doth the youthful general demean
His actions in these fortunes?
Pro. Excellent princess,
Your own fair eyes may soon report a truth
Unto your judgment, with what moderation,
Calmness of nature, measure, bounds, and limits
Of thankfulness and joy, he doth digest
Such amplitude of his success as would
In others, moulded of a spirit less clear,
Advance 'em to comparison with heaven:
But Ithocles—
Cal. Your friend—
Pro. He is so, madam,
In which the period of my fate consists:
He, in this firmament of honour, stands
Like a star fix'd, not mov'd with any thunder
Of popular applause or sudden lightning
Of self-opinion; he hath serv'd his country,
And thinks 'twas but his duty.
Crot. You describe
A miracle of man.

Amyc. Such, Crotolon,
On forfeit of a king's word, thou wilt find him.—
                                               [*Flourish.*
Hark, warning of his coming ! all attend him.

Enter ITHOCLES, *ushered in by the* Lords, *and followed
by* HEMOPHIL *and* GRONEAS.

Return into these arms, thy home, thy sanctuary,
Delight of Sparta, treasure of my bosom,
Mine own, own Ithocles!
    Ith.   Your humblest subject.
    Arm. Proud of the blood I claim an interest in,
As brother to thy mother, I embrace thee,
Right noble nephew.
    Ith.   Sir, your love's too partial.
    Crot. Our country speaks by me, who by thy valour,
Wisdom, and service, shares in this great action ;
Returning thee, in part of thy due merits,
A general welcome.
    Ith.   You exceed in bounty.
    Cal. Christalla, Philema, the chaplet. [*Takes the
        chaplet from them.*]—Ithocles,
Upon the wings of fame the singular
And chosen fortune of an high attempt
Is borne so past the view of common sight,
That I myself with mine own hands have wrought,
To crown thy temples, this provincial[5] garland :
Accept, wear, and enjoy it as our gift

---

[5] *this* provincial *garland:*] i.e. the wreath (of laurel) which she had prepared ; and which the ancients conferred on those who, like Ithocles, had added a *province* to the empire. These honorary chaplets or crowns were, as every schoolboy knows, composed of plants, leaves, or flowers, according to the nature of the service rendered. Thus we have the *provincial*, the civic, the mural, the obsidional, and various other garlands, all woven of different materials, and all appropriate to their respective wearers, "deserv'd, not purchas'd."

Deserv'd, not purchas'd.
Ith.   You're a royal maid.
Amyc. She is in all our daughter.
Ith.   Let me blush,
Acknowledging how poorly I have serv'd,
What nothings I have done, compar'd with th' honours
Heap'd on the issue of a willing mind;
In that lay mine ability, that only:
For who is he so sluggish from his birth,
So little worthy of a name or country,
That owes not out of gratitude for life
A debt of service, in what kind soever
Safety or counsel of the commonweath
Requires, for payment?
Cal.   He speaks truth.
Ith.   Whom heaven
Is pleas'd to style victorious, there to such
Applause runs madding, like the drunken priests
In Bacchus' sacrifices, without reason
Voicing the leader-on a demi-god;
Whenas, indeed, each common soldier's blood
Drops down as current coin in that hard purchase
As his whose much more delicate condition
Hath suck'd the milk of ease: judgment commands,
But resolution executes. I use not,
Before this royal presence, these fit slights[6]
As in contempt of such as can direct;
My speech hath other end; not to attribute
All praise to one man's fortune, which is strengthen'd
By many hands: for instance, here is Prophilus,
A gentleman—I cannot flatter truth—
Of much desert; and, though in other rank,

---

[6] *these fit* slights] i.e. these trifling services, to which I have adapted the slight or humble language which becomes them. It is the modesty of Ithocles which speaks.

Both Hemophil and Groneas were not missing
To wish their country's peace; for, in a word,
All there did strive their best, and 'twas our duty.
 Amyc. Courtiers turn soldiers!—We vouchsafe our
   hand: [*Hem. and Gron. kiss his hand.*
Observe your great example.
 Hem.   With all diligence.
 Gron. Obsequiously and hourly.
 Amyc.   Some repose
After these toils is[7] needful. We must think on
Conditions for the conquer'd; they expect 'em.
On!—Come, my Ithocles.
 Euph.   Sir, with your favour,
I need not a supporter.
  Pro.   Fate instructs me.
  [*Exit Amyc. attended, Ith., Cal., &c. As Chris.
   and Phil. are following Cal. they are detained
   by Hem. and Gron.*
 Chris. With me?
 Phil.   Indeed I dare not stay.
 Hem.   Sweet lady,
Soldiers are blunt,—your lip.   [*Kisses her.*
 Chris.   Fie, this is rudeness:
You went not hence such creatures.
 Gron.   Spirit of valour
Is of a mounting nature.
 Phil.   It appears so.—
In earnest, pray, how many men apiece[8]
Have you two been the death of?
 Gron.   'Faith, not many;
We were compos'd of mercy.
 Hem.   For our daring,

---

 [7] *is*] The 4to has "are." D.
 [8] *In earnest, pray, how many men apiece*] The 4to has "Pray in earnest, *how,*" &c.—Gifford printed "Pray [now], in earnest, how many men apiece." D.

You heard the general's approbation
Before the king.
  Chris.   You "*wish'd* your country's peace;"
That show'd your charity : where are your spoils,
Such as the soldier fights for?
  Phil.   They are coming.
  Chris. By the next carrier, are they not?
  Gron.   Sweet Philema,
When I was in the thickest of mine enemies,
Slashing off one man's head, another's nose,
Another's arms and legs,—
  Phil.   And all together.
  Gron. Then would I[9] with a sigh remember thee,
And cry, " Dear Philema, 'tis for thy sake
I do these deeds of wonder!"—dost not love me
With all thy heart now?
  Phil.   Now as heretofore.
I have not put my love to use; the principal
Will hardly yield an interest.
  Gron.   By Mars,
I'll marry thee!
  Phil.   By Vulcan, you're forsworn,
Except my mind do alter strangely.
  Gron.   One word.
  Chris. You lie beyond all modesty :—forbear me.
  Hem. I'll make thee mistress of a city; 'tis
Mine own by conquest.
  Chris.   By petition; sue for't
In forma pauperis.—City! kennel.—Gallants!
Off with your feathers, put on aprons, gallants;
Learn to reel, thrum, or trim a lady's dog,
And be good quiet souls of peace, hobgoblins!
  Hem. Christalla!

[9] *would I*] Gifford printed " I would." D.

Chris.   Practise to drill hogs, in hope
To share in th' acorns.—Soldiers! corncutters,
But not so valiant; they ofttimes draw blood,
Which you durst never do. When you have practis'd
More wit or more civility, we'll rank ye
I' th' list of men: till then, brave things-at-arms,
Dare not to speak to us,—most potent Groneas!—
  Phil. And Hemophil the hardy!—at your services.
                              [*Exeunt Chris. and Phil.*
  Gron. They scorn us, as they did before we went.
  Hem. Hang 'em! let us scorn them, and be revveng'd.
  Gron. Shall we?
  Hem.   We will: and when we slight them thus,
Instead of following them, they'll follow us;
It is a woman's nature.
  Gron.   'Tis a scurvy one.   [*Exeunt.*

Scene III. *The gardens of the palace. A grove.*

Enter TECNICUS, *and* ORGILUS *disguised like one of his Scholars.*

  Tec. Tempt not the stars; young man, thou canst
    not play
With the severity of fate: this change
Of habit and disguise in outward view
Hides not the secrets of thy soul within thee
From their quick-piercing eyes, which dive at all times
Down to thy thoughts: in thy aspéct I note
A consequence of danger.
  Org.   Give me leave,
Grave Tecnicus, without foredooming destiny,
Under thy roof to ease my silent griefs,

By applying to my hidden wounds the balm
Of thy oraculous lectures. If my fortune
Run such a crookèd by-way as to wrest
My steps to ruin, yet thy learnèd precepts
Shall call me back and set my footings straight.
I will not court the world.
　　　Tec.　　　　　　Ah, Orgilus,
Neglects in young men of delights and life
Run often to extremities; they care not
For harms to others who contemn their own.
　　　Org. But I, most learnèd artist, am not so much
At odds with nature that I grudge the thrift
Of any true deserver; nor doth malice
Of present hopes so check them with despair
As that I yield to thought of more affliction
Than what is incident to frailty: wherefore
Impute not this retirèd course of living
Some little time to any other cause
Than what I justly render,—th' information
Of an unsettled mind; as the effect
Must clearly witness.
　　　Tec.　　　　　Spirit of truth inspire thee!
On these conditions I conceal thy change,
And willingly admit thee for an auditor.—
I'll to my study.
　　　Org.　　　I to contemplations
In these delightful walks.　　　　　[*Exit Tec.*
　　　　　　　　　Thus metamorphos'd,
I may without suspicion hearken after
Penthea's usage and Euphranea's faith.
Love, thou art full of mystery! the deities
Themselves are not secure[10] in searching out

　　10　　　　　*the deities*
　　Themselves are not secure] i. e. *sure, certain:* they cannot depend on the results of their own omniscience in these inquiries.

The secrets of those flames, which, hidden, waste
A breast made tributary to the laws
Of beauty: physic yet hath never found
A remedy to cure a lover's wound.—
Ha! who are those that cross yon private walk
Into the shadowing grove in amorous foldings?

PROPHILUS *and* EUPHRANEA[11] *pass by arm in arm and whispering.*

My sister! O, my sister! 'tis Euphranea
With Prophilus: supported too! I would
It were an apparition! Prophilus
Is Ithocles his friend: it strangely puzzles me.

Re-enter PROPHILUS *and* EUPHRANEA.

Again! help me, my book; this scholar's habit
Must stand my privilege: my mind is busy,
Mine eyes and ears are open.
   [*Walks aside, pretending to read.*
Pro.   Do not waste
The span of this stol'n time, lent by the gods
For precious use, in niceness.[12] Bright Euphranea,
Should I repeat old vows, or study new,
For purchase of belief to my desires,—
   Org. [*aside*] Desires!
   Pro.   My service, my integrity,—
   Org. [*aside*] That's better.
   Pro.   I should but repeat a lesson
Oft conn'd without a prompter but thine eyes:

---

[11] *Prophilus and Euphranea*, &c.] The 4to has "Prophilus passeth ouer, supporting Euphrania, and whispering,"—where "supporting" seems to mean "with his arm round her waist." D.

[12]   *Do not waste*
   The span of this stol'n time, lent by the gods
   For precious use, in niceness.] i.e. in unnecessary preciseness, in starting trivial and unimportant objections.

My love is honourable.
 Org. [*aside*]   So was mine
To my Penthea, chastely honourable.
 Pro. Nor wants there more addition to my wish
Of happiness than having thee a wife;
Already sure of Ithocles, a friend
Firm and unalterable.
 Org. [*aside*]   But a brother
More cruel than the grave.
 Euph.   What can you look for,
In answer to your noble protestations,
From an unskilful maid, but language suited
To a divided mind?
 Org. [*aside*]   Hold out, Euphranea!
 Euph. Know, Prophilus, I never undervalu'd,
From the first time you mention'd worthy love,
Your merit, means, or person: it had been
A fault of judgment in me, and a dulness
In my affections, not to weigh and thank
My better stars that offer'd me the grace
Of so much blissfulness. For, to speak truth,
The law of my desires kept equal pace
With yours; nor have I left that resolution:
But only, in a word, whatever choice
Lives nearest in my heart must first procure
Consent both from my father and my brother,
Ere he can own me his.
 Org. [*aside*]   She is forsworn else.
 Pro. Leave me that task.
 Euph.   My brother, ere he parted
To Athens, had my oath.
 Org. [*aside*]   Yes, yes, he had, sure.
 Pro. I doubt not, with the means the court supplies,
But to prevail at pleasure.
 Org. [*aside*]   Very likely!

Pro. Meantime, best, dearest, I may build my
     hopes
On the foundation of thy constant sufferance
In any opposition.
     Euph.   Death shall sooner
Divorce life and the joys I have in living
Than my chaste vows from truth.
     Pro.   On thy fair hand
I seal the like.
     Org. [*aside*] There is no faith in woman.
Passion, O, be contain'd! my very heart-strings
Are on the tenters.
     Euph.   We are overheard.[13]
Cupid protect us! 'twas a stirring, sir,
Of some one near.
     Pro.   Your fears are needless, lady;
None have access into these private pleasures
Except some near in court, or bosom-student
From Tecnicus his oratory, granted
By special favour lately from the king
Unto the grave philosopher.
     Euph.   Methinks
I hear one talking to himself,—I see him.
     Pro. 'Tis a poor scholar, as I told you, lady.
     Org. [*aside*] I am discover'd.—[*Half aloud to him-
          self, as if studying*] Say it; is it possible,
With a smooth tongue, a leering countenance,
Flattery, or force of reason—I come t' ye, sir—

---

[13] Euph. *We are overheard.*] The 4to reads "*Sir*, we are overheard," which destroys both metre and rhythm. From the manner
in which this is printed in the old copy, I am almost persuaded that
the original stood thus;
          "We are overheard, *sir*.
     Cupid protect us! 'twas a stirring, *sure*,
     Of some one near."

[In the first of these lines I believe the true reading is "Sir, we are
o'erheard." D.]

To turn or to appease the raging sea?
Answer to that.—Your art! what art? to catch
And hold fast in a net the sun's small atoms?
No, no; they'll out, they'll out: ye may as easily
Outrun a cloud driven by a northern blast
As fiddle-faddle so! Peace, or speak sense.
    Euph. Call you this thing a scholar? 'las, he's lunatic.
    Pro. Observe him, sweet; 'tis but his recreation.
    Org. But will you hear a little? You're so tetchy,
You keep no rule in argument: philosophy
Works not upon impossibilities,
But natural conclusions.—Mew!—*absurd!*
The metaphysics are but speculations
Of the celestial bodies, or such accidents
As not mixt perfectly, in the air engender'd,
Appear to us unnatural; that's all.
Prove it; yet, with a reverence to your gravity,
I'll balk illiterate sauciness, submitting
My sole opinion to the touch of writers.
    Pro. Now let us fall in with him.
                                          [*They come forward.*
    Org.   Ha, ha, ha!
These apish boys, when they but taste the grammates[14]
And principles of theory, imagine
They can oppose their teachers. Confidence
Leads many into errors.
    Pro.   By your leave, sir.
    Euph. Are you a scholar, friend?

    [14] *when they but* taste *the* grammates] Orgilus affects the pedant-language of the schools. To *taste* is to touch lightly, to merely enter on: *grammates* seems to be a contemptuous diminutive for grammar, as grammatist is for grammarian.
    " Mew!—*absurd!*" which occurs just above, is a term of the schools, and is used when false conclusions are illogically deduced from the opponent's premises. See *Mass.* vol. iii. p. 280, where many [?] examples of the expression may be found.

Org.   I am, gay creature,
With pardon of your deities, a mushroom
On whom the dew of heaven drops now and then;
The sun shines on me too, I thank his beams!
Sometime[15] I feel their warmth; and eat and sleep.
  Pro. Does Tecnicus read to thee?
  Org.   Yes, forsooth,
He is my master surely; yonder door
Opens upon his study.
  Pro.   Happy creatures!
Such people toil not, sweet, in heats of state,
Nor sink in thaws of greatness: their affections
Keep order with the limits of their modesty;
Their love is love of virtue.—What's thy name?
  Org. Aplotes, sumptuous master, a poor wretch.
  Euph. Dost thou want anything?
  Org.   Books, Venus, books.
  Pro. Lady, a new conceit comes in my thought,
And most available for both our comforts.
  Euph. My lord,—
  Pro.   Whiles I endeavour to deserve
Your father's blessing to our loves, this scholar
May daily at some certain hours attend,
What notice I can write of my success,
Here in this grove, and give it to your hands;
The like from you to me: so can we never,
Barr'd of our mutual speech, want sure intelligence,
And thus our hearts may talk when our tongues cannot.
  Euph. Occasion is most favourable; use it.
  Pro. Aplotes, wilt thou wait us twice a-day,
At nine i' the morning and at four at night,
Here in this bower, to convey such letters
As each shall send to other? Do it willingly,

---

[15] *Sometime*] i.e. Sometimes (see my *Glossary to Shakespeare*).—
Gifford printed "Sometimes." D.

Safely, and secretly, and I will furnish
Thy study, or what else thou canst desire.
　Org. Jove, make me thankful, thankful, I beseech thee,
Propitious Jove! I will prove sure and trusty:
You will not fail me books?
　Pro.　　　　　　　　Nor aught besides
Thy heart can wish. This lady's name's Euphranea,
Mine Prophilus.
　Org.　　　I have a pretty memory;
It must prove my best friend. I will not miss
One minute of the hours appointed.
　Pro.　　　　　　　　Write
The books thou wouldst have bought thee in a note,
Or take thyself some money.
　Org.　　　　　　No, no money;
Money to scholars is a spirit invisible,
We dare not finger it: or books, or nothing.
　Pro. Books of what sort thou wilt: do not forget
Our names.
　Org.　　I warrant ye, I warrant ye.
　Pro. Smile, Hymen, on the growth of our desires;
We'll feed thy torches with eternal fires!
　　　　　　　　　[*Exeunt Pro. and Euph.*
　Org. Put out thy torches, Hymen, or their light
Shall meet a darkness of eternal night!
Inspire me, Mercury, with swift deceits.
Ingenious Fate has leapt into mine arms,
Beyond the compass of my brain.[16] Mortality
Creeps on the dung of earth, and cannot reach
The riddles which are purpos'd by the gods.
Great arts best write themselves in their own stories;
They die too basely who outlive their glories. [*Exit.*

　　　[16] *brain.*] Gifford printed "brains." D.

ACT II.

SCENE I. *A room in* BASSANES' *house.*

Enter BASSANES *and* PHULAS.

Bass. I'll have that window next the street damm'd-
up;
It gives too full a prospect to temptation,
And courts a gazer's glances: there's a lust
Committed by the eye, that sweats and travails,
Plots, wakes, contrives, till the deformèd bear-whelp,
Adultery, be lick'd into the act,
The very act: that light shall be damm'd-up;
D'ye hear, sir?
    Phu.   I do hear, my lord; a mason
Shall be provided suddenly.
    Bass.   Some rogue,
Some rogue of your confederacy,—factor
For slaves and strumpets!—to convey close packets
From this spruce springal and the t'other youngster;
That gaudy earwig, or my lord your patron,
Whose pensioner you are.—I'll tear thy throat out,
Son of a cat, ill-looking hound's-head, rip-up
Thy ulcerous maw, if I but scent a paper,
A scroll, but half as big as what can cover
A wart upon thy nose, a spot, a pimple,
Directed to my lady; it may prove
A mystical preparative to lewdness.
    Phu. Care shall be had: I will turn every thread
About me to an eye.—[*Aside*] Here's a sweet life!
    Bass. The city housewives, cunning in the traffic
Of chamber merchandise, set all at price
By wholesale; yet they wipe their mouths and simper,

Cull,[1] kiss, and cry "sweetheart," and stroke the head
Which they have branch'd; and all is well again!
Dull clods of dirt, who dare not feel the rubs
Stuck on the forehead.[2]
   Phu.   'Tis a villanous world;
One cannot hold his own in't.
   Bass.   Dames at court,
Who flaunt in riots, run another bias:
Their pleasure heaves the patient ass that suffers
Up on the stilts of office, titles, incomes;
Promotion justifies the shame, and sues for't.
Poor honour, thou art stabb'd, and bleed'st to death
By such unlawful hire! The country mistress
Is yet more wary, and in blushes hides
Whatever trespass draws her troth to guilt.
But all are false: on this truth I am bold,
No woman but can fall, and doth, or would.—
Now for the newest news about the city;
What blab the voices, sirrah?
   Phu.   O, my lord,
The rarest, quaintest, strangest, tickling news
That ever—
   Bass.   Hey-day! up and ride me, rascal!
What is't?
   Phu.   Forsooth, they say the king has mew'd
All his gray beard,[3] instead of which is budded
Another of a pure carnation colour,
Speckled with green and russet.

[1] *Cull,*] i.e. Embrace. This form of the word is occasionally found,—in Herrick, for instance.—Gifford printed the more usual one, "Coll." D.

[2] *the forehead.*] The 4to has "*the* fore-heads."—Qy. "*their* fore-heads"? D.

[3]   *the king has* mew'd
   All his gray beard,] This is falconers' language, and common to all our old writers. To *mew,* or rather *mue,* is to moult, to shed the feathers.

Bass.   Ignorant block!
Phu. Yes, truly; and 'tis talk'd about the streets,
That since Lord Ithocles came home, the lions
Never left roaring, at which noise the bears
Have danc'd[4] their very hearts out.
Bass.   Dance out thine too.
Phu. Besides, Lord Orgilus is fled to Athens
Upon a fiery dragon, and 'tis thought
He never can return.
Bass.   Grant it, Apollo!
Phu. Moreover, please your lordship, 'tis reported
For certain, that whoever is found jealous
Without apparent proof that's wife is wanton
Shall be divorc'd: but this is but she-news;
I had it from a midwife. I have more yet.
Bass. Antic, no more! idiots and stupid fools
Grate my calamities. Why to be fair
Should yield presumption of a faulty soul—
Look to the doors.
Phu.   The horn of plenty crest him!
                                        [*Aside, and exit.*
Bass. Swarms of confusion huddle in my thoughts
In rare distemper.—Beauty! O, it is
An unmatch'd blessing or a horrid curse.
She comes, she comes! so shoots the morning forth,
Spangled with pearls[5] of transparent dew.—
The way to poverty is to be rich,
As I in her am wealthy; but for her,
In all contents a bankrupt.

---

[4]   *the* lions
Never left roaring, at which noise the bears
Have danc'd, &c.] This must indeed have been "tickling news." The poet, however, was thinking of a spot much nearer home than Sparta.

[5] Spangled with *pearls*] See [note] p. 18.

Enter PENTHEA *and* GRAUSIS.

         Lov'd Penthea!
How fares my heart's best joy?
 Grau.   In sooth, not well,
She is so over-sad.
 Bass.   Leave chattering, magpie.—
Thy brother is return'd, sweet, safe, and honour'd
With a triumphant victory; thou shalt visit him:
We will to court, where, if it be thy pleasure,
Thou shalt appear in such a ravishing lustre
Of jewels above value, that the dames
Who brave it there, in rage to be outshin'd,
Shall hide them in their closets, and unseen
Fret in their tears; whiles every wondering eye
Shall crave none other brightness but thy presence.
Choose thine own recreations; be a queen
Of what delights thou fanciest best, what company,
What place, what times; do anything, do all things
Youth can command, so thou wilt chase these clouds
From the pure firmament of thy fair looks.
 Grau. Now 'tis well said, my lord.—What, lady!
  laugh,
Be merry; time is precious.
 Bass. [*aside*]   Furies whip thee!
 Pen. Alas, my lord, this language to your hand-
  maid
Sounds as would music to the deaf; I need
No braveries nor cost of art to draw
The whiteness of my name into offence:
Let such, if any such there are, who covet
A curiosity of admiration,
By laying-out their plenty to full view,
Appear in gaudy outsides; my attires
Shall suit the inward fashion of my mind;

From which, if your opinion, nobly plac'd,
Change not the livery your words bestow,
My fortunes with my hopes are at the highest.
 Bass. This house, methinks, stands somewhat too
   much inward,
It is too melancholy; we'll remove
Nearer the court: or what thinks my Penthea
Of the delightful island we command?
Rule me as thou canst wish.
 Pen.   I am no mistress:
Whither you please, I must attend; all ways
Are alike pleasant to me.
 Grau.   Island! prison;
A prison is as gaysome: we'll no islands;
Marry, out upon 'em! whom shall we see there?
Sea-gulls, and porpoises, and water-rats,
And crabs, and mews, and dog-fish; goodly gear
For a young lady's dealing,—or an old one's!
On no terms islands; I'll be stew'd first.
 Bass. [*aside to Grau.*]   Grausis,
You are a juggling bawd.—This sadness, sweetest,
Becomes not youthful blood.—[*Aside to Grau.*] I'll
   have you pounded.—
For my sake put on a more cheerful mirth;
Thou'lt mar thy cheeks, and make me old in griefs.—
[*Aside to Grau.*] Damnable bitch-fox!
 Grau.   I am thick of hearing,
Still, when the wind blows southerly.—What think ye,
If your fresh lady breed young bones, my lord!
Would not a chopping boy d'ye good at heart?
But, as you said—
 Bass. [*aside to Grau.*] I'll spit thee on a stake,
Or chop thee into collops!
 Grau.   Pray, speak louder.
Sure, sure the wind blows south still.

Pen. Thou prat'st madly.
Bass. 'Tis very hot; I sweat extremely.

Re-enter PHULAS.
Now?
Phu. A herd of lords, sir.
Bass. Ha!
Phu. A flock of ladies.
Bass. Where?
Phu. Shoals of horses.
Bass. Peasant, how?
Phu. Caroches
In drifts; th' one enter, th' other stand without, sir:
And now I vanish. [*Exit.*

Enter PROPHILUS, HEMOPHIL, GRONEAS, CHRISTALLA,
and PHILEMA.

Pro. Noble Bassanes!
Bass. Most welcome, Prophilus; ladies, gentlemen,
To all my heart is open; you all honour me,—
[*Aside*] A tympany swells in my head already,—
Honour me bountifully.—[*Aside*] How they flutter,
Wagtails and jays together!
Pro. From your brother,
By virtue of your love to him, I require
Your instant presence, fairest.
Pen. He is well, sir?
Pro. The gods preserve him ever! Yet, dear beauty,
I find some alteration in him lately,
Since his return to Sparta.—My good lord,
I pray, use no delay.
Bass. We had not needed
An invitation, if his sister's health
Had not fall'n into question.—Haste, Penthea,

Slack not a minute.—Lead the way, good Prophilus;
I'll follow step by step.
   Pro.   Your arm, fair madam.
                   [*Exeunt all but Bass. and Grau.*
   Bass. One word with your old bawdship : th' hadst
      been better
Rail'd at the saints thou worshipp'st[6] than have thwarted
My will : I'll use thee cursedly.
   Grau.   You dote,
You are beside yourself. A politician
In jealousy? no, you're too gross, too vulgar.
Pish, teach not me my trade; I know my cue :
My crossing you sinks me into her trust,
By which I shall know all; my trade's a sure one.
   Bass. Forgive me, Grausis, 'twas consideration
I relish'd not; but have a care now.
   Grau.   Fear not,
I am no new-come-to't.
   Bass.   Thy life's upon it,
And so is mine. My agonies are infinite.   [*Exeunt.*

SCENE II. *The palace.* ITHOCLES' *apartment.*

Enter ITHOCLES.

   Ith. Ambition! 'tis of viper's breed; it gnaws
A passage through the womb that gave it motion.
Ambition, like a seelèd dove, mounts upward,

---

   6 *th' hadst been better*] Altered by Gifford to "thou hadst better."
("*Thou hadst been better* have been born a dog," &c. Shakespeare's
Othello, act iii. sc. 3.) D.
   Rail'd at the saints *thou worshipp'st,* &c.] So I venture to give
the text. The 4to reads "the *sinnes* thou worshipp'st;" which is
manifestly wrong, because pure nonsense. If I am asked where
Grausis found her *saints,* I can only reply, where Phulas found his
dancing bears.

Higher and higher still,[7] to perch on clouds,
But tumbles headlong down with heavier ruin.
So squibs and crackers fly into the air,
Then, only breaking with a noise, they vanish
In stench and smoke. Morality, applied
To timely practice, keeps the soul in tune,
At whose sweet music all our actions dance :
But this is form['d] of books and school-tradition ;
It physics not the sickness of a mind
Broken with griefs : strong fevers are not eas'd
With counsel, but with best receipts and means;
Means, speedy means and certain ; that's the cure.

Enter ARMOSTES *and* CROTOLON.

Arm. You stick, Lord Crotolon, upon a point
Too nice and too unnecessary ; Prophilus
Is every way desertful. I am confident
Your wisdom is too ripe to need instruction
From your son's tutelage.

Crot.   Yet not so ripe,
My Lord Armostes, that it dares to dote
Upon the painted meat[8] of smooth persuasion,
Which tempts me to a breach of faith.

Ith.   Not yet
Resolv'd, my lord? Why, if your son's consent
Be so available, we'll write to Athens

---

[7] *Ambition, like a* seelèd *dove, mounts upward,*
Higher and higher still, &c.] To *seel* is to blind by sewing-up the eyelids. There is a similar allusion to that in the text in the *Arcadia;* "Now she brought them to see a *seeled dove,* who the blinder she was the higher she strove to reach." It is told in the *Gentleman's Recreation* that this wanton piece of cruelty is sometimes resorted to for *sport!* The poor dove, in the agonies of pain, soars, like the lark, as soon as dismissed from the hand, almost perpendicularly, and continues mounting till strength and life are totally exhausted, when she drops at the feet of her inhuman persecutors.

[8] *Upon the painted* meat] So the old copy: the author's word was not improbably "painted *bait.*"

For his repair to Sparta: the king's hand
Will join with our desires; he has been mov'd to't.
  Arm. Yes, and the king himself impórtun'd Cro-
    tolon
For a dispatch.
  Crot.   Kings may command; their wills
Are laws not to be question'd.
  Ith.   By this marriage
You knit an union so devout, so hearty,
Between your loves to me and mine to yours,
As if mine own blood had an interest in it;
For Prophilus is mine, and I am his.
  Crot. My lord, my lord!—
  Ith.   What, good sir? speak your thought.
  Crot. Had this sincerity been real once,
My Orgilus had not been now unwiv'd,
Nor your lost sister buried in a bride-bed:
Your uncle here, Armostes, knows this truth;
For had your father Thrasus liv'd,—but peace
Dwell in his grave! I've done.
  Arm.   You're bold and bitter.
  Ith. [*aside*] He presses home the injury; it smarts.—
No reprehensions, uncle; I deserve 'em.
Yet, gentle sir, consider what the heat
Of an unsteady youth, a giddy brain,
Green indiscretion, flattery of greatness,
Rawness of judgment, wilfulness in folly,
Thoughts vagrant as the wind and as uncertain,
Might lead a boy in years to:—'twas a fault,
A capital fault; for then I could not dive
Into the secrets of commanding love;
Since when experience, by th' extremes[9] in others,
Hath forc'd me to collect—and, trust me, Crotolon,

---

[9] *th' extremes*] The 4to has "the extremities." D.

I will redeem those wrongs with any service
Your satisfaction can require for current.
    Arm. Th' acknowledgment[10] is satisfaction:
What would you more?
    Crot.   I'm conquer'd : if Euphranea
Herself admit the motion, let it be so ;
I doubt not my son's liking.
    Ith.   Use my fortunes,
Life, power, sword, and heart,—all are your own.
    Arm. The princess, with your sister.

Enter CALANTHA, PENTHEA, EUPHRANEA, CHRISTALLA, PHILEMA, GRAUSIS, BASSANES, *and* PROPHILUS.

    Cal.   I present ye
A stranger here in court, my lord; for did not
Desire of seeing you draw her abroad,
We had not been made happy in her company.
    Ith. You are a gracious princess.—Sister, wedlock
Holds too severe a passion in your nature,
Which can engross all duty to your husband,
Without attendance on so dear a mistress.—
[*To Bass.*] 'Tis not my brother's pleasure, I presume,
T' immure her in a chamber.
    Bass.   'Tis her will ;
She governs her own hours.   Noble Ithocles,
We thank the gods for your success and welfare :
Our lady has of late been indispos'd,
Else we had waited on you with the first.
    Ith. How does Penthea now?
    Pen.   You best know, brother,
From whom my health and comforts are deriv'd.
    Bass. [*aside*] I like the answer well ; 'tis sad and
        modest.
There may be tricks yet, tricks.—Have an eye, Grausis!

---

[10] *Th' acknowledgment*] The 4to has " thy *acknowledgement.*" D.

Cal. Now, Crotolon, the suit we join'd in must not
Fall by too long demur.
  Crot.   'Tis granted, princess,
For my part.
  Arm.   With condition, that his son
Favour the contract.
  Cal.   Such delay is easy.—
The joys of marriage make thee, Prophilus,
A proud deserver of Euphranea's love,
And her of thy desert!
  Pro.   Most sweetly gracious!
  Bass. The joys of marriage are the heaven on earth,
Life's paradise, great princess, the soul's quiet,
Sinews of concord, earthly immortality,
Eternity of pleasures;—no restoratives
Like to a constant woman!—[*Aside*] But where is she?
'Twould puzzle all the gods but to create
Such a new monster.—I can speak by proof,
For I rest in Elysium; 'tis my happiness.
  Crot. Euphranea, how are you resolv'd, speak freely,
In your affections to this gentleman?
  Euph. Nor more nor less than as his love assures
    me;
Which—if your liking with my brother's warrants—
I cannot but approve in all points worthy.
  Crot. So, so!—[*To Pro.*] I know your answer.
  Ith.   'T had been pity
To sunder hearts so equally consented.

Enter HEMOPHIL.

  Hem. The king, Lord Ithocles, commands your
    presence;—
And, fairest princess, yours.
  Cal.   We will attend him.

Enter GRONEAS.

Gron. Where are the lords? all must unto the king
Without delay : the Prince of Argos—
Cal.   Well, sir?
Gron. Is coming to the court, sweet lady.
Cal.   How!
The Prince of Argos?
Gron.   'Twas my fortune, madam,
T' enjoy the honour of these happy tidings.
Ith. Penthea!—
Pen.   Brother?
Ith.   Let me an hour hence
Meet you alone within the palace-grove;
I have some secret with you.—Prithee, friend,
Conduct her thither, and have special care
The walks be clear'd of any to disturb us.
Pro. I shall.
Bass. [*aside*] How's that?
Ith.   Alone, pray be alone.—
I am your creature, princess.—On, my lords!
                                    [*Exeunt all but Bass.*
Bass. Alone! alone! what means that word *alone?*
Why might not I be there?—hum!—he's her brother.
Brothers and sisters are but flesh and blood,
And this same whoreson court-ease is temptation
To a rebellion in the veins;—besides,
His fine friend Prophilus must be her guardian :
Why may not he dispatch a business nimbly
Before the other come?—or—pandering, pandering
For one another,—be't to sister, mother,
Wife, cousin, anything,—'mongst youths of mettle
Is in request; it is so—stubborn fate!
But if I be a cuckold, and can know it,
I will be fell, and fell.

Re-enter GRONEAS.

Gron. My lord, you're call'd for.
Bass. Most heartily I thank ye. Where's my wife, pray?
Gron. Retir'd amongst the ladies.
Bass. Still I thank ye.
There's an old waiter with her; saw you her too?
Gron. She sits i' th' presence-lobby fast asleep, sir.
Bass. Asleep! asleep,[11] sir!
Gron. Is your lordship troubled?
You will not to the king?
Bass. Your humblest vassal.
Gron. Your servant, my good lord.
Bass. I wait your footsteps.
[*Exeunt.*

SCENE III. *The gardens of the palace. A grove.*

Enter PROPHILUS *and* PENTHEA.

Pro. In this walk, lady, will your brother find you:
And, with your favour, give me leave a little
To work a preparation. In his fashion
I have observ'd of late some kind of slackness
To such alacrity as nature [once]
And custom took delight in; sadness grows
Upon his recreations, which he hoards
In such a willing silence, that to question
The grounds will argue [little] skill in friendship,
And less good manners.
Pen. Sir, I'm not inquisitive
Of secrecies without an invitation.
Pro. With pardon, lady, not a syllable

[11] *asleep,*] The 4to has "sleepe." D.

SCENE III.   THE BROKEN HEART.   249

Of mine implies so rude a sense ; the drift—

Enter ORGILUS, *disguised as before.*

[*To Org.*] Do thy best
To make this lady merry for an hour.
 Org. Your will shall be a law, sir. [*Exit Pro.*
 Pen.   Prithee, leave me ;
I have some private thoughts I would account with ;
Use thou thine own.
 Org.   Speak on, fair nymph ; our souls
Can dance as well to music of the spheres
As any's who have feasted with the gods.
 Pen. Your school-terms are too troublesome.
 Org.   What heaven
Refines mortality from dross of earth
But such as uncompounded beauty hallows
With glorified perfection ?
 Pen.   Set thy wits
In a less wild proportion.
 Org.   Time can never
On the white table of unguilty faith
Write counterfeit dishonour ; turn those eyes,
The arrows of pure love, upon that fire,
Which once rose to a flame, perfum'd with vows
As sweetly scented as the incense smoking
On Vesta's altars, * * * * * *12

---

  12   *as the incense smoking*
  On Vesta's altars, * * * * * * &c.] It is greatly to be regretted that this apparently fine passage should have been so irreparably mutilated at the press. I have endeavoured to remedy the transpositions ; but who can hope to restore what was dropped ? It seems to me that Ford calls virgin tears *the holiest odours;* and the expression is beautiful and every way worthy of him. In the old copy, however, this, and indeed every other merit, is lost. It reads,

    '' as the incense smoking
   The holiest artars, virgin tears (like
   On Vesta's odours) sprinkled dews to feed 'em,
   And to increase," &c.

* * * the holiest odours, virgins' tears,
* * * * sprinkled, like dews, to feed them
And to increase their fervour.
  Pen.   Be not frantic.
  Org. All pleasures are but mere imagination,
Feeding the hungry appetite with steam
And sight of banquet, whilst the body pines,
Not relishing the real taste of food:
Such is the leanness of a heart divided
From intercourse of troth-contracted loves;
No horror should deface that precious figure
Seal'd with the lively stamp of equal souls.
  Pen. Away! some Fury hath bewitch'd thy tongue:
The breath of ignorance, that flies from thence,
Ripens a knowledge in me of afflictions
Above all sufferance.—Thing of talk, begone!
Begone, without reply!
  Org.   Be just, Penthea,
In thy commands; when thou send'st forth a doom
Of banishment, know first on whom it lights.
Thus I take off the shroud, in which my cares
Are folded up from view of common eyes.
            [*Throws off his scholar's dress.*
What is thy sentence next?
  Pen.   Rash man! thou lay'st
A blemish on mine honour, with the hazard
Of thy too-desperate life: yet I profess,
By all the laws of ceremonious wedlock,
I have not given admittance to one thought
Of female change since cruelty enforc'd
Divorce betwixt my body and my heart.
Why would you fall from goodness thus?
  Org.   O, rather
Examine me, how I could live to say
I have been much, much wrong'd. 'Tis for thy sake

I put on this imposture : dear Penthea,
If thy soft bosom be not turn'd to marble,
Thou'lt pity our calamities ; my interest
Confirms me thou art mine still.
  Pen.   Lend your hand ;
With both of mine I clasp it thus, thus kiss it,
Thus kneel before ye.   [*Pen. kneels.*
  Org. You instruct my duty. [*Org. kneels.*
  Pen. We may stand up. [*They rise.*] Have you aught
    else to urge
Of new demand? as for the old, forget it ;
'Tis buried in an everlasting silence,
And shall be, shall be ever : what more would ye ?
  Org. I would possess my wife ; the equity
Of very reason bids me.
  Pen.   Is that all ?
  Org. Why, 'tis the all of me, myself.
  Pen.   Remove
Your steps some distance from me :—at this space
A few words I dare change ; but first put on
Your borrow'd shape.[13]
  Org.   You are obey'd ; 'tis done.
       [*He resumes his disguise.*
  Pen. How, Orgilus, by promise I was thine
The heavens do witness ; they can witness too
A rape done on my truth : how I do love thee
Yet, Orgilus, and yet, must best appear
In tendering thy freedom ; for I find
The constant preservation of thy merit,
By thy not daring to attempt my fame
With injury of any loose conceit,

---

[13]   *but first put on*
 Your borrow'd shape.] This, as I have elsewhere observed, is the green-room term for a dress of disguise. In the opening of the next act, Orgilus, who had resumed his usual habit, is said to appear in his own *shape*.

Which might give deeper wounds to discontents.
Continue this fair race : then, though I cannot
Add to thy comfort, yet I shall more often
Remember from what fortune I am fall'n,
And pity mine own ruin.—Live, live happy,—
Happy in thy next choice, that thou mayst people
This barren age with virtues in thy issue!
And O, when thou art married, think on me
With mercy, not contempt! I hope thy wife,
Hearing my story, will not scorn my fall.—
Now let us part.

Org.   Part! yet advise thee better :
Penthea is the wife to Orgilus,
And ever shall be.

Pen.   Never shall nor will.

Org. How!

Pen.   Hear me; in a word I'll tell thee why.
The virgin-dowry which my birth bestow'd
Is ravish'd by another ; my true love
Abhors to think that Orgilus deserv'd
No better favours than a second bed.

Org. I must-not take this reason.

Pen.   To confirm it ;
Should I outlive my bondage, let me meet
Another worse than this and less desir'd,
If, of all men[14] alive, thou shouldst but touch
My lip or hand again!

Org.   Penthea, now
I tell ye, you grow wanton in my sufferance :
Come, sweet, thou'rt mine.

Pen.   Uncivil sir, forbear!
Or I can turn affection into vengeance ;
Your reputation, if you value any,

---

[14] *all men*] The 4to has "*all* the *men.*" D.

Lies bleeding at my feet. Unworthy man,
If ever henceforth thou appear in language,
Message, or letter, to betray my frailty,
I'll call thy former protestations lust,
And curse my stars for forfeit of my judgment.
Go thou, fit only for disguise, and walks,
To hide thy shame: this once I spare thy life.
I laugh at mine own confidence; my sorrows
By thee are made inferior to my fortunes.
If ever thou didst harbour worthy love,
Dare not to answer. My good Genius guide me,
That I may never see thee more!—Go from me!

Org. I'll[15] tear my veil of politic French off,
And stand up like a man resolv'd to do:
Action, not words, shall show me.—O Penthea!
[*Exit.*

Pen. He sigh'd my name, sure, as he parted from
me:
I fear I was too rough. Alas, poor gentleman!
He look'd not like the ruins of his youth,
But like the ruins of those ruins. Honour,
How much we fight with weakness to preserve thee!
[*Walks aside.*

Enter BASSANES *and* GRAUSIS.

Bass. Fie on thee! damn thee, rotten maggot, damn
thee!
Sleep? sleep at court? and now? Aches,[16] convulsions,
Imposthumes, rheums, gouts, palsies, clog thy bones
A dozen years more yet!

Grau.   Now you're in humours.

---

[15] *I'll*] The 4to has "I'e." D.

[16] *Aches,*] A dissyllable,—the word being pronounced in our author's days, and long after, "*aitches:*" see my *Gloss. to Shakespeare.* D.

Bass. She's by herself, there's hope of that; she's
    sad too;
She's in strong contemplation; yes, and fix'd:
The signs are wholesome.
    Grau.   Very wholesome, truly.
    Bass. Hold your chops, nightmare!—Lady, come;
    your brother
Is carried to his closet; you must thither.
    Pen. Not well, my lord?
    Bass.   A sudden fit; 'twill off;
Some surfeit or disorder.—How dost, dearest?
    Pen. Your news is none o' th' best.

                Re-enter PROPHILUS.

    Pro.   The chief of men,
The excellentest Ithocles, desires
Your presence, madam.
    Bass.   We are hasting to him.
    Pen. In vain we labour in this course of life
To piece our journey out at length, or crave
Respite of breath; our home is in the grave.
    Bass. Perfect philosophy!
    Pen.   Then let us care[17]
To live so, that our reckonings may fall even
When we're to make account.
    Pro.   He cannot fear
Who builds on noble grounds: sickness or pain
Is the deserver's exercise; and such
Your virtuous brother to the world is known.
Speak comfort to him, lady; be all gentle:

---

[17] Pen. *Then let us care*, &c.] The old copy gives this to Bassanes; but it is evidently the continuation of Penthea's ideas in the former speech, and to her therefore I have restored it. The answer of Prophilus, which is directed to Penthea, proves the necessity of the alteration.

Stars fall but in the grossness of our sight;
A good man dying, th' earth doth lose a light.
[*Exeunt.*

ACT III.

SCENE I. *The study of* TECNICUS.

Enter TECNICUS, *and* ORGILUS *in his usual dress.*

Tec. Be well advis'd; let not a resolution
Of giddy rashness choke the breath of reason.
   Org. It shall not, most sage master.
   Tec.   I am jealous;[1]
For if the borrow'd shape so late put on
Inferr'd a consequence, we must conclude
Some violent design of sudden nature
Hath shook that shadow off, to fly upon
A new-hatch'd execution. Orgilus,
Take heed thou hast not, under our integrity,
Shrouded unlawful plots; our mortal eyes
Pierce not the secrets of your heart,[2] the gods
Are only privy to them.
   Org.   Learnèd Tecnicus,
Such doubts are causeless; and, to clear the truth
From misconceit, the present state commands me.
The Prince of Argos comes himself in person
In quest of great Calantha for his bride,
Our kingdom's heir; besides, mine only sister,
Euphranea, is dispos'd to Prophilus;
Lastly, the king is sending letters for me

---

[1] *I am* jealous;] i.e. I am *fearful, suspicious*, of it: a Scotticism; and probably once common to most of our remote provinces.
[2] *heart,*] The 4to has "hearts." D.

To Athens, for my quick repair to court:
Please to accept these reasons.
　Tec.　　　　　　　Just ones, Orgilus,
Not to be contradicted: yet beware
Of an unsure foundation; no fair colours
Can fortify a building faintly jointed.
I have observ'd a growth in thy aspéct
Of dangerous extent, sudden, and—look to't—
I might add, certain—
　Org.　　　　　　　My aspéct! could art
Run through mine inmost thoughts, it should not sift
An inclination there more than what suited
With justice of mine honour.
　Tec.　　　　　　　I believe it.
But know then, Orgilus, what honour is:
Honour consists not in a bare opinion
By doing any act that feeds content,
Brave in appearance, 'cause we think it brave;
Such honour comes by accident, not nature,
Proceeding from the vices of our passion,
Which makes our reason drunk: but real honour
Is the reward of virtue, and acquir'd
By justice, or by valour which for basis
Hath justice to uphold it.　He then fails
In honour, who for lucre or revenge[3]
Commits thefts, murders,[4] treasons, and adulteries,
With suchlike, by intrenching on just laws,
Whose sovereignty is best preserv'd by justice.
Thus, as you see how honour must be grounded
On knowledge, not opinion,—for opinion
Relies on probability and accident,
But knowledge on necessity and truth,—

---

[3] *who for lucre or revenge*] The 4to has "for lucre *of* revenge." The context shows that this can scarcely be the genuine reading.
[4] *murders*,] Gifford printed "murther." D.

SCENE I.   THE BROKEN HEART.   257

I leave thee to the fit consideration
Of what becomes the grace of real honour,
Wishing success to all thy virtuous meanings.
   Org. The gods increase thy wisdom, reverend
      oracle,
And in thy precepts make me ever thrifty!
   Tec. I thank thy wish.   [*Exit Org.*
                  Much mystery of fate
Lies hid·in that man's fortunes; curiosity
May lead his actions into rare attempts :—
But let the gods be moderators still;
No human power can prevent their will.

         Enter ARMOSTES *with a casket.*
From whence come ye?
   Arm.   From King Amyclas,—pardon
My interruption of your studies.—Here,
In this seal'd box, he sends a treasure [to you],
Dear to him as his crown : he prays your gravity,
You would examine, ponder, sift, and bolt
The pith and circumstance of every tittle
The scroll within contains.
   Tec.   What is't, Armostes?
   Arm. It is the health of Sparta, the king's life,
Sinews and safety of the commonwealth;
The sum of what the oracle deliver'd
When last he visited the prophetic temple
At Delphos: what his reasons are, for which,
After so long a silence, he requires
You[r] counsel now, grave man, his majesty
Will soon himself acquaint you with.
   Tec.   Apollo [*He takes the casket.*
Inspire my intellect!—The Prince of Argos
Is entertain'd?
   Arm.   He is; and has demanded
   VOL. I.   S

Our princess for his wife; which I conceive
One special cause the king impórtunes you
For resolution of the oracle.

Tec. My duty to the king, good peace to Sparta,
And fair day to Armostes!

Arm. Like to Tecnicus! [*Exeunt.*

SCENE II. *The palace.* ITHOCLES' *apartment.*

Soft music. A song within, during which PROPHILUS, BASSANES,
PENTHEA, and GRAUSIS *pass over the stage.* BASSANES *and*
GRAUSIS *re-enter softly, and listen in different places.*

SONG.

Can you paint a thought? or number
Every fancy in a slumber?
Can you count soft minutes roving
From a dial's point by moving?
Can you grasp a sigh? or, lastly,
Rob a virgin's honour chastly?
    No, O, no! yet you may
      Sooner do both that and this,
      This and that, and never miss,
    Than by any praise display
      Beauty's beauty; such a glory,
      As beyond all fate, all story,
        All arms, all arts,
        All loves, all hearts,
      Greater than those or they,
      Do, shall, and must obey.

Bass. All silent, calm, secure.—Grausis, no creaking?
No noise? dost [thou] hear nothing?

Grau.   Not a mouse,
Or whisper of the wind.
Bass.   The floor is matted;
The bedposts sure are steel or marble.—Soldiers
Should not affect, methinks, strains so effeminate:
Sounds of such delicacy are but fawnings
Upon the sloth of luxury, they heighten
Cinders of covert lust up to a flame.
    Grau. What do you mean, my lord?—speak low;
        that gabbling
Of yours will but undo us.
    Bass.   Chamber-combats
Are felt, not heard.
    Pro. [*within*]   He wakes.
    Bass.   What's that?
    Ith. [*within*]   Who's there?
Sister?—All quit the room else.
    Bass.   'Tis consented!

        Re-enter PROPHILUS.

    Pro. Lord Bassanes, your brother would be private,
We must forbear; his sleep hath newly left him.
Please ye withdraw.
    Bass.   By any means; 'tis fit.
    Pro. Pray, gentlewoman, walk too.
    Grau.   Yes, I will, sir. [*Exeunt.*

The Scene opens; ITHOCLES *is discovered in a chair,*
    and PENTHEA *beside him.*

    Ith. Sit nearer, sister, to me; nearer yet:
We had one father, in one womb took life,
Were brought up twins together, yet have liv'd
At distance, like two strangers: I could wish
That the first pillow whereon I was cradled
Had prov'd to me a grave.

Pen. You had been happy:
Then had you never known that sin of life
Which blots all following glories with a vengeance,
For forfeiting the last will of the dead,
From whom you had your being.
    Ith. Sad Penthea,
Thou canst not be too cruel; my rash spleen
Hath with a violent hand pluck'd from thy bosom
A love-blest[5] heart, to grind it into dust;
For which mine's now a-breaking.
    Pen. Not yet, heaven,
I do beseech thee! first let some wild fires
Scorch, not consume it! may the heat be cherish'd
With desires infinite, but hopes impossible!
    Ith. Wrong'd soul, thy prayers are heard.
    Pen. Here, lo, I breathe,
A miserable creature, led to ruin
By an unnatural brother!
    Ith. I consume
In languishing affections for that trespass;
Yet cannot die.
    Pen. The handmaid to the wages
Of country toil drinks the untroubled streams[6]
With leaping kids and with the bleating lambs,
And so allays her thirst secure; whiles I
Quench my hot sighs with fleetings of my tears.
    Ith. The labourer doth eat his coarsest bread,
Earn'd with his sweat, and lies[7] him down to sleep;

---

[5] *love-blest*] The 4to has "*louer-blest.*" D.
[6]   *The handmaid to the wages*
Of country toil drinks the untroubled *streams*] There is a slight confusion in the old copy, arising from two of the words being shuffled out of their place; it reads,

"the handmaid to the wages
The untroubled of country toil, drinks streams."

[7] *lies*] Gifford printed "lays." D.

While[8] every bit I touch turns in digestion
To gall as bitter as Penthea's curse.
Put me to any penance for my tyranny,
And I will call thee merciful.
　　Pen.　　　　　　　　Pray kill me,
Rid me from living with a jealous husband;
Then we will join in friendship, be again
Brother and sister.—Kill me, pray; nay, will ye?
　　Ith. How does thy lord esteem thee?
　　Pen.　　　　　　　　　Such an one
As only you have made me; a faith-breaker,
A spotted whore :—forgive me, I am one—
In act,[9] not in desires, the gods must witness.
　　Ith. Thou dost belie thy friend.
　　Pen.　　　　　　　I do not, Ithocles;
For she that's wife to Orgilus, and lives
In known adultery with Bassanes,
Is at the best a whore.　Wilt kill me now?
The ashes of our parents will assume
Some dreadful figure, and appear to charge
Thy bloody guilt, that hast betray'd their name
To infamy in this reproachful match.
　　Ith. After my victories abroad, at home
I meet despair; ingratitude of nature
Hath made my actions monstrous : thou shalt stand
A deity, my sister, and be worshipp'd
For thy resolvèd martyrdom; wrong'd maids
And married wives shall to thy hallow'd shrine
Offer their orisons, and sacrifice
Pure turtles, crown'd with myrtle; if thy pity
Unto a yielding brother's pressure lend
One finger but to ease it.
　　Pen.　　　　　　O, no more!

[8] *While*] The 4to has "Which." D.
[9] *act,*] The 4to has "art." D.

Ith. Death waits to waft me to the Stygian banks,
And free me from this chaos of my bondage;
And[9] till thou wilt forgive, I must endure.
   Pen. Who is the saint you serve?
   Ith.   Friendship, or [nearness]
Of birth[10] to any but my sister, durst not
Have mov'd that question; 'tis a secret, sister,
I dare not murmur to myself.
   Pen.   Let me,
By your new protestations I conjure ye,
Partake her name.
   Ith.   Her name?—'tis—'tis—I dare not.
   Pen. All your respects are forg'd.
   Ith.   They are not.—Peace!
Calantha is—the princess[11]—the king's daughter—
Sole heir of Sparta.—Me, most miserable!
Do I now love thee? for my injuries
Revenge thyself with bravery, and gossip
My treasons to the king's ears, do :—Calantha

   [9] *And*] Qy. "But"? D.
   [10]   *Friendship, or [nearness]*
   Of birth, &c.] A word has been dropt here, and I have taken
that which has been suggested, though doubtful of its genuineness;
the pointing too seems defective. Ithocles appears to allude to Prophilus in the first instance. In the next line, for "*as* a secret," I
read, with more confidence, "*'tis* a secret." [In the third line Gifford,
by some mistake, printed "this *question*." D.]
   [11]   *Peace!*
   Calantha is—the princess, &c.] "I have ventured," Mr. Weber
says, "to make an alteration here [viz. "Calantha *'tis:* the princess,"
&c.]. The old copy reads, 'Calantha *is* the princess,' &c., which is
neither unknown to Penthea nor to the reader." Pity that such
sagacity should be thrown away! Penthea had pressed her brother
for the name of his mistress, which, after repeated attempts, he declares he dares not utter: on which she taxes him with want of affection to herself; and he then, with all the delicacy of respectful feeling,
after an injunction of silence, replies, as in the text,
               "Peace!
   Calantha is—the princess—the king's daughter—
   Sole heir of Sparta:"—
(her claims progressively rising in dignity)—to show the hopeless
nature of his love. What now becomes of Mr. Weber's poor vul-
garism—"Calantha *'tis*"?

Knows it not yet, nor Prophilus, my nearest.
 Pen. Suppose you were contracted to her, would it not
Split even your very soul to see her father
Snatch her out of your arms against her will,
And force her on the Prince of Argos?
 Ith.   Trouble not
The fountains of mine eyes with thine own story;
I sweat in blood for't.
 Pen.   We are reconcil'd.
Alas, sir, being children, but two branches
Of one stock, 'tis not fit we should divide:
Have comfort, you may find it.
 Ith.   Yes, in thee;
Only in thee, Penthea mine.
 Pen.   If sorrows
Have not too much dull'd my infected brain,
I'll cheer invention for an active strain.
 Ith. Mad man! why have I wrong'd a maid so excellent!

BASSANES *rushes in with a poniard, followed by* PROPHILUS, GRONEAS, HEMOPHIL, *and* GRAUSIS.

 Bass. I can forbear no longer; more, I will not:
Keep off your hands, or fall upon my point.—
Patience is tir'd; for, like a slow-pac'd ass,
Ye ride my easy nature, and proclaim
My sloth to vengeance a reproach and property.
 Ith. The meaning of this rudeness?
 Pro.   He's distracted.
 Pen. O, my griev'd lord!—
 Gau.   Sweet lady, come not near him;
He holds his perilous weapon in his hand
To prick he cares not whom nor where,—see, see, see!

Bass. My birth is noble: though the popular blast
Of vanity, as giddy as thy youth,
Hath rear'd thy name up to bestride a cloud,
Or progress[12] in the chariot of the sun,
I am no clod of trade, to lackey pride,
Nor, like your slave of expectation, wait
The baudy hinges of your doors, or whistle
For mystical conveyance to your bed-sports.
   Gron. Fine humours! they become him.
   Hem.   How he stares,
Struts, puffs, and sweats! most admirable lunacy!
   Ith. But that I may conceive the spirit of wine
Has took possession of your soberer custom,
I'd say you were unmannerly.
   Pen.   Dear brother!—
   Bass. Unmannerly!—mew, kitling!—smooth formality
Is usher to the rankness of the blood,
But impudence bears up the train. Indeed, sir,
Your fiery mettle, or your springal blaze
Of huge renown, is no sufficient royalty
To print upon my forehead the scorn, "cuckold."
   Ith. His jealousy has[13] robb'd him of his wits;
He talks he knows not what.
   Bass.   Yes, and he knows
To whom he talks; to one that franks his lust
In swine-security[14] of bestial incest.

---

   [12] *progress*] This passage is not without curiosity as tending to prove that some of the words now supposed to be Americanisms were in use among our ancestors, and crossed the Atlantic with them. It is not generally known that Ford's county (Devonshire) supplied a very considerable number of the earlier settlers in the Colonies.

   [13] *has*] Gifford printed "hath." D.

   [14]   *to one that* franks *his lust*
   In swine-security, &c.] In this coarse speech Bassanes alludes to the small enclosures (*franks*, as distinguished from styes) in which

Ith. Ha, devil!
Bass.   I will haloo't; though I blush more
To name the filthiness than thou to act it.
Ith. Monster!   [*Draws his sword.*
Pro.   Sir, by our friendship—
Pen.   By our bloods—
Will you quite both undo us, brother?
Grau.   Out on him!
These are his megrims, firks, and melancholies.
Hem. Well said, old touch-hole.
Gron.   Kick him out at doors.
Pen. With favour, let me speak.—My lord, what slackness
In my obedience hath deserv'd this rage?
Except humility and silent[15] duty
Have drawn on your unquiet, my simplicity
Ne'er studied your vexation.
Bass.   Light of beauty,
Deal not ungently with a desperate wound!
No breach of reason dares make war with her
Whose looks are sovereignty, whose breath is balm:

---

boars were fattened. As these animals were dangerous when full-fed, it was necessary to shut them up alone. The distinction is not always observed by our old dramatists; but in general the extreme of grossness and sensuality is conveyed by the words *franked up*.—It is not easy to comprehend the character of Bassanes as the poet has drawn him; and, in truth, it may almost be doubted whether, when he sat down to write, he had fully embodied in his own mind the *person* he intended to produce. The gloomy discontent of Penthea at her ill-assorted marriage is evidently not calculated to tranquillise the suspicious terrors of her doting husband; and his sudden transitions from the most frantic jealousy to all the impotence of childish fondness, from wanton outrage to whining and nauseous repentance, may not therefore be thought altogether unnatural: but Ford has also represented him as shrewd, sentimental, and even impassioned; at one period with a mind habitually weak and unsound, and at another with a vigorous understanding, broken indeed and disjointed, but occasionally exhibiting in its fragments traits of its original strength.

[15] *silent*] The 4to has "sinlent." D.

O, that I could preserve thee in fruition
As in devotion !
   Pen.   Sir, may every evil
Lock'd in Pandora's box shower, in your presence,
On my unhappy head, if, since you made me
A partner in your bed, I have been faulty
In one unseemly thought against your honour !
   Ith. Purge not his griefs, Penthea.
   Bass.   Yes, say on,
Excellent creature !—[*To Ith.*] Good, be not a hindrance
To peace and praise of virtue.—O, my senses
Are charm'd with sounds celestial !—On, dear, on:
I never gave you one ill word ; say, did I ?
Indeed I did not.
   Pen.   Nor, by Juno's forehead,
Was I e'er guilty of a wanton error.
   Bass. A goddess ! let me kneel.
   Grau.   Alas, kind animal !
   Ith. No ; but for penance.
   Bass.   Noble sir, what is it ?
With gladness I embrace it; yet, pray let not
My rashness teach you to be too unmerciful.
   Ith. When you shall show good proof that manly
       wisdom,
Not oversway'd by passion or opinion,
Knows how to lead [your] judgment, then this lady,
Your wife, my sister, shall return in safety
Home, to be guided by you ; but, till first
I can out of clear evidence approve it,
She shall be my care.
   Bass.   Rip my bosom up,
I'll stand the execution with a constancy;
This torture is insufferable.
   Ith.   .Well, sir,

I dare not trust her to your fury.
  Bass.   But
Penthea says not so.
  Pen.   She needs no tongue
To plead excuse who never purpos'd wrong.
                [*Exit with Ith. and Pro.*
  Hem. Virgin of reverence and antiquity,
Stay you behind.
          [*To Grau. who is following Pen.*
  Gron. The court wants not your diligence.
              [*Exeunt Hem. and Gron.*
  Grau. What will you do, my lord? my lady's gone;
I am denied to follow.
  Bass.   I may see her,
Or speak to her once more?
  Grau.   And feel her too, man;
Be of good cheer, she's your own flesh and bone.
  Bass. Diseases desperate must find cures alike.
She swore she has been true.
  Grau.   True, on my modesty.
  Bass. Let him want truth who credits not her
      vows!
Much wrong I did her, but her brother infinite;
Rumour will voice me the contempt of manhood,
Should I run on thus: some way I must try
To outdo art, and jealousy decry.[16]
                    [*Exeunt.*

---

[16] *To outdo art, and jealousy* decry.] The old copy reads, "To outdo art, and *cry a* jealousy." This is undoubtedly corrupt. I have, I believe, by a slight transposition of the dislocated words, restored the meaning, if not the expression, of the author.

SCENE III. *A room in the palace.*

Flourish. Enter AMYCLAS, NEARCHUS *leading* CALANTHA, AR-
MOSTES, CROTOLON, EUPHRANEA, CHRISTALLA, PHILEMA,
and AMELUS.

Amyc. Cousin of Argos, what the heavens have
    pleas'd,
In their unchanging counsels, to conclude
For both our kingdoms' weal, we must submit to:
Nor can we be unthankful to their bounties,
Who, when we were even creeping to our grave,[16]
Sent us a daughter, in whose birth our hope
Continues of succession. As you are
In title next, being grandchild to our aunt,
So we in heart desire you may sit nearest
Calantha's love; since we have ever vow'd
Not to enforce affection by our will,
But by her own choice to confirm it gladly.

    Near. You speak the nature of a right just father.
I come not hither roughly to demand
My cousin's thraldom, but to free mine own:
Report of great Calantha's beauty, virtue,
Sweetness, and singular perfections, courted
All ears to credit what I find was publish'd
By constant truth; from which, if any service
Of my desert can purchase fair construction,
This lady must command it.

    Cal.   Princely sir,
So well you know how to profess observance,
That you instruct your hearers to become
Practitioners in duty; of which number
I'll study to be chief.

    Near.   Chief, glorious virgin,
In my devotion,[17] as in all men's wonder.

[16] *grave,*] The 4to has "graues;" and so Gifford. D.
[17] *devotion,*] The 4to has "devotions." D.

Amyc. Excellent cousin, we deny no liberty;
Use thine own opportunities.—Armostes,
We must consult with the philosophers;
The business is of weight.
Arm.   Sir, at your pleasure.
Amyc. You told me, Crotolon, your son's return'd
From Athens: wherefore comes he not to court,
As we commanded?
Crot.   He shall soon attend
Your royal will, great sir.
Amyc.   The marriage
Between young Prophilus and Euphranea
Tastes of too much delay.
Crot.   My lord,—
Amyc.   Some pleasures
At celebration of it would give life
To th' entertainment of the prince our kinsman;
Our court wears gravity more than we relish.
Arm. Yet the heavens smile on all your high attempts,
Without a cloud.
Crot.   So may the gods protect us!
Cal. A prince a subject?
Near.   Yes, to beauty's sceptre;
As all hearts kneel, so mine.
Cal.   You are too courtly.

Enter ITHOCLES, ORGILUS, *and* PROPHILUS.

Ith. Your safe return to Sparta is most welcome:
I joy to meet you here, and, as occasion
Shall grant us privacy, will yield you reasons
Why I should covet to deserve the title
Of your respected friend; for, without compliment,
Believe it, Orgilus, 'tis my ambition.

Org. Your lordship may command me, your poor servant.

Ith. [*aside*] So amorously close![18]—so soon!—my heart!

Pro. What sudden change is next?

Ith.   Life to the king!
To whom I here present this noble gentleman,
New come from Athens : royal sir, vouchsafe
Your gracious hand in favour of his merit.
                [*The King gives Org. his hand to kiss.*
Crot. [*aside*] My son preferr'd by Ithocles!

Amyc.   Our bounties
Shall open to thee, Orgilus ; for instance,—
Hark in'thine ear,—if, out of those inventions
Which flow in Athens, thou hast there engross'd
Some rarity of wit,[19] to grace the nuptials
Of thy fair sister, and renown our court
In th' eyes of this young prince, we shall be debtor
To thy conceit : think on't.

Org.   Your highness honours me.

Near. My tongue and heart are twins.

Cal.   A noble birth,
Becoming such a father.—Worthy Orgilus,
You are a guest most wish'd for.

Org.   May my duty
Still rise in your opinion, sacred princess!

Ith. Euphranea's brother, sir ; a gentleman
Well worthy of your knowledge.

Near.   We embrace him,

---

[18] *close!*] The 4to has "*close,* close." D.

[19]   *if thou hast there* engross'd
Some rarity of wit, &c.] i. e. if thou hast possessed thyself of, mastered, so as to bring away:—the king seems inclined rather to tax the memory of Orgilus than his imagination. It [*engross*] occurs in the very same sense in *Love's Sacrifice,* act iv. sc. 1.

Proud of so dear acquaintance.
Amyc. All prepare
For revels and disport; the joys of Hymen,
Like Phœbus in his lustre, put to flight
All mists of dulness, crown the hours with gladness:
No sounds but music, no discourse but mirth!
 Cal. Thine arm, I prithee, Ithocles.—Nay, good
My lord, keep on your way; I am provided.
 Near. I dare not disobey.
 Ith.   Most heavenly lady!
            [*Exeunt.*

SCENE IV. *A room in the house of* CROTOLON.

Enter CROTOLON *and* ORGILUS.

 Crot. The king hath spoke his mind.
 Org.   His will he hath;
But were it lawful to hold plea against
The power of greatness, not the reason, haply
Such undershrubs as subjects sometimes might
Borrow of nature justice, to inform
That license sovereignty holds without check
Over a meek obedience.
 Crot.   How resolve you
Touching your sister's marriage? Prophilus
Is a deserving and a hopeful youth.
 Org. I envy not his merit, but applaud it;
Could wish[20] him thrift in all his best desires,
And with a willingness inleague our blood
With his, for purchase of full growth in friendship.
He never touch'd on any wrong that malic'd
The honour of our house nor stirr'd our peace;
Yet, with your favour, let me not forget

---

[20] *wish*] The 4to has "with." D.

Under whose wing he gathers warmth and comfort,
Whose creature he is bound, made, and must live so.

Crot. Son, son, I find in thee a harsh condition ;[21]
No courtesy can win it, 'tis too rancorous.

Org. Good sir, be not severe in your construction;
I am no stranger to such easy calms
As sit in tender bosoms: lordly Ithocles
Hath grac'd my entertainment in abundance;
Too humbly hath descended from that height
Of arrogance and spleen which wrought the rape
On griev'd Penthea's purity; his scorn
Of my untoward fortunes is reclaim'd
Unto a courtship, almost to a fawning :—
I'll kiss his foot, since you will have it so.

Crot. Since I will have it so! friend, I will have it so,
Without our ruin by your politic plots,
Or wolf of hatred snarling in your breast.
You have a spirit, sir, have ye? a familiar
That posts i' th' air for your intelligence?
Some such hobgoblin hurried you from Athens,
For yet you come unsent for.

Org.   If unwelcome,
I might have found a grave there.

Crot.   Sure, your business
Was soon dispatch'd, or your mind alter'd quickly.

Org. 'Twas care, sir, of my health cut short my journey;
For there a general infection

---

[21] *I find in thee a harsh* condition,] i.e. temper, disposition. The word occurs in the same sense in all our old writers, and in none more frequently than Ford. The line above,

"I envy not his merit, but applaud it,"

is a close translation of Virgil's "Non equidem invideo, miror magis." The deep dissimulation, the deadly resentment of Orgilus are powerfully marked in this scene.

Threatens a desolation.
Crot. And I fear
Thou hast brought back a worse infection with thee,—
Infection of thy mind; which, as thou say'st,
Threatens the desolation of our family.

Org. Forbid it, our dear Genius! I will rather
Be made a sacrifice on Thrasus' monument,
Or kneel to Ithocles his son in dust,
Than woo a father's curse. My sister's marriage
With Prophilus is from my heart confirm'd;
May I live hated, may I die despis'd,
If I omit to further it in all
That can concern me!

Crot. I have been too rough.
My duty to my king made me so earnest;
Excuse it, Orgilus.

Org. Dear sir!—

Crot. Here comes
Euphranea, with Prophilus and Ithocles.

Enter PROPHILUS, EUPHRANEA, ITHOCLES, GRONEAS,
and HEMOPHIL.

Org. Most honour'd!—ever famous!

Ith. Your true friend;
On earth not any truer.—With smooth eyes
Look on this worthy couple; your consent
Can only make them one.

Org. They have it.—Sister,
Thou pawn'dst to me an oath, of which engagement
I never will release thee, if thou aim'st
At any other choice than this.

Euph. Dear brother,
At him, or none.

Crot. To which my blessing's added.

Org. Which, till a greater ceremony perfect,—

Euphranea, lend thy hand,—here, take her, Prophilus:
Live long a happy man and wife; and further,
That these in presence may conclude an omen,
Thus for a bridal song I close my wishes:

> *Comforts lasting, loves increasing,*
> *Like soft hours never ceasing;*
> *Plenty's pleasure, peace complying,*
> *Without jars, or tongues envying;*
> *Hearts by holy union wedded,*
> *More than theirs by custom bedded;*
> *Fruitful issues; life so grac'd,*
> *Not by age to be defac'd,*
> *Budding, as the year ensu'th,*
> *Every spring another youth:*
> *All what thought can add beside*
> *Crown this bridegroom and this bride!*

Pro. You have seal'd joy close to my soul.—Euphranea,
Now I may call thee mine.
    Ith.   I but exchange
One good friend for another.
    Org.   If these gallants
Will please to grace a poor invention
By joining with me in some slight device,
I'll venture on a strain my younger days
Have studied for delight.
    Hem.   With thankful willingness
I offer my attendance.
    Gron.   No endeavour
Of mine shall fail to show itself.
    Ith.   We will
All join to wait on thy directions, Orgilus.
    Org. O, my good lord, your favours flow towards
A too unworthy worm;—but as you please;

I am what you will shape me.
Ith.   A fast friend.
Crot. I thank thee, son, for this acknowledgment;
It is a sight of gladness.
Org.   But my duty.   [*Exeunt.*

SCENE V. CALANTHA'S *apartment in the palace.*

Enter CALANTHA, PENTHEA, CHRISTALLA, *and* PHILEMA.

Cal. Whoe'er would speak with us, deny his entrance;
Be careful of our charge.
Chris.   We shall, madam.[22]
Cal. Except the king himself, give none admittance;
Not any.
Phil. Madam, it shall be our care.
            [*Exeunt Chris. and Phil.*
Cal. Being alone, Penthea, you have granted
The opportunity you sought, and might
At all times have commanded.
Pen.   'Tis a benefit
Which I shall owe your goodness even in death for:
My glass of life, sweet princess, hath few minutes
Remaining to run down; the sands are spent;
For by an inward messenger I feel
The summons of departure short and certain.
Cal. You feed too much your melancholy.
Pen.   Glories
Of human greatness are but pleasing dreams
And shadows soon decaying: on the stage
Of my mortality my youth hath acted
Some scenes of vanity, drawn out at length

[22] *We shall, madam.*] Qy. "Madam, we shall"? D.

By varied pleasures, sweeten'd in the mixture,
But tragical in issue : beauty, pomp,
With every sensuality our giddiness
Doth frame an idol, are unconstant friends,
When any troubled passion makes assault
On the unguarded castle of the mind.
    Cal. Contemn not your condition for the proof
Of bare opinion only : to what end
Reach all these moral texts ?
    Pen.   To place before ye
A perfect mirror, wherein you may see
How weary I am of a lingering life,
Who count the best a misery.
    Cal.   Indeed
You have no little cause ; yet none so great
As to distrust a remedy.
    Pen.   That remedy
Must be a winding-sheet, a fold of lead,
And some untrod-on corner in the earth.—
Not to detain your expectation, princess,
I have an humble suit.
    Cal.   Speak ; I enjoy it.[23]
    Pen. Vouchsafe, then, to be my executrix,
And take that trouble on ye to dispose
Such legacies as I bequeath impartially ;
I have not much to give, the pains are easy ;
Heaven will reward your piety, and thank it
When I am dead ; for sure I must not live ;
I hope I cannot.
    Cal.   Now, beshrew thy sadness,
Thou turn'st me too much woman.   [*Weeps.*
    Pen. [*aside*]   Her fair eyes
Melt into passion.—Then I have assurance
Encouraging my boldness. In this paper

    [23] *I enjoy it.*] I take pleasure in it. [Qy. "*I* enjoin *it*" ? D.]

My will was character'd; which you, with pardon,
Shall now know from mine own mouth.
 Cal.   Talk on, prithee;
It is a pretty earnest.
 Pen.   I have left me
But three poor jewels to bequeath. The first is
My Youth; for though I am much old in griefs,
In years I am a child.
 Cal.   To whom that [jewel]?
 Pen. To virgin-wives, such as abuse not wedlock
By freedom of desires, but covet chiefly
The pledges of chaste beds for ties of love,
Rather than ranging of their blood; and next
To married maids, such as prefer the number
Of honourable issue in their virtues
Before the flattery of delights by marriage:
May those be ever young!
 Cal.   A second jewel
You mean to part with?
 Pen.   'Tis my Fame, I trust
By scandal yet untouch'd: this I bequeath
To Memory, and Time's old daughter, Truth.
If ever my unhappy name find mention
When I am fall'n to dust, may it deserve
Beseeming charity without dishonour!
 Cal. How handsomely thou play'st with harmless
    sport
Of mere imagination! speak the last.
I strangely like thy will.
 Pen.   This jewel, madam,
Is dearly precious to me; you must use
The best of your discretion to employ
This gift as I intend it.
 Cal.   Do not doubt me.
 Pen. 'Tis long agone since first I lost my heart:

Long I have[24] liv'd without it, else for certain
I should have given that too; but instead
Of it, to great Calantha, Sparta's heir,
By service bound and by affection vow'd,
I do bequeath, in holiest rites of love,
Mine only brother, Ithocles.
   Cal.   What saidst thou?
   Pen. Impute not, heaven-blest lady, to ambition
A faith as humbly perfect as the prayers
Of a devoted suppliant can endow it:
Look on him, princess, with an eye of pity;
How like the ghost of what he late appear'd
He moves before you.
   Cal.   Shall I answer here,
Or lend my ear too grossly?
   Pen.   First his heart
Shall fall in cinders, scorch'd by your disdain,
Ere he will dare, poor man, to ope an eye
On these divine looks, but with low-bent thoughts
Accusing such presumption; as for words,
He dares not utter any but of service:
Yet this lost creature loves ye.—Be a princess
In sweetness as in blood; give him his doom,
Or raise him up to comfort.
   Cal.   What new change
Appears in my behaviour, that thou dar'st
Tempt my displeasure?
   Pen.   I must leave the world
To revel [in] Elysium, and 'tis just
To wish my brother some advantage here;
Yet, by my best hopes, Ithocles is ignorant
Of this pursuit: but if you please to kill him,
Lend him one angry look or one harsh word,

---

[24] *I have*] Gifford printed "have I." D.

And you shall soon conclude how strong a power
Your absolute authority holds over
His life and end.
Cal. You have forgot, Penthea,
How still I have a father.
Pen. But remember
I am a sister, though to me this brother
Hath been, you know, unkind, O, most unkind!
Cal. Christalla, Philema, where are ye?—Lady,
Your check lies in my silence.

Re-enter CHRISTALLA *and* PHILEMA.

Chris.
Phil. } Madam, here.

Cal. I think ye sleep, ye drones: wait on Penthea
Unto her lodging.—[*Aside*] Ithocles? wrong'd lady!
Pen. My reckonings are made even; death or fate
Can now nor strike too soon nor force too late.
[*Exeunt.*

ACT IV.

SCENE I. *The palace.* ITHOCLES' *apartment.*

Enter ITHOCLES *and* ARMOSTES.

Ith. Forbear your inquisition: curiosity
Is of too subtle and too searching nature,
In fears of love too quick, too slow of credit.—
I am not what you doubt me.
Arm. Nephew, be, then,
As I would wish;—all is not right.—Good heaven
Confirm your resolutions for dependence

On worthy ends, which may advance your quiet!
Ith. I did the noble Orgilus much injury,
But griev'd Penthea more : I now repent it,—
Now, uncle, now; this "now" is now too late.
So provident is folly in sad issue,
That after-wit, like bankrupts' debts, stand[s] tallied,
Without all possibilities of payment.
Sure, he's an honest, very honest gentleman;
A man of single meaning.[1]
    Arm.   I believe it:
Yet, nephew, 'tis the tongue informs our ears;
Our eyes can never pierce into the thoughts,
For they are lodg'd too inward:—but I question
No truth in Orgilus.—The princess, sir.
    Ith. The princess! ha!
    Arm.   With her the Prince of Argos.

    Enter NEARCHUS, *leading* CALANTHA; AMELUS,
                CHRISTALLA, PHILEMA.

    Near. Great fair one, grace my hopes with any instance
Of livery,[2] from th' allowance of your favour;
This little spark—
                [*Attempts to take a ring from her finger.*
    Cal.   A toy!
    Near.   Love feasts on toys,
For Cupid is a child;—vouchsafe this bounty:
It cannot be denied.[3]

---

[1] *A man of* single *meaning.*] i.e. plain, open, sincere, unreserved. It appears, notwithstanding the disavowal of Armostes, that he did not altogether adopt the fatal error of his nephew.

[2]   *grace my hopes with any instance*
Of livery] i.e. favour me with some *badge*, some ornament from your person, to show that you have condescended to enrol me among your servants. This was the language of courtship, and was derived from the practice of distinguishing the followers and retainers of great families by the badge or crest of the house.

[3] *be denied.*] The 4to has "beny'd." D.

Cal.   You shall not value,
Sweet cousin, at a price, what I count cheap;
So cheap, that let him take it who dares stoop for't,
And give it at next meeting to a mistress:
She'll thank him for't, perhaps.
          [*Casts the ring before Ithocles, who takes it up.*
Ame.   The ring, sir, is
The princess's; I could have took it up.
     Ith. Learn manners, prithee. — To the blessèd
          owner,
Upon my knees—   [*Kneels and offers it to Calantha.*
Near.   You're saucy.
Cal.   This is pretty!
I am, belike, "a mistress"—wondrous pretty!—
Let the man keep his fortune, since he found it;
He's worthy on't.—On, cousin!
               [*Exeunt Near. Cal. Chris. and Phil.*
     Ith. [*to Ame.*]   Follow, spaniel;
I'll force ye to a fawning else.
     Ame.   You dare not. [*Exit.*
     Arm. My lord, you were too forward.
     Ith.   Look ye, uncle,
Some such there are whose liberal contents
Swarm without care in every sort of plenty;
Who after full repasts can lay them down
To sleep; and they sleep, uncle: in which silence
Their very dreams present 'em choice of pleasures,
Pleasures—observe me, uncle—of rare object;
Here heaps of gold, there increments of honours,
Now change of garments, then the votes of people;
Anon varieties of beauties, courting,
In flatteries of the night, exchange of dalliance:
Yet these are still but dreams. Give me felicity
Of which my senses waking are partakers,
A real, visible, material happiness;

And then, too, when I stagger in expectance
Of the least comfort that can cherish life.—
I saw it, sir, I saw it; for it came
From her own hand.
    Arm.   The princess threw it t'ye.
    Ith. True; and she said—well I remember what—
Her cousin prince would beg it.
    Arm.   Yes, and parted
In anger at your taking on't.
    Ith.   Penthea,
O, thou hast pleaded with a powerful language!
I want a fee to gratify thy merit;
But I will do—
    Arm.   What is't you say?
    Ith.   In anger!
In anger let him part; for could his breath,
Like whirlwinds, toss such servile slaves as lick
The dust his footsteps print into a vapour,
It durst not stir a hair of mine, it should not;
I'd rend it up by th' roots first. To be anything
Calantha smiles on, is to be a blessing
More sacred than a petty prince of Argos
Can wish to equal or in worth or title.
    Arm. Contain yourself, my lord: Ixion, aiming
To embrace Juno, bosom'd but a cloud,
And begat Centaurs; 'tis an useful moral:
Ambition hatch'd in clouds of mere opinion
Proves but in birth a prodigy.
    Ith.   I thank ye;
Yet, with your license, I should seem uncharitable
To gentler fate, if, relishing the dainties
Of a soul's settled peace, I were so feeble
Not to digest it.
    Arm.   He deserves small trust
Who is not privy-counsellor to himself.

SCENE I.   THE BROKEN HEART.   283

Re-enter NEARCHUS *and* AMELUS, *with* ORGILUS.

Near. Brave me?
Org. Your excellence mistakes his temper;
For Ithocles in fashion of his mind
Is beautiful, soft, gentle, the clear mirror
Of absolute perfection.
Ame. Was't your modesty[4]
Term'd any of the prince's servants "spaniel"?
Your nurse, sure, taught you other language.
Ith.   Language!
Near. A gallant man-at-arms is here, a doctor
In feats of chivalry, blunt and rough-spoken,
Vouchsafing not the fustian of civility,
Which [less] rash spirits style good manners.[5]
Ith.   Manners!
Org. No more, illustrious sir; 'tis matchless Itho-
    cles.
Near. You might have understood who I am.
Ith.   Yes,
I did; else—but the presence calm'd th' affront—
You're cousin to the princess.
Near.   To the king too;
A certain instrument that lent supportance
To your colossic greatness—to that king too,

---

[4] *your* modesty] This is an appellative, like "your sovereignty" in *Hamlet*, about which so much nonsense has been written. [Here, no doubt, Gifford is right as to "*your modesty:*" but when, in a note on Jonson's *Works*, vol. v. p. 352, he asserted that, in the following line of *Hamlet*, act i. sc. 4,
    "Which might deprive your sovereignty of reason,"
"*sovereignty*" was "merely a title of respect," he was utterly mistaken: see my *Gloss. to Shakespeare*, sub "*deprive.*" D.]
[5] *Which* [less] *rash spirits style good manners.*] The 4to reads, "Which rash spirits style good manners." The want of rhythm alone, even if the expression were not, as it is, devoid of congruity and sense, would suffice to show that something is defective. I have made the best guess I could, and, at all events, given a shadow of meaning to the words.

You might have added.
Ith.   There is more divinity
In beauty than in majesty.
Arm.   O fie, fie!
Near. This odd youth's pride turns heretic in loyalty.
Sirrah! low mushrooms never rival cedars.
                              [*Exeunt Near. and Ame.*
Ith. Come back!—What pitiful dull thing am I
So to be tamely scolded at! come back!—
Let him come back, and echo once again
That scornful sound of *mushroom!* painted colts[6]—
Like heralds' coats gilt-o'er with crowns and sceptres—
May bait a muzzled lion.
Arm.   Cousin, cousin,
Thy tongue is not thy friend.
Org.   In point of honour
Discretion knows no bounds. Amelus told me
'Twas all about a little ring.
Ith.   A ring
The princess threw away, and I took up:
Admit she threw't to me, what arm of brass
Can snatch it hence? No; could he grind the hoop
To powder, he might sooner reach my heart
Than steal and wear one dust on't.—Orgilus,
I am extremely wrong'd.
Org.   A lady's favour
Is not to be so slighted.
Ith.   Slighted!
Arm.   Quiet
These vain unruly passions, which will render ye

---

[6] *painted* colts, &c.] Our old writers used *colt* (probably from the boisterous gambols of this animal) for a compound of rudeness and folly. The meaning of the text is sufficiently obvious; but it would seem that there is also an allusion to some allegorical representation of this kind in "the painted cloth."

Into a madness.
   Org.   Griefs will have their vent.[7]

        Enter TECNICUS *with a scroll.*

   Arm. Welcome; thou com'st in season, reverend
      man,
To pour the balsam of a suppling[8] patience
Into the festering wound of ill-spent fury.
   Org. [*aside*] What makes he here?
   Tec.   The hurts are yet but mortal,
Which shortly will prove deadly.[9] To the king,
Armostes, see in safety thou deliver
This seal'd-up counsel; bid him with a constancy
Peruse the secrets of the gods.—O Sparta,
O Lacedæmon! double-nam'd, but one
In fate: when kingdoms reel,—mark well my saw,—
Their heads must needs be giddy. Tell the king
That henceforth he no more must inquire after
My agèd head; Apollo wills it so:
I am for Delphos.
   Arm.   Not without some conference

---

    [7] The extraordinary success with which the revengeful spirit of Orgilus is maintained through every scene is highly creditable to the poet's skill. There is not a word spoken by him which does not denote a deep and dangerous malignity, couched in the most sarcastic and rancorous language. The bitterness of gall, the poison of asps, lurk under every compliment, which nothing but the deep repentance and heartfelt sincerity of Ithocles could possibly prevent him from feeling and detecting.
    [8] *suppling*] The 4to has "supplying." D.
    [9]   *The hurts are yet but* mortal,
  Which shortly will prove deadly.] There are few words so frequently confounded by the press of our poet's time as *but* and *not:* a mistake of this kind seems to have taken place here, and for "*but*" we should perhaps read "*not*," i.e. the wounds, though yet *not* mortal, will speedily prove so. Otherwise it is not easy to discover how the author distinguished the last word from "deadly;" unless, indeed, he adopted the vulgar phraseology of his native place, and used "*mortal*" in the sense of very great, extreme, &c.

With our great master?
  Tec.   Never more to see him :
A greater prince commands me.—Ithocles,
   When youth is ripe, and age from time doth part,
   The Lifeless Trunk shall wed the Broken Heart.
  Ith. What's this, if understood?
  Tec.   List, Orgilus;
Remember what I told thee long before,
These tears shall be my witness.
  Arm.   'Las, good man!
  Tec.
   Let craft with courtesy a while confer,
   Revenge proves its own executioner.
  Org. Dark sentences are for Apollo's priests;
I am not Œdipus.
  Tec.   My hour is come;
Cheer up the king; farewell to all.—O Sparta,
O Lacedæmon!   [*Exit.*
  Arm.   If prophetic fire
Have warm'd this old man's bosom, we might construe
His words to fatal sense.
  Ith.   Leave to the powers
Above us the effects of their decrees;
My burthen lies within me : servile fears
Prevent no great effects.—Divine Calantha!
  Arm. The gods be still propitious!
                             [*Exeunt Ith. and Arm.*
  Org.   Something oddly
The book-man prated, yet he talk'd it weeping;
   Let craft with courtesy a while confer,
   Revenge proves its own executioner.
Con it again;—for what? It shall not puzzle me;
'Tis dotage of a wither'd brain.—Penthea
Forbade me not her presence; I may see her,

And gaze my fill. Why see her, then, I may,
When, if I faint to speak—I must be silent. [*Exit.*

SCENE II. *A room in* BASSANES' *house.*

Enter BASSANES, GRAUSIS, *and* PHULAS.

Bass. Pray, use your recreations, all the service
I will expect is quietness amongst ye;
Take liberty at home, abroad, at all times,
And in your charities appease the gods,
Whom I, with my distractions, have offended.
  Grau. Fair blessings on thy heart!
  Phu. [*aside*]   Here's a rare change!
My lord, to cure the itch, is surely gelded;
The cuckold in conceit hath cast his horns.
  Bass. Betake ye to your several occasions;
And wherein I have heretofore been faulty,
Let your constructions mildly pass it over;
Henceforth I'll study reformation,—more
I have not for employment.
  Grau.   O, sweet man!
Thou art the very Honeycomb of Honesty.
  Phu. The Garland of Good-will.[10]—Old lady, hold
    up
Thy reverend snout, and trot behind me softly,
As it becomes a moil[11] of ancient carriage.
          [*Exeunt Grau. and Phu.*
  Bass. Beasts, only capable of sense, enjoy
The benefit of food and ease with thankfulness;

---

[10] The Honeycomb of Honesty, like the "Garland of Good-will," was probably one of the popular miscellanies of the day. The quaint and alliterative titles to these collections of ballads, stories, jests, &c. gave every allusion to them an air of pleasantry, and perhaps excited a smile on the stage.
[11] *moil*] i.e. mule.—Altered by Gifford to "mule." D.

Such silly creatures, with a grudging, kick not
Against the portion nature hath bestow'd :
But men, endow'd with reason and the use
Of reason, to distinguish from the chaff
Of abject scarcity the quintessence,
Soul, and elixir of the earth's abundance,
The treasures of the sea, the air, nay, heaven,
Repining at these glories of creation
Are verier beasts than beasts; and of those beasts
The worst am I : I, who was made a monarch
Of what a heart could wish for,—a chaste wife,—
Endeavour'd what in me lay to pull down
That temple built for adoration only,
And level't in the dust of causeless scandal.
But, to redeem a sacrilege so impious,
Humility shall pour, before the deities
I have incens'd, a largess[11] of more patience
Than their displeasèd altars can require :
No tempests of commotion shall disquiet
The calms of my composure.

Enter ORGILUS.

 Org.   I have found thee,
Thou patron of more horrors than the bulk
Of manhood, hoop'd about with ribs of iron,
Can cram within thy breast : Penthea, Bassanes,
Curs'd by thy jealousies,—more, by thy dotage,—
Is left a prey to words.
 Bass.   Exercise
Your trials for addition to my penance ;
I am resolv'd.
 Org. Play not with misery
Past cure : some angry minister of fate hath
Depos'd the empress of her soul, her reason,

---

[11] *largess*] The 4to has "largenesse." D.

From its most proper throne; but, what's the miracle
More new, I, I have seen it, and yet live!
    Bass. You may delude my senses, not my judgment;
'Tis anchor'd into a firm resolution;
Dalliance of mirth or wit can ne'er unfix it:
Practise yet further.[12]
    Org.   May thy death of love to her
Damn all thy comforts to a lasting fast
From every joy of life! Thou barren rock,
By thee we have been split in ken of harbour.

    Enter PENTHEA *with her hair loose,* ITHOCLES, PHILEMA, *and* CHRISTALLA.

    Ith. Sister, look up; your Ithocles, your brother,
Speaks t'ye; why do you weep? dear, turn not from me.—
Here is a killing sight; lo, Bassanes,
A lamentable object!
    Org.   Man, dost see't?
Sports are more gamesome; am I yet in merriment?
Why dost not laugh?
    Bass.   Divine and best of ladies,
Please to forget my outrage; mercy ever
Cannot but lodge under a roof[13] so excellent:
I have cast off that cruelty of frenzy
Which once appear'd imposture,[14] and then juggled
To cheat my sleeps of rest.
    Org.   Was I in earnest?
    Pen. Sure, if[15] we were all Sirens, we should sing pitifully,

---

[12] *Practise yet further.*] i. e. try all your vexations upon me.
[13] *roof*] The 4to has "root." D.
[14] *imposture,*] The 4to has "Impostors." D.
[15] *Sure, if,* &c.] Some slight corruption here. D.

VOL. I.   U

And 'twere a comely music, when in parts
One sung another's knell: the turtle sighs
When he hath lost his mate; and yet some say
He must be dead first: 'tis a fine deceit
To pass away in a dream! indeed, I've slept
With mine eyes open a great while. No falsehood
Equals a broken faith; there's not a hair
Sticks on my head but, like a leaden plummet,
It sinks me to the grave: I must creep thither;
The journey is not long.
 Ith.   But thou, Penthea,
Hast many years, I hope, to number yet,
Ere thou canst travel that way.
 Bass.   Let the sun[16] first
Be wrapp'd up in an everlasting darkness,
Before the light of nature, chiefly form'd
For the whole world's delight, feel an eclipse
So universal!
 Org. Wisdom, look ye, begins
To rave!—art thou mad too, antiquity?
 Pen. Since I was first a wife, I might have been
Mother to many pretty prattling babes;
They would have smil'd when I smil'd, and for certain
I should have cried when they cried:—truly, brother,
My father would have pick'd me out a husband,
And then my little ones had been no bastards;
But 'tis too late for me to marry now,
I am past child-bearing; 'tis not my fault.
 Bass. Fall on me, if there be a burning Ætna,
And bury me in flames! sweats hot as sulphur
Boil through my pores! affliction hath in store
No torture like to this.
 Org.   Behold a patience!

---

[16] *sun*] The 4to has "Swan." D.

Lay-by thy whining gray dissimulation,[17]
Do something worth a chronicle; show justice
Upon the author of this mischief; dig out
The jealousies that hatch'd this thraldom first
With thine own poniard : every antic rapture
Can roar as thine does.
    Ith.   Orgilus, forbear.
    Bass. Disturb him not; it is a talking motion[18]
Provided for my torment. What a fool am I
To bandy[19] passion! ere I'll speak a word,
I will look on and burst.
    Pen.   I lov'd you once. [*To Org.*
    Org. Thou didst, wrong'd creature : in despite of
            malice,
For it I[20] love thee ever.
    Pen.   Spare your hand;
Believe me, I'll not hurt it.
    Org.   My heart too.[21]
    Pen. Complain not though I wring it hard : I'll
        kiss it;

[17] *Lay-by thy whining gray dissimulation,*] This beautiful expression is happily adopted by Milton, the great plunderer of the poetical hive of our old dramatists;

        " He ended here; and Satan, bowing low
          His gray dissimulation," &c.   *Par. Reg.*

It would appear from the next speech that the unsuspicious Ithocles supposed Orgilus to address Bassanes in this rant in order to incite him to wreak vengeance on himself for his cruelty to Penthea; but the covert object of it is evidently Ithocles.
    [18] *motion*] i.e. puppet : see note, p. 97. D.
    [19] *bandy*] The 4to has "bawdy;" which Gifford retained. D.
    [20] *I*] Gifford printed "I'll." D.
    [21] Org. *My heart too.*] Here is some mistake of the press, which I cannot pretend to rectify. The 4to reads,

        "*Org. Paine* my heart *to*
        Complaine not," &c.

I have little doubt that a line has been dropt, containing the conclusion of Orgilus' speech and the commencement of Penthea's, whose name does not appear in the text. My arrangement pretends to nothing more than rendering the passage intelligible.

O, 'tis a fine soft palm!—hark, in thine ear;
Like whom do I look, prithee?—nay, no whispering.
Goodness! we had been happy; too much happiness
Will make folk proud, they say—but that is he—
                                    [*Pointing to Ith.*
And yet he paid for't home; alas, his heart
Is crept into the cabinet of the princess;
We shall have points[22] and bride-laces. Remember,
When we last gather'd roses in the garden,
I found my wits; but truly you lost yours.
That's he, and still 'tis he.   [*Again pointing to Ith.*
    Ith.   Poor soul, how idly
Her fancies guide her tongue!
    Bass. [*aside*]   Keep in, vexation,
And break not into clamour.
    Org. [*aside*]   She has tutor'd me;[23]
Some powerful inspiration checks my laziness.—
Now let me kiss your hand, griev'd beauty.
    Pen.   Kiss it.—
Alack, alack, his lips be wondrous cold;
Dear soul, 'has lost his colour: have ye seen
A straying heart? all crannies! every drop
Of blood is turnèd to an amethyst,
Which married bachelors hang in their ears.
    Org. Peace usher her into Elysium!—
If this be madness, madness is an oracle.
                                    [*Aside, and exit.*
    Ith. Christalla, Philema, when slept my sister,
Her ravings are so wild?
    Chris.   Sir, not these ten days.
    Phil. We watch by her continually; besides,

    [22] *points*] i.e. tagged laces, used in dress. D.
    [23] *She has tutor'd me;*] i.e. by repeatedly pointing out Ithocles to his resentment. What plan of vengeance Orgilus had previously meditated we know not; but the deep and irresistible pathos of this most afflicting scene evidently gives a deadly turn to his wrath.

We can not any way pray her to eat.
  Bass. O, misery of miseries!
  Pen. Take comfort;
You may live well, and die a good old man :
By yea and nay, an oath not to be broken,
If you had join'd our hands once in the temple,—
'Twas since my father died, for had he liv'd
He would have done't,—I must have call'd you father.—
O, my wreck'd honour![24] ruin'd by those tyrants,
A cruel brother and a desperate dotage.
There is no peace left for a ravish'd wife
Widow'd by lawless marriage; to all memory
Penthea's, poor Penthea's name is strumpeted :
But since her blood was season'd by the forfeit
Of noble shame with mixtures of pollution,
Her blood—'tis just—be henceforth never heighten'd
With taste of sustenance ! starve; let that fulness
Whose plurisy hath fever'd faith and modesty—
Forgive me; O, I faint !
    [*Falls into the arms of her Attendants.*
  Arm. Be not so wilful,
Sweet niece, to work thine own destruction.
  Ith. Nature
Will call her daughter monster !—What ! not eat?
Refuse the only ordinary means
Which are ordain'd for life? Be not, my sister,
A murderess to thyself.—Hear'st thou this, Bassanes?

[24] *O, my wreck'd honour!* &c.] The transition of Penthea from the wandering insanity which had marked the previous part of her discourse to the deep but composed melancholy of what follows, is surely too sudden, and may seem to throw some suspicion on the reality—not of her sufferings and despair, for these are too strongly marked for doubt, but of her aberration of mind; and indeed it cannot be concealed that this lovely and interesting woman has a spice of selfishness in her grief, and approaches somewhat too nearly to Orgilus in the unforgiving part of his character. Even her last words are expressive of resentment.

Bass. Foh! I am busy; for I have not thoughts
Enow to think : all shall be well anon.
'Tis tumbling in my head ; there is a mastery
In art to fatten and keep smooth the outside,
Yes, and to comfort-up the vital spirits
Without the help of food, fumes or perfumes,
Perfumes or fumes. Let her alone ; I'll search out
The trick on't.
 Pen.   Lead me gently ; heavens reward ye.
Griefs are sure friends ; they leave without control
Nor cure nor comforts for a leprous soul.
    [*Exit, supported by Chris. and Phil.*
Bass. I grant ye ; and will put in practice instantly
What you shall still admire : 'tis wonderful,
'Tis super-singular, not to be match'd ;
Yet, when I've done't, I've done't :—ye shall all thank
  me.   [*Exit.*
 Arm. The sight is full of terror.
 Ith.   On my soul
Lies such an infinite clog of massy dulness,
As that I have not sense enough to feel it.—
See, uncle, th' angry[25] thing returns again ;
Shall's welcome him with thunder? we are haunted,
And must use exorcism to conjure down
This spirit of malevolence.
 Arm.   Mildly, nephew.

    Enter NEARCHUS *and* AMELUS.

Near. I come not, sir, to chide your late disorder,
Admitting that th' inurement to a roughness
In soldiers of your years and fortunes, chiefly
So lately prosperous, hath not yet shook off
The custom of the war in hours of leisure ;

---

[25] *th' angry*] The 4to has "*th'* augury." D.

Nor shall you need excuse, since you're to render
Account to that fair excellence, the princess,
Who in her private gallery expects it
From your own mouth alone : I am a messenger
But to her pleasure.
  Ith.   Excellent Nearchus,
Be prince still of my services, and conquer
Without the combat of dispute ; I honour ye.
  Near. The king is on a sudden indispos'd,
Physicians are call'd for ; 'twere fit, Armostes,
You should be near him.
  Arm.   Sir, I kiss your hands.
          [*Exeunt Ith. and Arm.*
  Near. Amelus, I perceive Calantha's bosom
Is warm'd with other fires than such as can
Take strength from any fuel of the love
I might address to her : young Ithocles,
Or ever I mistake, is lord ascendant
Of her devotions ; one, to speak him truly,
In every disposition nobly fashion'd.
  Ame. But can your highness brook to be so rivall'd,
Considering th' inequality of the persons ?
  Near. I can, Amelus ; for affections injur'd
By tyranny or rigour of compulsion,
Like tempest-threaten'd trees unfirmly rooted,
Ne'er spring to timely growth : observe, for instance,
Life-spent Penthea and unhappy Orgilus.
  Ame. How does your grace determine?
  Near.   To be jealous
In public of what privately I'll further ;
And, though they shall not know, yet they shall find it.
             [*Exeunt.*

SCENE III. *An apartment in the palace.*

Enter the King, *led by* HEMOPHIL *and* GRONEAS, *followed by* ARMOSTES *with a box*, CROTOLON, *and* PROPHILUS. *The* King *is placed in a chair.*

Amyc. Our daughter is not near?
Arm. She is retir'd, sir,
Into her gallery.
Amyc. Where's the prince our cousin?
Pro. New walk'd into the grove, my lord.
Amyc. All leave us
Except Armostes, and you, Crotolon;
We would be private.
Pro. Health unto your majesty!
[*Exeunt Pro. Hem. and Gron.*
Amyc. What! Tecnicus is gone?
Arm. He is, to Delphos;
And to your royal hands presents this box.
Amyc. Unseal it, good Armostes; therein lie
The secrets of the oracle; out with it:
[*Arm. takes out the scroll.*
Apollo live our patron! Read, Armostes.
Arm. [*reads*]
> *The plot in which the Vine takes root*
> *Begins to dry from head to foot;*
> *The stock, soon withering, want of sap*
> *Doth cause to quail the Budding Grape:*
> *But from the neighbouring Elm a dew*
> *Shall drop, and feed the plot anew.*

Amyc. That is the oracle: what exposition
Makes the philosopher?
Arm. This brief one only.
[*Reads*]
> *The plot is Sparta, the dried Vine the king;*
> *The quailing Grape his daughter; but the thing*

*Of most importance, not to be reveal'd,
Is a near prince, the Elm: the rest conceal'd.*
                                   TECNICUS.

    Amyc. Enough; although the opening of this riddle
Be but itself a riddle, yet we construe
How near our labouring age draws to a rest:
But must Calantha quail too? that young grape
Untimely budded! I could mourn for her;
Her tenderness hath yet deserv'd no rigour
So to be cross'd by fate.
    Arm.   You misapply, sir,—
With favour let me speak it,—what Apollo
Hath clouded in hid sense: I here conjecture
Her marriage with some neighbouring prince, the dew
Of which befriending elm shall ever strengthen
Your subjects with a sovereignty of power.
    Crot. Besides, most gracious lord, the pith of oracles
Is to be then digested when th' events
Expound their truth, not brought as soon to light
As utter'd; Truth is child of Time: and herein
I find no scruple, rather cause of comfort,
With unity of kingdoms.
    Amyc.   May it prove so,
For weal of this dear nation!—Where is Ithocles?—
Armostes, Crotolon, when this wither'd vine
Of my frail carcass, on the funeral pile
Is fir'd into its ashes, let that young man
Be hedg'd about still with your cares and loves:
Much owe I to his worth, much to his service.—
Let such as wait come in now.
    Arm.   All attend here!

    Enter CALANTHA, ITHOCLES, PROPHILUS, ORGILUS,
        EUPHRANEA, HEMOPHIL, *and* GRONEAS.

    Cal. Dear sir! king! father!

Ith. O, my royal master!
Amyc. Cleave not my heart, sweet twins of my life's
    solace,
With your forejudging fears; there is no physic
So cunningly restorative to cherish
The fall of age, or call back youth and vigour,
As your consents in duty: I will shake off
This languishing disease of time, to quicken
Fresh pleasures in these drooping hours of sadness.
Is fair Euphranea married yet to Prophilus?
    Crot. This morning, gracious lord.
    Org. This very morning;
Which, with your highness' leave, you may observe too.
Our sister looks, methinks, mirthful and sprightly,
As if her chaster fancy could already
Expound the riddle of her gain in losing
A trifle maids know only that they know not.
Pish! prithee, blush not; 'tis but honest change
Of fashion in the garment, loose for strait,
And so the modest maid is made a wife:
Shrewd business—is't not, sister?
    Euph. You are pleasant.
    Amyc. We thank thee, Orgilus; this mirth becomes
        thee.
But wherefore sits the court in such a silence?
A wedding without revels is not seemly.
    Cal. Your late indisposition, sir, forbade it.
    Amyc. Be it thy charge, Calantha, to set forward
The bridal sports, to which I will be present;
If not, at least consenting.—Mine own Ithocles,
I have done little for thee yet.
    Ith. You've built me
To the full height I stand in.
    Cal. [*aside*] Now or never!—
May I propose a suit?

Amyc.   Demand, and have it.
Cal. Pray, sir, give me this young man, and no
  further
Account him yours than he deserves in all things
To be thought worthy mine : I will esteem him
According to his merit.
  Amyc.   Still thou'rt my daughter,
Still grow'st upon my heart.—[*To Ith.*] Give me thine
  hand ;—
Calantha, take thine own ; in noble actions
Thou'lt find him firm and absolute.—I would not
Have parted with thee, Ithocles, to any
But to a mistress who is all what I am.
  Ith. A change, great king, most wish'd for, 'cause
    the same.
  Cal. [*aside to Ith.*] Thou'rt mine. Have I now kept
    my word?
  Ith. [*aside to Cal.*]   Divinely.
  Org. Rich fortunes guard, the[26] favour of a princess
Rock thee, brave man, in ever-crownèd plenty !
You're minion of the time ; be thankful for it.—
[*Aside*] Ho! here's a swing in destiny—apparent !
The youth is up on tiptoe, yet may stumble.
  Amyc. On to your recreations.—Now convey me
Unto my bed-chamber : none on his forehead
Wear a distemper'd look.
  All.   The gods preserve ye !
  Cal. [*aside to Ith.*] Sweet, be not from my sight.
  Ith. [*aside to Cal.*]   My whole felicity !
          [*Amyc. is carried out. Exeunt all but
            Ith., who is detained by Org.*
  Org. Shall I be bold, my lord?
  Ith.   Thou canst not, Orgilus.
Call me thine own ; for Prophilus must henceforth

---

[26] *the*] The 4to has "to." D.

Be all thy sister's : friendship, though it cease not
In mairiage, yet is oft at less command
Than when a single freedom can dispose it.
  Org. Most right, my most good lord, my most
    great lord,
My gracious princely lord,—I might add, royal.
  Ith. Royal! a subject royal?
  Org.   Why not, pray, sir?
The sovereignty of kingdoms in their nonage
Stoop'd to desert, not birth; there's as much merit
In clearness of affection as in puddle
Of generation : you have conquer'd love
Even in the loveliest; if I greatly err not,
The son of Venus hath bequeath'd his quiver
To Ithocles his manage,[27] by whose arrows
Calantha's breast is open'd.
  Ith.   Can't be possible?
  Org. I was myself a piece of suitor once,
And forward in preferment too; so forward,
That, speaking truth, I may without offence, sir,
Presume to whisper that my hopes, and—hark ye—
My certainty of marriage stood assur'd
With as firm footing—by your leave—as any's
Now at this very instant—but—
  Ith.   'Tis granted :
And for a league of privacy between us,
Read o'er my bosom and partake a secret;
The princess is contracted mine.
  Org.   Still, why not?
I now applaud her wisdom : when your kingdom
Stands seated in your will secure and settled,
I dare pronounce you will be a just monarch;
Greece must admire and tremble.

---

[27] *To Ithocles his manage,*] Here Gifford, not perceiving that
"Ithocles his" was equivalent to "*Ithocles's,*" printed "*To Ithocles*
to *manage.*" D.

Ith.   Then the sweetness
Of so imparadis'd a comfort, Orgilus!
It is to banquet with the gods.
    Org.   The glory
Of numerous children, potency of nobles,
Bent knees, hearts pav'd to tread on!
    Ith.   With a friendship
So dear, so fast as thine.
    Org.   I am unfitting
For office; but for service—
    Ith.   We'll distinguish
Our fortunes merely in the title; partners
In all respects else but the bed.
    Org.   The bed!
Forfend it Jove's own jealousy!—till lastly
We slip down in the common earth together;
And there our beds are equal; save some monument
To show this was the king, and this the subject.—
                                 [*Soft sad music.*
List, what sad sounds are these,—extremely sad ones?
    Ith. Sure, from Penthea's lodgings.
    Org.   Hark! a voice too.

                      Song *within.*

      O, no more, no more, too late
         Sighs are spent; the burning tapers
      Of a life as chaste as fate,
         Pure as are unwritten papers,
    Are burnt out: no heat, no light
    Now remains; 'tis ever night.
      Love is dead; let lovers' eyes,
         Lock'd in endless dreams,
         Th' extremes of all extremes,
      Ope no more, for now Love dies,
    Now Love dies,—implying
    Love's martyrs must be ever, ever dying.

Ith. O, my misgiving heart!
Org. A horrid stillness
Succeeds this deathful air; let's know the reason:
Tread softly; there is mystery in mourning. [*Exeunt.*

SCENE IV. *Apartment of* PENTHEA *in the same.*

PENTHEA *discovered in a chair, veiled;* CHRISTALLA *and* PHILEMA *at her feet mourning. Enter two* Servants *with two other chairs, one with an engine.*[28]

Enter ITHOCLES *and* ORGILUS.

First Serv. [*aside to Org.*] 'Tis done; that on her right hand.

---

[28] *Enter two Servants with two chairs, one with an* engine.] This *engine*, as it is here called, in correspondence with the homely properties of our old theatres, was merely a couple of movable arms added to the common chair. The contrivance itself is of early date, and, if Pausanias ([*Attica*], c. 20) is to be trusted, of celestial origin. Vulcan, he tells us, in order to be revenged of Juno for turning him out of heaven, insidiously presented her with a golden throne with hidden springs, which prevented her, after being seated upon it, from rising up again. It appears that Bacchus alone of all the gods had influence enough with the sooty artist to persuade him to liberate her:—the exquisite moral of which, I presume, is, that people are sometimes good-humoured in their cups. Ford, however, brought no golden chair from Olympus: he found his simple contrivance not only on the stage, but (where his predecessors probably found it) in *Bandello* (Nov. 27, part iv.) [Nov. i. Parte iv. vol. ix. p. 13, ed. Milano, 1814], where it is described at length, and Deodati is entrapped by il Turchi, precisely as Ithocles is here by Orgilus, and then stabbed with a dagger.

The author of *The Devil's Charter* (1607), where this chair is also introduced, appears from the following lines to have been aware of the passage in Pausanias:—but he [Barnaby Barnes] was evidently a scholar;

"Enter Lucretia, with a *chair* in her hand, which she sets on the stage."
It was not a very ponderous "machine," as the reader sees.

"*Luc.* I have devised such a curious snare
As jealous Vulcan never yet devis'd,
To grasp his armes, unable to resist
Death's instrument inclosed in these hands."

And accordingly Gismond sits down, is "grasped," like Ithocles, and stabbed without resistance by his wife; who retires, as she en-

Org. Good: begone.
            [*Exeunt Servants.*
Ith. Soft peace enrich this room!
Org. How fares the lady?
Phil. Dead!
Chris.   Dead!
Phil.   Starv'd!
Chris.   Starv'd!
Ith.   Me miserable!
Org.   Tell us
How parted she from life.
    Phil. She call'd for music,
And begg'd some gentle voice to tune a farewell
To life and griefs: Christalla touch'd the lute;
I wept the funeral song.
    Chris. Which scarce was ended
But her last breath seal'd-up these hollow sounds,
"O, cruel Ithocles and injur'd Orgilus!"
So down she drew her veil, so died.
    Ith.   So died!
    Org. Up! you are messengers of death; go from
            us;   [*Chris. and Phil. rise.*
Here's woe enough to court without a prompter:
Away; and—hark ye—till you see us next,
No syllable that she is dead.—Away,
Keep a smooth brow.   [*Exeunt Chris. and Phil.*
                My lord,—
    Ith.   Mine only sister!
Another is not left me.
    Org. Take that chair;
I'll seat me here in this: between us sits

---

tered, "with the *chair* in her hand." [In quoting Barnes's tragedy Gifford has somewhat altered the wording of the stage-directions, and in Lucretia's speech has (rightly) substituted "*instrument*" for "instruments." D.]

The object of our sorrows; some few tears
We'll part among us : I perhaps can mix
One lamentable story to prepare 'em.—
There, there; sit there, my lord.
    Ith.   Yes, as you please.
    [*Sits down, the chair closes upon him.*
What means this treachery?
    Org.   Caught! you are caught,
Young master; 'tis thy throne of coronation,
Thou fool of greatness! See, I take this veil off;
Survey a beauty wither'd by the flames
Of an insulting Phaëthon, her brother.
    Ith. Thou mean'st to kill me basely?
    Org.   I foreknew
The last act of her life, and train'd thee hither
To sacrifice a tyrant to a turtle.
You dreamt of kingdoms, did ye? how to bosom
The delicacies of a youngling princess;
How with this nod to grace that subtle courtier,
How with that frown to make this noble tremble,
And so forth; whiles Penthea's groans and tortures,
Her agonies, her miseries, afflictions,
Ne'er touch'd upon your thought: as for my injuries,
Alas, they were beneath your royal pity;
But yet they liv'd, thou proud man, to confound thee.
Behold thy fate; this steel !   [*Draws a dagger.*
    Ith.   Strike home! A courage
As keen as thy revenge shall give it welcome :
But prithee faint not; if the wound close up,
Tent it with double force, and search it deeply.
Thou look'st that I should whine and beg compassion,
As loth to leave the vainness of my glories;
A statelier resolution arms my confidence,
To cozen thee of honour; neither could I
With equal trial of unequal fortune

By hazard of a duel; 'twere a bravery
Too mighty for a slave intending murder.
On to the execution, and inherit
A conflict with thy horrors.
    Org.   By Apollo,
Thou talk'st a goodly language! for requital
I will report thee to thy mistress richly:
And take this peace along; some few short minutes
Determin'd, my resolves shall quickly follow
Thy wrathful ghost; then, if we tug for mastery,
Penthea's sacred eyes shall lend new courage.
Give me thy hand: be healthful in thy parting
From lost mortality! thus, thus I free it. [*Stabs him.*
    Ith. Yet, yet, I scorn to shrink.
    Org.   Keep up thy spirit:
I will be gentle even in blood; to linger
Pain, which I strive to cure, were to be cruel.
    [*Stabs him again.*
    Ith. Nimble in vengeance, I forgive thee. Follow
Safety, with best success; O, may it prosper!—
Penthea, by thy side thy brother bleeds;
The earnest of his wrongs to thy forc'd faith.
Thoughts of ambition, or delicious banquet
With beauty, youth, and love, together perish
In my last breath, which on the sacred altar
Of a long-look'd-for peace—now—moves—to heaven.
    [*Dies.*
    Org. Farewell, fair spring of manhood! henceforth welcome
Best expectation of a noble sufferance.
I'll lock the bodies safe, till what must follow
Shall be approv'd.—Sweet twins, shine stars for ever!—
In vain they build their hopes whose life is shame:
No monument lasts but a happy name.
    [*Locks the door, and exit.*

ACT V.

SCENE I. *A room in* BASSANES' *house.*

Enter BASSANES.

Bass. Athens—to Athens I have sent, the nursery
Of Greece for learning and the fount of knowledge;
For here in Sparta there's not left amongst us
One wise man to direct; we're all turn'd madcaps.
'Tis said Apollo is the god of herbs,
Then certainly he knows the virtue of 'em:
To Delphos I have sent too. If there can be
A help for nature, we are sure yet.

Enter ORGILUS.

Org. Honour
Attend thy counsels ever!
Bass. I beseech thee
With all my heart, let me go from thee quietly;
I will not aught to do with thee, of all men.
The doubles of a hare,—or, in a morning,
Salutes from a splay-footed witch,—to drop
Three drops of blood at th' nose just and no more,—
Croaking of ravens, or the screech of owls,
Are not so boding mischief as thy crossing
My private meditations: shun me, prithee;
And if I cannot love thee heartily,
I'll love thee as well as I can.
Org. Noble Bassanes,
Mistake me not.
Bass. Phew! then we shall be troubled.
Thou wert ordain'd my plague—heaven make me thankful,

And give me patience too, heaven, I beseech thee.

    Org. Accept a league of amity; for henceforth,
I vow, by my best Genius, in a syllable,
Never to speak vexation: I will study
Service and friendship, with a zealous sorrow
For my past incivility towards ye.

    Bass. Hey-day, good words, good words! I must believe 'em,
And be a coxcomb for my labour.

    Org.   Use not
So hard a language; your misdoubt is causeless:
For instance, if you promise to put on
A constancy of patience, such a patience
As chronicle or history ne'er mention'd,
As follows not example, but shall stand
A wonder and a theme for imitation,
The first, the index pointing to a second,[1]
I will acquaint ye with an unmatch'd secret,
Whose knowledge to your griefs shall set a period.

    Bass. Thou canst not, Orgilus; 'tis in the power
Of the gods only: yet, for satisfaction,
Because I note an earnest in thine utterance,
Unforc'd and naturally free, be resolute
The virgin-bays shall not withstand the lightning
With a more careless danger than my constancy
The full of thy relation; could it move
Distraction in a senseless marble statue,
It should find me a rock: I do expect now
Some truth of unheard moment.

    Org.   To your patience

---

[1] It may be just necessary to observe that Orgilus alludes to the *index-hand* (☞) so common in the margin of our old books, and which served to direct the reader's attention to such passages as the author wished to recommend to particular notice. "Be *resolute*," in the next speech, must be understood in the old sense of be *persuaded, assured,* &c.

You must add privacy, as strong in silence
As mysteries lock'd-up in Jove's own bosom.
　Bass. A skull hid in the earth a treble age
Shall sooner prate.
　Org.　　　　Lastly, to such direction
As the severity of a glorious action
Deserves to lead your wisdom and your judgment,
You ought to yield obedience.
　Bass.　　　　　　　With assurance
Of will and thankfulness.
　Org.　　　　　　　With manly courage
Please, then, to follow me.
　Bass.　　　Where'er, I fear not. [*Exeunt.*

SCENE II. *A state-room in the palace.*

A flourish. Enter EUPHRANEA, *led by* GRONEAS *and* HEMOPHIL;
PROPHILUS, *led by* CHRISTALLA *and* PHILEMA; NEARCHUS
supporting CALANTHA; CROTOLON *and* AMELUS.

　Cal. We miss our servant Ithocles and Orgilus;
On whom attend they?
　Crot.　　　　My son, gracious princess,
Whisper'd some new device, to which these revels
Should be but usher; wherein I conceive
Lord Ithocles and he himself are actors.
　Cal. A fair excuse for absence: as for Bassanes,
Delights to him are troublesome: Armostes
Is with the king?
　Crot.　　　He is.
　Cal.　　　　　　On to the dance!—
Cousin, hand you the bride;[2] the bridegroom must be

---

[2] *Cousin, hand you the bride;*] I have omitted "*dear*" before
"*Cousin*," which reduced the line to mere prose, and could scarcely
therefore come from the author.

Intrusted to my courtship. Be not jealous,
Euphranea ; I shall scarcely prove a temptress.—
Fall to our dance.

THE REVELS.

Music. NEARCHUS *dances with* EUPHRANEA, PROPHI-
LUS *with* CALANTHA, CHRISTALLA *with* HEMOPHIL,
PHILEMA *with* GRONEAS.

They dance the first change; during which ARMOSTES
enters.

Arm. [*whispers Cal.*] The king your father's dead.
Cal. To the other change.
Arm.   Is't possible ?

They dance the second change.

Enter BASSANES.

Bass. [*whispers Cal.*]   O, madam !
Penthea, poor Penthea's starv'd.
Cal.   Beshrew thee !—
Lead to the next.
Bass.   Amazement dulls my senses.

They dance the third change.

Enter ORGILUS.

Org. [*whispers Cal.*] Brave Ithocles is murder'd,
  murder'd cruelly.
Cal. How dull this music sounds ! Strike up more
  sprightly ;
Our footings are not active like our heart,
Which treads the nimbler measure.
Org.   I am thunderstruck.

The last change.

Cal. So ! let us breathe awhile. [*Music ceases.*]—
         Hath not this motion

Rais'd fresher colour³ on our⁴ cheeks?
  Near.   Sweet princess,
A perfect purity of blood enamels
The beauty of your white.
  Cal.   We all look cheerfully:
And, cousin, 'tis methinks a rare presumption
In any who prefer our lawful pleasures
Before their own sour censure, t' interrupt
The custom of this ceremony bluntly.
  Near. None dares, lady.
  Cal. Yes, yes; some hollow voice deliver'd to me
How that the king was dead.
  Arm.   The king is dead:
That fatal news was mine; for in mine arms
He breath'd his last, and with his crown bequeath'd ye
Your mother's wedding-ring; which here I tender.
  Crot. Most strange!
  Cal. Peace crown his ashes! We are queen, then.
  Near. Long live Calantha! Sparta's sovereign queen!
  All. Long live the queen!
  Cal.   What whisper'd Bassanes?
  Bass. That my Penthea, miserable soul,
Was starv'd to death.
  Cal.   She's happy; she hath finish'd
A long and painful progress.—A third murmur
Pierc'd mine unwilling ears.
  Org.   That Ithocles
Was murder'd;—rather butcher'd, had not bravery
Of an undaunted spirit, conquering terror,
Proclaim'd his last act triumph over ruin.
  Arm. How! murder'd!
  Cal.   By whose hand?

---

³ *colour*] Gifford printed "colours." D.
⁴ *our*] The 4to has "your." D.

Org.   By mine; this weapon
Was instrument to my revenge: the reasons
Are just, and known; quit him of these, and then
Never liv'd gentleman of greater merit,
Hope or abiliment to steer a kingdom.
    Crot. Fie, Orgilus!
    Euph.   Fie, brother!
    Cal.   You have done it?
    Bass. How it was done let him report, the forfeit
Of whose allegiance to our laws doth covet
Rigour of justice; but that done it is
Mine eyes have been an evidence of credit
Too sure to be convinc'd.[5] Armostes, rent[6] not
Thine arteries with hearing the bare circumstances
Of these calamities; thou'st lost a nephew,
A niece, and I a wife: continue man still;
Make me the pattern of digesting evils,
Who can outlive my mighty ones, not shrinking
At such a pressure as would sink a soul
Into what's most of death, the worst of horrors.
But I have seal'd a covenant with sadness,
And enter'd into bonds without condition,
To stand these tempests calmly; mark me, nobles,
I do not shed a tear, not for Penthea!
Excellent misery!
    Cal.   We begin our reign
With a first act of justice: thy confession,
Unhappy Orgilus, dooms thee a sentence;
But yet thy father's or thy sister's presence
Shall be excus'd.—Give, Crotolon, a blessing
To thy lost son;—Euphranea, take a farewell;—

---

[5] *Mine eyes have been an evidence of credit
    Too sure to be* convinc'd.] It may be necessary to observe that *convince* is used here in the primitive sense of *conquered, overthrown.* In modern terms, "my evidence is too true to be confuted."
[6] *rent*] Gifford printed "rend." See note, p. 194. D.

And both be gone.
Crot. [*to. Org.*] Confirm thee noble sorrow
In worthy resolution !
Euph. Could my tears speak,
My griefs were slight.
Org. All goodness dwell amongst ye !
Enjoy my sister, Prophilus : my vengeance
Aim'd never at thy prejudice.
Cal. Now withdraw.
[*Exeunt Crot. Pro. and Euph.*
Bloody relater of thy stains in blood,
For that thou hast reported him, whose fortunes
And life by thee are both at once snatch'd from him,
With honourable mention, make thy choice
Of what death likes thee best; there's all our bounty.—
But to excuse delays, let me, dear cousin,
Intreat you and these lords see execution
Instant before ye part.
Near. Your will commands us.
Org. One suit, just queen, my last : vouchsafe your
clemency,
That by no common hand I be divided
From this my humble frailty.
Cal. To their wisdoms
Who are to be spectators of thine end
I make the reference : those that are dead
Are dead ; had they not now died, of necessity
They must have paid the debt they ow'd to nature
One time or other.—Use dispatch, my lords ;
We'll suddenly prepare our coronation.
[*Exeunt Cal. Phil. and Chris.*
Arm. 'Tis strange these tragedies should never touch on
Her female pity.
Bass. She has a masculine spirit :

SCENE II. THE BROKEN HEART. 313

And wherefore should I pule, and, like a girl,
Put finger in the eye? let's be all toughness,
Without distinction betwixt sex and sex.
 Near. Now, Orgilus, thy choice?
 Org.   To bleed to death.
 Arm. The executioner?
 Org.   Myself, no surgeon;
I am well skill'd in letting blood. Bind fast
This arm, that so the pipes may from their conduits
Convey a full stream; here's a skilful instrument:
        [*Shows his dagger.*
Only I am a beggar to some charity
To speed me in this execution
By lending th' other prick to th' tother[7] arm,
When this is bubbling life out.
 Bass.   I am for ye;
It most concerns my art, my care, my credit.—
Quick fillet both his[8] arms.
 Org.   Gramercy, friendship!
Such courtesies are real which flow cheerfully
Without an expectation of requital.
Reach me a staff in this hand. [*They give him a staff.*]
      —If a proneness
Or custom in my nature from my cradle
Had been inclin'd to fierce and eager bloodshed,
A coward guilt, hid in a coward quaking,
Would have betray'd me to ignoble flight[9]
And vagabond pursuit of dreadful safety:
But look upon my steadiness, and scorn not
The sickness of my fortune, which since Bassanes
Was husband to Penthea had lain bed-rid.
We trifle time in words:—thus I show cunning

  [7] *to th' tother*] Gifford printed "*to th'* other:" but Ford doubtless wrote as in the 4to. D.
  [8] *his*] The 4to has "this." D.
  [9] *Would have betray'd* me *to ignoble flight*] For "*me*" the old copy reads "*fame.*"

In opening of a vein too full, too lively.
        [*Pierces the vein with his dagger.*
Arm. Desperate courage!
Near.   Honourable infamy![10]
Hem. I tremble at the sight.
Gron.   Would I were loose!
Bass. It sparkles like a lusty wine new broach'd;
The vessel must be sound from which it issues.—
Grasp hard this other stick—I'll be as nimble—
But prithee, look not pale—have at ye! stretch out
Thine arm with vigour and unshak[en][11] virtue.
                                [*Opens the vein.*
Good! O, I envy not a rival, fitted
To conquer in extremities: this pastime
Appears majestical; some high-tun'd poem
Hereafter shall deliver to posterity
The writer's glory and his subject's triumph.
How is't, man?—droop not yet.
Org.   I feel no palsies.
On a pair-royal do I wait in death;
My sovereign, as his liegeman; on my mistress,
As a devoted servant; and on Ithocles,
As if no brave, yet no unworthy enemy:
Nor did I use an engine to entrap
His life, out of a slavish fear to combat
Youth, strength, or cunning;[12] but for that I durst not
Engage the goodness of a cause on fortune,
By which his name might have outfac'd my vengeance.

[10] Near. *Honourable infamy!*] The 4to gives this speech to Orgilus, the only person on the stage to whom it cannot possibly belong. It does not misbecome Nearchus, who has hitherto said nothing. I need not observe how improperly the concluding part of the next speech [but two] is put into the mouth of Bassanes; who might surely have been restored to reason without trenching on the confines of honourable feeling and sentimental dignity.

[11] *and unshak*[en]] So Gifford.—The 4to has "*and* vnshooke." Qy. "*and* with unshook"? D.

[12] *Youth, strength, or* cunning;] i.e. practical skill in the use of arms. See [note], p. 134.

O, Tecnicus, inspir'd with Phœbus' fire!
I call to mind thy augury, 'twas perfect;
Revenge proves its own executioner.
When feeble man is bending to his mother,
The dust he was first fram'd on, thus he totters.
    Bass. Life's fountain is dried up.
    Org.   So falls the standard[13]
Of my prerogative in being a creature!
A mist hangs o'er mine eyes, the sun's bright splendour
Is clouded in an everlasting shadow;
Welcome, thou ice, that sitt'st about my heart,
No heat can ever thaw thee.   [*Dies.*
    Near.   Speech hath left him.
    Bass. He has[14] shook hands with time; his funeral
        urn
Shall be my charge: remove the bloodless body.
The coronation must require attendance;
That past, my few days can be but one mourning.
                                         [*Exeunt.*

SCENE III. *A temple.*

An altar covered with white; two lights of virgin wax upon it. Recorders,[15] *during which enter Attendants bearing* ITHOCLES *on a hearse, in a rich robe, with a crown on his head, and place him on the one side of the altar. After which enter* CALANTHA *in white, crowned, attended by* EUPHRANEA, PHILEMA, *and* CHRISTALLA, *also in white;* NEARCHUS, ARMOSTES, CROTOLON, PROPHILUS, AMELUS, BASSANES, HEMOPHIL, *and* GRONEAS. CALANTHA *kneels before the altar, the* Ladies *kneeling behind her, the rest stand off. The recorders cease during her devotions. Soft music.* CALANTHA *and the rest rise, doing obeisance to the altar.*

    Cal. Our orisons are heard; the gods are merciful.—

---

[13] *standard*] The 4to has "Standards." D.
[14] *has*] Gifford printed "hath." D.
[15] *Recorders*] i. e. a sort of flutes or flageolets. D.

Now tell me, you whose loyalties pay tribute
To us your lawful sovereign, how unskilful
Your duties or obedience is to render
Subjection to the sceptre of a virgin,
Who have been ever fortunate in princes
Of masculine and stirring composition.
A woman has enough to govern wisely
Her own demeanours, passions, and divisions.
A nation warlike and inur'd to practice
Of policy and labour cannot brook
A feminate authority : we therefore
Command your counsel, how you may advise us
In choosing of a husband, whose abilities
Can better guide this kingdom.
 Near.   Royal lady,
Your law is in your will.
 Arm.   We have seen tokens
Of constancy too lately to mistrust it.
 Crot. Yet, if your highness settle on a choice
By your own judgment both allow'd and lik'd of,
Sparta may grow in power, and proceed
To an increasing height.
 Cal.   Hold you the same mind?
 Bass. Alas, great mistress, reason is so clouded
With the thick darkness of my infinite[16] woes,
That I forecast nor dangers, hopes, or safety.
Give me some corner of the world to wear out
The remnant of the minutes I must number,
Where I may hear no sounds but sad complaints
Of virgins who have lost contracted partners ;
Of husbands howling that their wives were ravish'd
By some untimely fate ; of friends divided
By churlish opposition ; or of fathers

---

[16] *infinite*] The 4to has ;" infinites." D.

Weeping upon their children's slaughter'd carcasses;
Or daughters groaning o'er their fathers' hearses;
And I can dwell there, and with these keep consort
As musical as theirs. What can you look for
From an old, foolish, peevish, doting man
But craziness of age?
 Cal. Cousin of Argos,—
 Near.   Madam?
 Cal.   Were I presently
To choose you for my lord, I'll open freely
What articles I would propose to treat on
Before our marriage.
 Near.   Name them, virtuous lady.
 Cal. I would presume you would retain the royalty
Of Sparta in her own bounds; then in Argos
Armostes might be viceroy; in Messene
Might Crotolon bear sway; and Bassanes—
 Bass. I, queen! alas, what I?
 Cal.   Be Sparta's marshal:
The multitudes of high employments could not
But set a peace to private griefs. These gentlemen,
Groneas and Hemophil, with worthy pensions,
Should wait upon your person in your chamber.—
I would bestow Christalla on Amelus,
She'll prove a constant wife; and Philema
Should into Vesta's Temple.
 Bass.   This is a testament!
It sounds not like conditions on a marriage.
 Near. All this should be perform'd.
 Cal.   Lastly, for Prophilus,
He should be, cousin, solemnly invested
In all those honours, titles, and preferments
Which his dear friend and my neglected husband
Too short a time enjoy'd.
 Pro.   I am unworthy

To live in your remembrance.
Euph. Excellent lady!
Near. Madam, what means that word, "neglected husband"?
Cal. Forgive me:—now I turn to thee, thou shadow
Of my contracted lord! Bear witness all,
I put my mother['s] wedding-ring upon
His finger; 'twas my father's last bequest.
  [*Places a ring on the finger of Ithocles.*
Thus I new-marry him whose wife I am;
Death shall not separate us. O, my lords,
I but deceiv'd your eyes with antic gesture,
When one news straight came huddling on another
Of death! and death! and death! still I danc'd forward;
But it struck home, and here, and in an instant.
Be such mere women, who with shrieks and outcries
Can vow a present end to all their sorrows,
Yet live to court new pleasures,[17] and outlive them:
They are the silent griefs which cut the heart-strings;
Let me die smiling.
Near. 'Tis a truth too ominous.
Cal. One kiss on these cold lips, my last! [*Kisses Ith.*]—Crack, crack!—
Argos now's Sparta's king.—Command the voices
Which wait at th' altar now to sing the song
I fitted for my end.
Near. Sirs, the song!

DIRGE.

Cho. *Glories, pleasures, pomps, delights, and ease,*
  Can but please

---

[17] *Yet live to* court *new pleasures,* &c.] For "*court,*" which I have ventured to introduce, the old copy reads "*vow;*" evidently an erroneous repetition of the word which occurs in the verse immediately above it.

SCENE III.   THE BROKEN HEART.   319

      [*Th'*] *outward senses, when the mind*
      Is [*or*] *untroubled*¹⁸ *or by peace refin'd.*
First voice. *Crowns may flourish and decay,*
      Beauties shine, but fade away.
Second. *Youth may revel, yet it must*
      Lie down in a bed of dust.
Third. *Earthly honours flow and waste,*
      Time alone doth change and last.
Cho. *Sorrows mingled with contents prepare*
      Rest for care;
      Love only reigns in death; though art
      Can find no comfort for a BROKEN
      HEART. [*Calantha dies.*
 Arm. Look to the queen!
 Bass.   Her "heart is broke" indeed.
O, royal maid, would thou hadst miss'd this part!
Yet 'twas a brave one. I must weep to see
Her smile in death.
 Arm.   Wise Tecnicus! thus said he;
When youth is ripe, and age from time doth part,
The Lifeless Trunk shall wed the Broken Heart.
'Tis here fulfill'd.
 Near. I am your king.

---

¹⁸ This fine dirge has sustained some injury from the press. The old copy shows that a word has dropt from the commencement of the third verse, and there is an evident confusion in that which follows it. I can only reduce it to some tolerable meaning by reading "*or*" before "*untroubled*" instead of "*not.*" There are few situations on the stage so dramatically striking as this, or wrought up with such heart-rending pathos; but it is purchased at the expense of nature and probability, which are wantonly violated in the preparatory scene. No audience of the present day would support a sight so dreadfully fantastic as the continuance of the revels amidst such awful intelligence as reaches Calantha in quick succession. Those of the poet's age, however, had firmer nerves,—and they needed them: the caterers for their amusements were mighty in their profession, and cared little how highly the passions of the spectators were wound up by the tremendous exhibitions to which they accustomed them, as they had ever some powerful stroke of nature or of art at command to compose or justify them.

All. Long live Nearchus, King of Sparta!

Near. Her last will
Shall never be digress'd from : wait in order
Upon these faithful lovers, as becomes us.—
The counsels of the gods are never known
Till men can call th' effects of them their own.

[*Exeunt.*

EPILOGUE.

WHERE noble judgments and clear eyes are fix'd
To grace endeavour, there sits truth, not mix'd
With ignorance ; those censures may command
Belief which talk not till they understand.
Let some say, "This was flat;" some, "Here the scene
Fell from its height;" another, "That the mean
Was ill observ'd in such a growing passion
As it transcended either state or fashion:"
Some few may cry, " 'Twas pretty well," or so,
"But—" and there shrug in silence : yet we know
Our writer's aim was in the whole addrest
Well to deserve of all, but please the best ;
Which granted, by th' allowance of this strain
The BROKEN HEART may be piec'd-up again.

END OF VOL. I.

www.ingramcontent.com/pod-product-compliance
Lightning Source LLC
Chambersburg PA
CBHW020104020526
44112CB00033B/919